The Poetry of T. S. ELIOT

The Poetry

of

T. S. ELIOT

by

D. E. S. MAXWELL

UNIVERSITY PAPERBACK

BARNES & NOBLE, INC.
Publishers • Booksellers • Since 1873

Published in 1952 by Routledge & Kegan Paul Ltd.

Reprinted by Barnes & Noble, Inc.

First Printing, 1961

L. C. Catalogue Card Number: 61-17767

Printed in the United States of America

Contents

Acknowledgments

Acknowledgment is due to Mr. T. S. Eliot and Messrs. Faber and Faber for permission to make the quotations from Mr. Eliot's prose and poetry.

The Poetry of T. S. ELIOT

Chapter One

The Critical Background

(1)

FROM 1900 until the first world war, poetry in England wandered for the most part along the country paths opened up by the nineteenth-century romantics, unaware that the paths had become ruts, and that a more suitable track was now the pavement. New forces were appearing, but their influence was small, and on the Georgians, who commanded what popular favour for poetry there was, non-existent. Eliot's earliest undergraduate poetry has a Georgian tinge, but the mésalliance was brief, and it was his later reaction to their work that led to his formulating the literary theories from which all his poetry since has derived. To discover these it is necessary to go to his criticism, for there, 'at the back of the poet's mind, if not as his ostensible purpose, he is always trying to defend the kind of poetry he is writing, or to formulate the kind he wants to write.' (*The Music of Poetry*, p. 8). Valuable as an introduction to the theory is a study of Eliot's opinion of Georgian practice, for this not only initiated his search for a literary philosophy, but also provided it immediately with one of its components, a demand for a greater esotericism in poetry.

While it is impossible to frame any satisfactory definition of poetry, a reasonably accurate distinction between different kinds of poetry can be made. Such distinction is that between poetry with an immediate popular appeal, and poetry which will command only a limited audience. The former need not be worthless, but when written during the decadence of a tradition the chances are that it will not be the greatest poetry. For its essential qualities involve nothing that could be considered a necessary part of greatness. Its tendency is to dispense with subtlety, metrical, linguistic, intellectual, or emotional. Briefly stated, its essential is that it should express an easily grasped thought in simple language and strongly emphasised, little varied metre.

Of this kind is Georgian poetry, which though it began as a revolt produced no effective or durable novelty. It was an attempt to revitalise the failing romantic tradition, without infusing into this process anything foreign to that tradition. The result was an intensified enervation. Brooke's rather spiritless Shelleyan philosophy may be mentioned as a symptom of the decay. In these lines:

> *There the Eternals are, and there*
> *The Good, the Lovely, and the True,*
> *And Types, whose earthly copies were*
> *The foolish broken things we knew:*

the weak rhythmical pattern robs the poetry of force, and lends it a languid quality far removed from the movement of Shelley's verse. The revolt of the Georgians was no more than a restatement of 'what had already been said perfectly', justifying itself as a revolt by restating not the immediately preceding poetry but that coming earlier in the tradition. As C. Day Lewis has expressed it, 'The Georgian poets, a sadly pedestrian rabble, flocked along the roads their fathers had built, pointing out to each other the beauty spots, and ostentatiously drinking small beer in a desperate attempt to prove their virility.' (*A Hope for Poetry*, p. 2.) Nominally a protest against the changing civilisation, the movement's protest consisted in avoiding awareness of the changes.

That the Georgians recognised the changing nature of civilisation cannot be denied. Instead, however, of so adapting their poetry as to make it a fit medium for the expression of the changed circumstances—and this was the really important issue of their time—they continued to play with subjects having a preconceived and rather facile emotional appeal. It was purely a poetry of escape, concerned with the romance of far-off lands, the sea, and of a sentimentalised English countryside, fixed firmly at three o'clock on a sunny afternoon before the first world war.

2

'Love in country lanes, the song of birds, moonlight—these the poet, playing for safety, and the critic trying to find something safe to praise, will deem the sure cards in the poetic pack' (Ford Madox Hueffer: Preface to the *Collected Poems*). Such poetry was motivated by the 'sub-Wordsworthian ideals of those who wrote verse which was fashionable from 1900 until about five years ago' (Edith Sitwell: 'Experiment in Poetry', an essay in *Tradition and Experiment in Present-day Literature*, 1929, p. 95).

Wordsworth had wrought a great and significant change in English poetry at the end of the eighteenth century: his experiments eventually became a part of the English literary tradition. But even with Tennyson and his contemporaries the initial force had lost its vitality. Swinburne's poetry was a playing with the music of words, tending to divorce them from their relations with the objects which they represent. 'It is in fact the word which gives him the thrill, not the object.' Eliot admits Swinburne's genius, but contends that it was not one which could provide a satisfactory model for a generation 'struggling to digest and express new objects . . . new feelings, new aspects' (Swinburne as Poet, *The Sacred Wood*, p. 150). This, then, is the test of a tradition—its relevance to contemporary circumstances. It is this which will decide 'what in the past is worth preserving, and what should be rejected',[1] as far as the immediate practical needs of poetry are concerned. Eliot finds even in the greatest romantic poetry no help for the modern poet. The disembodied convolutions of Swinburne's poetry and the escapism of the Georgians were equally symptoms of the same disease—decadence of the tradition. The Georgian experiment indicated the intensity of the decadence, and showed the extent to which the romantic tradition was unrelated to the artistic problems of the time.

On being told that his writing of indecent verse and prose offended against 'the serious ideal of correctness', Pope replied that there was a distinction between work and play. With such a distinction Eliot would very probably agree, and this should be borne in mind in any consideration of his comments on Georgian poetry. Quite obviously he does not take it seriously. An article in the *Egoist* (September, 1917) is not unfavourable to the school, and its conclusion is a fair summary of the outlook: 'It is a limited

1. *Points of View*, p. 22

genre: but it is a legitimate bypath of poetry. It has been done best, perhaps, by Henri Bataille. Only in something harder can great passion be expressed; the vague is a more dangerous path for poetry than the arid.' In March of the following year, however, his verdict is much less favourable: 'The serious writer of verse must be prepared to cross himself with the best verse of other languages, and the best prose of all languages. In Georgian poetry there is no such crossing visible; it is inbred.' He goes on to summarise the Georgian subject catalogue as 'rainbows, cuckoos, daffodils and timid hares.' Finally this comment written in May 1919, may be taken as a product of his dictum that '. . . we must learn to take literature seriously' (*Egoist*, April, 1918): 'Keats, Shelley and Wordsworth punish us from their graves with the annual scourge of the Georgian anthology.'

It may be assumed from this that Eliot ultimately decided the prolific inbreeding of Georgian poetry to constitute a danger to the future of any better poetry, to militate against the creation of a public that would take literature seriously'. Eliot's attitude at this time was that of Dryden, which he discusses in *The Use of Poetry*: 'But Dryden, . . . was writing in a form which had not grown out of popular tradition or popular requirements, a form the acceptance of which had therefore to come by diffusion through a small society' (p. 22). It is because such a diffusion in Eliot's time was hindered by the writings of the Georgians that Eliot grows less patient with their wanderings through the 'legitimate bypath'. They were then a luxury that poetry could not afford.

As Michael Roberts has indicated (*Critique of Poetry*), the Georgians were accepted immediately because of the amount of immediately recognisable poetic technique in their work. Debased romantic technique that was establishing a public that demanded certain things of their poets—obvious rhythms, and a restriction of subject to what seemed indisputably 'poetic'. This public would accept Keats's nightingale as a symbol of escape, but could not see the same significance in Prufrock's lobster, as their sensibility had become too narrowly canalised. Because the poets did nothing to alter this state of affairs, poetry became as formalised as it had at the end of the eighteenth century. The audience was large for this poetry, which was no more than continual limited variation on restricted themes, expressed in stereotyped formal patterns. It was

4

'flat and thin, or shallow and shadowless . . . an evasion like the phrase, "Not at Home" ' (Edith Sitwell: *Aspects of Modern Poetry*, p. 73). As the majority will always prefer evasion, and as the evasion was musically expressed, the poetry was popular. Simultaneously the audience for any better poetry diminished.

Undoubtedly there were other causes. 'Again, the fact of universal elementary education is inimical to poetry. It has tended to depress the culture of the minority below the point at which a full understanding of poetry becomes possible, without raising the culture of the majority to that point. . . . I am not claiming poetry as the preserve of the intellectual: that it has undoubtedly become so seems to me a thoroughly unfortunate state of affairs . . .' (C. Day Lewis: *A Hope for Poetry*, p. 31). It can be seen that the causes of the diminished interest in poetry are complex, and perhaps more a matter of social than of artistic history. The Georgians, however, failed to adapt poetry to a changed environment when it should have been obvious that radical change was demanded, and are at least partially responsible for the decline of interest in good poetry. This is the great danger of popular, exoteric poetry.

That there is a considerable substance in these charges against the Georgians must be immediately obvious. They are condemned for not doing what they should have done, and for doing badly what they did do. The question of their failure to widen poetic themes requires elaboration. Certain of Brooke's poems seem to escape the eternal round of pretty-prettiness, even at times to recognise that there is an urban, as well as a rural civilisation. 'A Channel Passage', for example, is outside the usual limits:

> *Now there's a choice—heartache or tortured liver!*
> *A sea-sick body, or a you-sick soul!*
> *Do I forget you? Retchings twist and tie me,*
> *Old meat, good meals, brown gobbets, up I throw.*
> *Do I remember? Acrid return and slimy,*
> *The sobs and slobbers of a last year's woe.*
> *And still the sick ship rolls. 'Tis hard, I tell ye,*
> *To choose 'Twixt love and nausea, heart and belly.*

Yet these coarse posturings represent only the semblance of an escape, imperfectly engineered. Even without the forced archaisms, the unpleasing turn of phrase in the second line, the poem would be basically an imperfect conception, the reverse of pretty-pretty: ugly-ugly. It is an unconvincing, overhearty, and completely purposeless portrayal of the physically nauseating. Unconvincing and purposeless because, taking this peculiarly revolting subject, the poem fails to suggest in it significance of any order, to leave the listener feeling that here is the crystallisation of some experience essential to a coherent design. The vices of superficial pictorialism become even more apparent here than in Brooke's more usual versifications of rural excursions.

Similarly with 'Jealousy':

> . . . you, that loved young life and clean, must tend
> A foul sick fumbling dribbling body and old,
> When his rare lips hang flabby and can't hold
> Slobber, and you're enduring that worst thing,
> Senility's queasy furtive love-making,
> And searching those dear eyes for human meaning,
> Propping the bald and helpless head, and cleaning
> A scrap that life's flung by, and love's forgotten.

This over-emphasised rhetoric involves a subject and treatment as superficially unpleasant as the others were superficially pleasant. Essentially, the objection to the Georgians was that their poetic world was incomplete, excluding any concepts of Good and Evil, in fact of any spiritual significance whatever. They deal rather with a world of 'niceness' and 'not-niceness'. Faulty manipulation of detail assured frequent failure of the poetry even on this level of perception. The bald head in Brooke's poem is overwhelmed in the preceding tirade, and achieves no particular effect. In contrast the nuances of 'The Love Song of J. Alfred Prufrock' have a more forceful impact than all Brooke's elaborate description:

> And though I have wept and fasted, wept and prayed,
> Though I have seen my head (grown slightly bald) brought in upon
>   a platter,
> I am no prophet—and here's no great matter.

The shift here from penance to baldness is a device of wit that reveals Prufrock's consciousness and suggests the values of his middle age more tellingly than could such elaboration as Brooke's.

So in turning to the unpleasant Brooke merely added another decoration to his poetry, which remained unaffected by the changing relationship of man to his surroundings, by the faster and more complex rhythms of modern life. What was required was that a perception of this should enter into the essence of poetry, and become an integral part of it. Realism is not to be superimposed on an unchanged outlook and manner of expression: by littering one's verse with omnibuses instead of stage-coaches, for instance. 'The Lady of Shalott' would not become an expression of contemporary life if one were to replace the lady's barge by a motor-boat, any more than a mention of the Black Death might have been supposed to make Chaucer's poetry more truly a mirroring of its time. The state of mind created by awareness of the plague and its effects is not absent from *The Canterbury Tales* and some analogous influence should be exercised in today's poetry by the time's characteristics.

Brooke's 'The Great Lover' gains nothing of the new mood by the intrusion of 'the keen unpassioned beauty of a great machine': this is realism romanticised, unrelated to anything deeper in contemporary life than the impermanent decorative paraphernalia of mechanism. A more subtle and a more valid influence is exercised by the age on Eliot's:

> *Inside my brain a dull tom-tom begins*
> *Absurdly hammering a prelude of its own,*
> *Capricious monotone.*

In the texture of these lines are implicit the idiom and the rhythms of modern life, and they become a living element in the whole. Similarly these lines from *The Waste Land*:[1]

> *At the violet hour, when the eyes and back*
> *Turn upward from the desk, when the human engine waits*
> *Like a taxi throbbing waiting, . . .*

1. More generally in *The Waste Land* can be seen the intrusion of fragmentary café conversation, permeated by spasmodic gramophone music, vague in the incoherent tissue of sound. The increased spread of largely unheard music in modern life accounts for a great deal of the incidental music to Eliot's poems. See Chapter Four, section (i), where this is considered in greater detail.

are innovatory not because they mention a taxi, but because the human component of urban life is deeply related to—almost identified with—what most intimately informs its daily activity, the rhythm of its life, in lines that subtly catch the essence of that rhythm, the unending monotony of pulsing machines. Brooke's fugitive realisations that his poetry failed to take account of the profound changes in life are wrongly directed, and the romanticism that veils and distorts his landscapes sentimentalises too his realism, never potently embodied in his verse. Always his poetry is of the surface. In Chapter Three will be considered the way in which Eliot uses some of the surface characteristics of modern urban civilisation to probe far beneath the surface.

Brooke's fall from critical favour is comparatively recent. The same is true of Housman. Writing in the *New Statesman and Nation* in 1923 (14th July, p. 423) F. L. Lucas placed Housman among 'our three main poets', describing him as 'perfectly original'. Originality is precisely what the experimenters denied to Housman, along with his reputation as a classical poet. Here again, it is the iconoclasts who saw clearly, and we must wonder that a reputation for originality could rest on so slight a foundation. Housman's poetry derives, if ancestry must be assigned, not from the English Augustans, nor from the Greek and Roman poets, but from particular instances in decadent romanticism. More precisely, the greater part of his poetry is a reiteration of the Omar Khayyam sentiment, and can be localised even to these lines of Hood:

> *I remember, I remember,*
> *The fir trees dark and high*
> *I used to think their slender tops*
> *Were close against the sky:*
>
> *It was a childish ignorance,*
> *But now 'tis little joy*
> *To know I'm further off from heaven*
> *Than when I was a boy.*

Divided into two quatrains the verse becomes pure Housman, in form and in mood, lacking only the extra dolorous line that is Housman's sole technical innovation. Other parallels are easily found:

> *Awake! for Morning in the bowl of night*
> *Has flung the stone that puts the stars to flight:*
> *And lo! the hunter of the East has caught*
> *The Sultan's Turret in a Noose of Light.*

> *Wake: the silver dusk returning*
> *Up the beach of darkness brims*
> *And the ship of sunrise burning*
> *Strands upon the eastern rims.*

In these verses only the conventions of imagery differ.[1] The structure of each is the same: exhortation followed by two metaphors descriptive of daybreak.

Further parallels[2] add nothing to the consideration of Housman's originality, for in the verse from Hood is contained the major part of all that Housman ever said. This theme, distributed throughout his poetry, is repeated in,

> *Far in a western brookland*
> *That bred me long ago*
> *The poplars stand and tremble*
> *By pools I used to know.*
> (*Shropshire Lad*, LII.)

A thin cynicism—'the still sad music of infirmity', as Eliot has said in another connexion—is added in other verses:

> *O never fear, man, nought's to dread,*
> *Look not left nor right:*
> *In all the endless road you tread*
> *There's nothing but the night.* (LX)

The cynicism, as much as the regret and the nostalgia, is ill-defined, incapable of producing in the listener any deep-seated reaction. It can become, even, vaguely soothing, with its suggestion of man's fortitude under a blind fate. There is nothing here to disturb poetry or poetry-readers from a comfortable assurance, any

1. There is of course no copyright in Dawn. Nevertheless Housman's diction and imagery do not reveal a poetic sensibility formed by the peculiarities of the twentieth century, perfectly original in its re-creation of the surrounding world.

2. For example, Housman's 'Epitaph on an Army of Mercenaries' seems but a slight variation on the theme of the *Rubaiyat*, LII.

9

more than would after-dinner conversation about the existence of God shake the self-made man's faith in his own unaided ability.

This is not to demand didacticism of poetry, to say that its purpose is simply to rebuke the normal man's unwillingness to question his 'certain certainties'. Yet something of this nature should be involved in any poetry described as perfectly original, as a medium newly adapted to the expression of new outlooks and influences. Neither in what it says nor in the way it says it does Housman's verse show any awareness of changes. Nor does it go any way towards expressing them, and showing them in relation to what is permanent in man. We may reasonably suspect that Housman's originality was seen only by pseudo-traditionalists anxious to avoid anything more revolutionary than a cynicism producing sweetly sentimental emotional reactions. On this point—whether or not Housman does represent an outlook profoundly changed by profound changes—there can be no doubt that *A Shropshire Lad* and *Last Poems* are inadequate.

As poems of the countryside there is merit in some of Housman's lyrics. The same kind of thing, however, had been done much more successfully by earlier poets. In the countryside of the *Shropshire Lad* there is generally a lack of precision. We cannot answer the question, 'What are those blue remembered hills?', for indeed they are nowhere in particular. It is mainly this lack of definition that shows Housman to be no classicist. He does not convince that for him the milieux had any interest in their own right, and they become rather the centres of vague emotional diffusion. This vagueness is reflected in the words he uses. 'Silver' and 'Gold' are the most frequently used for description, occurring often either in cliché or in an unconvincing context:

> 'Ah, Spring was sent for lass and lad,
>   'Tis now the blood runs gold'   (V)
> 'O I shall be stiff and cold
>   When I forget you, hearts of gold.'   (XLII)
> '. . . all the brooks ran gold'   (LIV)
> 'The silver dust' of dawn   (XXVI)
> 'silver waters'   (XLII)

From this metallic imagery results a haze that envelops the landscapes and produces a crop of related words: 'Glimmering sheep' (IX); 'Glimmering weirs' (LII); 'the vanes of Shrewsbury gleam' (XXVIII);

> *This is the land of lost content*
> *I see it* shining *plain*   (XL)

There is in this very limited range of imagery, beyond which Housman rarely strays, no vivid evocation of particular scenes. Without this, regional pictorial nature poetry must largely fail of its object.

The strength of Eliot's reaction against these failings must have affected the form which his poetry was to take. His readiness to absorb the influences discussed in the third chapter springs directly from their being essentially more esoteric in appeal. The tradition to which the Georgians belonged, and for which Eliot had never found sympathy, had been so treated that any expansion of its scope had become impossible. It seemed that generally its practitioners lacked skill even within their limits, that the consistent playing for popularity had utterly enervated the tradition. And an isolated exception could not divert its direction, nor manipulate it to contain the growing complexity of events.

A kinder verdict on these poets is given by Alan Pryce-Jones (*Penguin New Writing*, No. 35, p. 100): 'They tried to offer not greatness but delight. And sometimes they succeeded.' Sometimes indeed they did, and if the other judgment seems harsh, it is because these poets tried to offer not only 'not greatness', but a delight largely illusory, and in their time an unworthy sidetracking of poetry's needs. That, and their failure to be sufficiently expert within their own chosen field. With one exception. And this exception also showed that indeed the tradition was incapable of satisfying the necessity for change.

Walter de la Mare's poetry creates a world of fantasy that has the completeness and cohesion of a dream. Only when we wake from dreaming do we see that the outlines were blurred, the values abnormal, the logic of all dreams, by waking standards, irrational. To suppose that dreams are invariably peaceful and soothing is of course quite erroneous. There can be too an overwhelming fear, a sense of utter helplessness, of an evil never clearly seen and incapable of definition. These phantasms are exquisitely caught in de la Mare's poetry. The states summoned up in his poems range beyond

> . . . *the quiet steeps of dreamland,*
> *The waters of no more pain*   ('Nod')

to 'the sullen courts of sleep' ('Sunk Lyonesse'). In the latter occur normality's frightening changes to, in one poem, inexplicable journeyings down endless stairways, just outdistancing pursuing shapes—'The Feckless Dinner Party'. This poem moves with extreme skill from the opening chit-chat to the terrors of the end. Here the dreamers do not waken—the most chilling fear of all uneasy sleep—and there is left only, in the shadowy abandoned house,

> *He who misled them all—the butler Toomes.*

This utilisation of the macabre deepens and completes de la Mare's dream world. A feeling of awe and wonder ('The Scribe'), the presence of mystery and terror ('The Listeners'), mingle with delicate traceries of beauty ('The Snowdrop'), in his poetry. Archaisms do not jar in this world as they do in almost all other Georgian poetry; and again in contrast, de la Mare's technical virtuosity is beyond question.

A sense of mystery is at the roots of all romantic poetry. Something of it must be present in poetry of any tradition that is to be called great. But it is most strongly accentuated—sometimes at the expense of other important attributes—in the romantic school. It is from this tradition that poetry such as de la Mare's must inevitably derive its sustenance. To the use of completely subjective symbolism in verse purporting to have elements of realism one may reasonably object. In dream one does not demand exactness, and even those of de la Mare's poems which seem to begin in actuality ('The Feckless Dinner Party') merge imperceptibly into dream. This is not an attempt to construct a dream world from, or to superimpose it on, actual waking experience. It is an exploration of the world of dreams that exists in its own right.

> *'Hearken! 'Tis news I cry!'*
> *The shades drift by . . .*
> *'Strange and wondrous things:*
> *A four-foot Beast upon Wings,*

> *Thieves in a burning Mill,*
> *An empty Cross on a Hill,*
> *Ravin of swine in Beauty's places,*
> *And a Woman with two Faces!*
> *News!—News! I call. . . .'*

The symbols here are personal, and in their context one can ask no other kind. But this symbolism, and the poetry of which it is a part, excludes reality entirely, and is because of this incomplete. Its only fitting subject is the phantoms of the mind, and there is no hope that a virile line of realistic poetry, envisaging modern urban civilisation as part of its scope, might be developed from it. De la Mare had exploited superbly the last vein of the tradition. The nature of his success emphasised its limitations.

In the failure of most of the Georgians, and in the success of de la Mare, we see implied Eliot's reasons for seeking esotericism. We see too the cause of his belief that only through the poet's willingness to accept as his aim dissemination of his work through a small group, might poetry regain some of its lost powers, and absorb vital new influences. It is some measure of the Georgian influence that de la Mare, associated with them, became in the public imagination reduced to the position of poet to beguile the nursery. Even good poetry became popular for reasons that had little to do with its real worth.

To describe poetry as good begs more questions than it answers. It may be said, however, that formally it blends the three aspects of poetry defined by Ezra Pound: '(1) Melopoeia, to wit, poetry which moves by its music, whether it be a music in words or an aptitude for, or suggestion of, accompanying music; (2) Imagism, or poetry wherein the feelings of painting and sculpture are predominant . . .; and there is, thirdly, logopoeia, or poetry that is akin to nothing but language, which is a dance of intelligence among words and ideas and modifications of ideas and words' (from a review of *Others: An Anthology. Little Review*, March, 1918). Something of each of these will be found in good poetry. Such poetry too, must resolve the distinctive characteristics of its own time—which are temporary—into universality, must show them as part of a greater pattern. Its ability to do this makes it at once individual and yet conformable to the pattern of tradition.

Further, it demands from the reader concentration and intellectual acuity as well as sensuous receptivity. So good poetry will always be more esoteric than will second-rate.

At the time when Eliot began to write a degree of esotericism, voluntarily sought, even greater than usual was required, in reaction to the exotericism of the preceding age. 'I sometimes think that our own time, with its elaborate equipment of science and psychological analysis is even less fitted than the Victorian age to appreciate poetry as poetry' (T. S. Eliot: Introductory Essay to *'London' and 'The Vanity of Human Wishes'*). Realising this, Eliot abandoned the popular methods of the Georgians in favour of esotericism. An appeal to a smaller audience willing to make the effort required for appreciation of the 'new' poetry, rather than to 'the average human being' who 'no longer cares to feel the keen edge of life, to have freshness in vision or zest and savour in the senses. He prefers to face life in the armour of boredom and cynicism, fending off despair with the brazen shield of dissipation. . . . But rich or poor, it is the same fever to escape from reality—above all from art, which is the mirror in which the reality of life is accentuated' (Herbert Read: *Politics of the Unpolitical*, p. 101). This is not an isolated reaction. Valéry too has protested against the facility demanded by the reading public (*Nouvelle Revue Française*, May, 1932). Partly, then, the esotericism of Eliot's poetry is sought voluntarily, in protest against the demands of a public kept in being in England by Georgian poetry, and in the hope of finding or creating an audience which, though smaller, would at least realise that poetry makes demands of the reader as well as of the poet.

Nor was it solely in reaction against the preceding poetry that Eliot chose the way of esotericism. 'We can only say that it appears likely that poets in our civilisation, as it exists at present, must be difficult. Our civilisation comprehends great variety and complexity, and this variety and complexity, playing upon a refined sensibility, must produce various and complex results. The poet must become more and more comprehensive, more allusive, more indirect, in order to force, to dislocate if necessary, language into his meaning' (T. S. Eliot: 'The Metaphysical Poets', *Selected Essays*, p. 289). Quite apart from the shortcomings of Georgian poetry, it was inevitable that the poetry coming after it should have been esoteric, 'cultivating all the possibilities of words as a medium',[1] and, 'when the speech of one sense is insufficient to convey (the) entire meaning, (using) the language of another'.[2] That it should, in other words, be esoteric because of its necessity to create new devices essential to the expression of entirely new conditions.

We may discern, then, the causes of esotericism in Eliot's poetry. Firstly, the uselessness of wide appeal to an audience incapable of full appreciation, the result of social factors, and of Georgian usage with its debased playing on the lowest artistic responses of a large audience. Instead of this the poet appeals to a small public in the hope that by a process of diffusion his work may reach, and be fully appreciated by, a large part of society. Secondly, the demands of a civilisation infinitely more complex than in any previous era, whose mirroring in art requires the resurrection of lost and the development of new artistic devices. Esotericism, that is, was at once a discipline for the easier desires of the artist and of the audience, and a necessary result of the conditions in which the poet's sensibility had to operate.

Only a detailed examination of Eliot's poems can reveal the effect on his art of this doctrine of esotericism, the kind of poetry which it has produced, and the measure of its success. This will bring to light more of Eliot's sources, and the use to which he puts them, for from these sources comes much that, because of desuetude and unfamiliarity, could have, at least in the beginning, only a limited appeal. Before this, the critical background must be completed by tracing the line which Eliot followed in trying to find new directions to lead away from the devitalised poetry that was the artistic nourishment of his time. Behind all Eliot's poetry is the critical sense which led him to examine the past for a new source of strength, and from his examination to produce a traditionalism very different from the barren laissez-faire of most of his contemporaries. Georgian poetry was merely the ultimate development of a tradition with which Eliot was entirely out of sympathy. It is by finding why he considered romanticism fallacious that we may decide what else might best fulfil his demands.

1. Edith Sitwell: *Poetry and Criticism*, p. 23.
2. Ibid., p. 18.

(II)

It was in the first quarter of this century that the dangers inherent in romantic literary doctrine first became apparent, though only to a minority. All the different kinds of romantic had been united by their belief that a work of art was fundamentally an expression of the artist's personality, and that allegiance was owed not to any external authority but to the dictates of the poet's inner voice. Shelley found 'a principle within the human being . . . which acts otherwise than in a lyre, and produces not melody alone, but harmony, by an internal adjustment of the sounds and the motions thus excited to the impressions which excite them' (*Defence of Poetry*). Wordsworth looked on poetry, as Longinus looked on sublimity, as the echo of a great soul, 'the spontaneous overflow of powerful feelings', its laws formulated by the poet's own powerful desires and sensations, his 'undisciplined squads of emotion' (*East Coker: Four Quartets*, p. 22). In the beginning this did not produce anarchy; it resulted in the variety that was needed after classical decadence. Nevertheless, it is obvious that if supreme authority for the individual is to be vested in the caprices of his own individuality, then the absence of any common external authority may result eventually in a loss of stability. As excess of restraint had led to death, excess of liberty might well lead to license. Because the first romantics after the Augustan tradition—Wordsworth, Coleridge, Shelley and Keats—had been men of genius, the experiment was successful. But to continue the experiment through generations of lesser men was for poetry to condemn itself to 'fitful and transient bursts of literary brilliance' (T. S. Eliot: *Points of View*, p. 85). With the dying of the first revolutionary passion, the inner voices lost their force. Underlying the doctrine was the assumption that man's innate goodness would in the end overcome his weakness. Godwin in political theory and Shelley in his poetry both proclaimed the perfectibility of man. On this assumption romantic theory can be justified. For if man is perfectible then he must contain within himself at least the seeds of the perfect ethic and the perfect art: to follow the guidance of an inner voice is therefore unimpeachable, and the important thing in a work of art is not the object considered, but what the author felt about the object. This is the romantic fallacy.

During the uneasy years around the first world war, this assumption had begun to lose its attractiveness. To the minds of many it seemed to have caused, in art and in the social order, a complete lack of cohesion. There was no striving towards a common end, for things had become ends in themselves: efficiency and speed were justified by their existence, and it was not thought that they should be subordinated to higher interests, or indeed that anything higher should even exist. Men were

> *Dividing the stars into common and preferred,*
> *Engaged in devising the perfect refrigerator,*
> *Engaged in working out a rational morality,*
> *Engaged in printing as many books as possible,*

and forgetting 'the way to the Temple' (choruses from *The Rock: Collected Poems*, p. 167). For Eliot in particular the revolt against romanticism involved the rejection of the liberal doctrine which held man's chief end to be the complete development of his personality. Here again the emphasis was on egotism rather than on self-restraint. This will be considered in detail in the examination of his poems. At the moment, however, we are concerned with the purely literary aspect of his revolt.

Eliot's rejection of the romantic faith is fundamental.[1] He refuses to accept their basic tenet that the sole authority for the artist is his inner voice, the appetites of his personality. Not even for the first products of this theory, in the nineteenth century, can he find enthusiasm. It is with approval that he quotes Arnold's condemnation of the group: it 'proceeded without having its proper data', and this makes 'Byron so empty of matter, Shelley so incoherent'.[2] Eliot believes that romantic poetry is for 'those who demand of poetry a day-dream, or a metamorphosis of their own feeble desires and lusts, or what they believe to be "intensity" of passion' (Introductory Essay to *'London' and 'The Vanity of Human Wishes'*). Art based on the romantic fallacy will become

1. See, *The Sacred Wood*, p. 32: 'there is no place for it (romanticism) in letters.'
2. See the introduction to *The Sacred Wood*, pp. xi–xii.

> *music which we seize*
> *To body forth our own vacuity.*
> ('Conversation Galante': *Collected Poems*, p. 33.)

What is important is not 'what the author felt', for this makes poetry no more than 'a collection of psychological data about the minds of poets' (Preface: *The Sacred Wood*, p. ix).

In *After Strange Gods* Eliot spoke of D. H. Lawrence as having 'had no guidance except the Inner Light, the most untrustworthy and deceitful guide that ever offered itself to wandering humanity' (p. 59). This condemnation of artistic self-sufficiency Eliot had already elaborated in 'The Function of Criticism'. Here the inner voice is dismissed as 'an old principle which has been formulated in the now familiar phrase of "doing as one likes" '(*Selected Essays*, p. 26). If the critic's aim is to find common principles among men, objective standards by which art may be judged— and this, says Eliot, is his aim—then he cannot simply 'do as he likes'. For this must inevitably result in the multiplication rather than in the resolving into order of critical standards; and, *a fortiori*, of the standards of creative work. The romantic fallacy has resulted in a destruction of belief in central authority to which all men might owe allegiance, in objective standards by which men might agree to judge art, and in any inspiration other than the shiftings of personality through which adult, orderly art might be created.

From this it can be seen that what is wanted is cohesion, which can be achieved only by dependence on objective authority. That Eliot, in his comments on romantic poetry, should refer frequently to the Augustans, is revealing. He couples the two in order to emphasise that the classical school achieved 'an elegance and a dignity absent from the popular and pretentious verse of of the Romantic poets' (Preface to *Homage to John Dryden*). Even more important is his opinion that the difference between the two schools is that 'between the complete and the fragmentary, the adult and the immature, the orderly and the chaotic' ('The Function of Criticism': *Selected Essays*, p. 26). Beyond doubt, Eliot desires the order and completeness of classical poetry. The task of the critic is to discover an objective authority that will enable the poet to produce such poetry, to escape from the expression of personality to the expression of something more universal. And, as with the Augustans, the necessary wisdom is to be found in past attempts, for

'. . . *here upon earth you have the reward of the good and ill that was done by those who have gone before you.*'
(Choruses from *The Rock: Collected Poems*, p. 163.)

The poet's struggle is to discover what

> *By strength and submission, has already been discovered*
> *Once or twice, or several times by men whom one cannot hope*
> *To emulate—but there is no competition—*
> *There is only the fight to recover what has been lost*
> *And found and lost again and again: and now under conditions*
> *That seem unpropitious.*

(*East Coker: Four Quartets*, p. 22.)

For such a struggle, the weapons must be found in what Blunden calls 'the stores of tradition'.

This brief discussion is intended only to indicate the nature of the romantic fallacy, and to sketch Eliot's reasons for rejecting it. That his rejection implies not a denial of the worth of man's inner longings, as the humanists suggest, but the need for objective standards by which they may be correctly orientated, will be shown in the following sections of this chapter. Enough has been said to suggest that contemporary society could offer no ground for the discovery of such standards. Romantic egotism was to give way to the classical principle of faith in the value of tradition, at precisely the time when such a change of heart was most needed.

(III)

Edith Sitwell prefaces her *Poetry and Criticism* with a quotation from Abraham Cowley: 'A war-like, various, and a tragical age is best to write of, but worst to write in.' There can be few ages to which Cowley's description would be more applicable than it is to this. The political hysteria of the inter-war years was paralleled by a wild outburst of artistic experiment justified by its 'modernity' and the extent to which it broke with tradition. That modernity is a relative term, and that experiment conducted on such a basis could establish nothing but chaos, does not seem to have occurred to its exponents. Their argument, if they had an argument, was that as life was chaotic, it was chaos that art must express. This can be justified. But one does not express chaos by creating it, as one does not recreate in a literary work an observed atmosphere of boredom by boring the reader. When, towards the end of *The Waste Land*, Eliot says,

> *These fragments I have shored against my ruins,*

he implies, by his allusion to the quotations from the dead authors throughout the poem, that the ruins of traditional ethics and artistic standards that form the modern world's spiritual store are to be rebuilt be synthesising the peculiarities of the modern world with the universality that can be found in tradition.

In Julien Benda's description of contemporary French society Eliot sees an analysis capable of a wider application: 'On entrevoit le jour où la bonne société française repudiera encore le peu qu'elle supporte aujourd'hui d'idées et d'organisation dans l'art . . .' (*The Sacred Wood*, p. 45). The destruction of belief in organisation in art, and the sacrifice to emotional appeals of its rational qualities are not confined to French society. These maladies are widespread, and tradition, 'the common inheritance'[1] of all artists, offers to them the medium through which they may attain a sense of community, and hence the creation of order out of chaos. A sense of community is essential to a mature, authoritative art, capable of revealing the hidden significances in, and the connexions between, the disparate elements of reality. Art, the end of which is to show that coherence and meaning exist where none appeared, must first achieve coherence itself. It is as true of artistic endeavour as it is of the religious life, that,

> *There is no life that is not in community.*
> (Choruses from *The Rock: Collected Poems*, p. 164.)

Although there is the possibility that such a community of feeling may be attained without conscious effort, 'our instincts of tidiness imperatively command us not to leave to the haphazard of the

---

1. When, in 'Tradition and the Individual Talent,' Eliot says, 'Tradition cannot be inherited', he means rather the sense of tradition.

unconscious what we can attempt to do consciously' ('The Function of Criticism': *Selected Essays*, p. 24).

If, as Eliot says in *After Strange Gods* (p. 48), the struggle of our time is to 're-establish a vital connexion between the individual and the race', then the struggle in art is to make the poet aware of 'the mind of Europe . . . a mind which he learns in time to be much more important than his own private mind' ('Tradition and the Individual Talent': *Selected Essays*, p. 16). That is, to establish here as well a link between the individual and something outside him, and greater than him, of which he is a part. The race can be distinguished by its habits as a race, formed by the experience of past generations. So the mind of Europe is a universal mind by virtue of its involving all the philosophy and all the art of the dead writers. Of this universal mind tradition is the expression. In this lies the universal quality of tradition, for the collective mind of Europe, with its immense variety of thought, can appeal equally to all. It may be asked how, in this authority that is to produce cohesion, order can exist among such variety. Let us assume for the moment that it does. Then the advantage of submission to the authority of tradition is that poets will express not their own personality, but their personality universalised by its experience of the mind of Europe, 'the accumulated wisdom of time' ('The Function of Criticism': *Selected Essays*, p. 29).

In 'Tradition and the Individual Talent' Eliot speaks of the critical tendency 'to insist on those aspects of his (the poet's) work in which he least resembles anyone else. In those aspects or parts of his work we pretend to find what is the peculiar essence of the man' (*Selected Essays*, p. 14). If a poet's essential personality is expressed in this way then his personality is just those things which differentiate him from others. Eliot does not agree that this is what should be expressed in poetry. It is the operation in each poet's individuality of the collective mind that orientates correctly the desires of his personality, puts them in a proper perspective, and tells the poet how best they may be satisfied. As he progresses he will come to realise that his personal desires may be satisfied not by disordered experiment, based on the expression of those things which emphasise his division from others, but by experiment founded on the methods recorded in tradition, adapted to his needs and to the needs of his time. He will learn, therefore, that the important thing, the thing that will be of greatest relevance both to him and to his time, is not any virtue that may be within him. It is the wisdom that he can glean from 'what has already been discovered', and from his attempts

> to recover what has been lost
> And found and lost again and again.

That is to say, he will become the voice not so much of his private self as of the mind of Europe. It is in this way that, 'The progress of the artist is a continual self-sacrifice, a continual extinction of personality' (Tradition and the Individual Talent': *Selected Essays*, p. 17).

Despite the 'extinction of personality', there is a place given in this theory of poetry to the poet's personality. All that the doctrine attempts, is to indicate to the poet an atmosphere in which his private feelings and desires, his innate abilities, may profitably operate. A passage from 'Religion and Literature', explains much of the idea: 'Wide Reading . . . is valuable because in the process of being affected by one powerful personality after another, we cease to be dominated by any one, or by any small number. The very different views of life, co-habiting in our minds, affect each other, and our own personality asserts itself and gives each a place in some arrangement peculiar to ourselves' (*Points of View*, p. 18). The poet can obtain awareness of the mind of Europe by wide reading in traditional literature. This does not exactly extinguish his own personality, but replaces it by his own personality as affected by his experience of the dead writers and the varied wisdom which their work involves. In this way he not only has what we may call his poetic personality formed by the collective mind, but by his work adds to the store of that mind. This he does because in his reading he composes a re-arrangement of the relative values of the collective mind's thought peculiar to himself, and to the self that is being gradually formed by the interaction between his mind and the collective mind. This concept will be more clearly defined when we consider the nature of tradition—and it is this that will make apparent how unity can exist in the variety of the mind of Europe. Before this we may summarise what has already been established.

The chaos in poetry is to be resolved by the establishment of a community among artists. This will come from their common submission to the authority of poetic tradition, the expression of the mind of Europe. It reveals the history of metrical innovation: and in this is involved much else of significance to poetry. From the interaction between the poet's personality and the mind of Europe will result a poetic personality that, while retaining a certain individuality, a peculiar interpretation of the values of the collective mind, will be able to speak sanely and authoritatively because its individuality is not based solely on the poet's ego. In this way the poet becomes a medium capable of relating, 'the accumulated wisdom of time' to the problems of this unsettled age, and will be better able, because of this, to see the pattern into which the chaos may be resolved. We can

> take heart for the future
> Remembering the past.
> (Choruses from *The Rock: Collected Poems*, p. 175.)

(IV)

Evidently a theory laying such importance on tradition must have something in common with Augustan literary doctrine. The differences, however, are more revealing, as they help to define the exact nature of Eliot's view.

The eighteenth-century classicists made little attempt to analyse the nature of the tradition to which they delegated such authority. For them there was no question of arguing terms with the past, of deciding which of a variety of directions should be taken. But then they did not have so wide and so confusing a choice of traditions.[1] Nor, in an age of comparative certainty, were they so troubled by social and artistic insecurity, by the prospect of gods become 'a heap of broken images'.

Authority was vested, broadly speaking, in the Greek and Roman authors, in Aristotle and in Horace. These were accepted without question as having formulated the laws by which poetry

1. See 'Poetry Today', an essay by Louis MacNeice in *The Arts Today*, where he says: 'The problem is especially difficult for us because, unlike our more parochial predecessors, we have so many Pasts and Presents to choose from.'

must be created, without which poetry could not exist. To put it like that is to over-simplify, for Pope recognised—though grudgingly and with reservations—the genius of Shakespeare, who was not bound by the 'ancient rules'. Nevertheless as there is a difference between Augustan and Modern Classicism, it is on this issue that the distinction must be made. Because Eliot, who is the supreme example of the modern classicist, questions tradition, makes demands of it, and asserts propositions about its nature in a way that the earlier school did not. His acceptance of the worth of tradition is not so unquestioning nor so facile as was Pope's. And one can sense in his more self-conscious acceptance a greater urgency, a feeling that as the romantic doctrine had failed, it was essential to be assured of the vitality, the capacity to undergo change, of the authority that was to replace it.

It is perhaps because Eliot is an American that he is unable to accept the European tradition as a matter of course, despite his obvious desire to find an authority greater and more stable than the compulsions of personality. His writings on 'the scattered fragments of American literature' are small in number, but sufficient to indicate what he finds lacking in the American tradition. In a review in the *Athenaeum* he remarks that 'it is inevitable that any work on American literature should contain a great deal of stuffing', and that 'the great figures of American literature are peculiarly isolated' ('American Literature'; a review by T. S. Eliot, *Athenaeum*, 25th April, 1919). That he should emphasise their isolation, the fragmentary nature of the literature which they compose, is suggestive. We may deduce that Eliot found no ordered pattern in the literary tradition of his native country. American writers have been essentially individualist: Eliot finds them unsatisfactory not because America has failed to produce any great writers, but because the great writers that it did produce form no ordered pattern, did not grow one from the other so as to form a continuous, inevitable line of descent. The literary tradition of America lacks coherence. As Eliot has said elsewhere, 'Three or four great novelists do not make a literature' (Notes: *Criterion*, October, 1923).

The American tradition, then, offered to him no authority to which he could attach his creative belief. For this reason he turned to the European tradition, which was not his natural inheritance. Despite this, his attitude to it differs from that of many other Americans during the 1920's. The extreme American viewpoint was that of Gorham B. Munson who in an essay on T. S. Eliot (July, 1924) drew a distinction between decayed European culture and an America of great vitality and 'high spiritual potentiality', the implication being that the contemporary artist should seek his inspiration in the new rather than in the old world. Herbert Read, criticising this essay in *Criterion* during the period of Eliot's association with the paper, pointed out that in America more than in any other country could be seen the symptoms of Europe's disease. That is, an 'imperialism of mechanical powers—power without vision, intelligence or moral design'. The conclusion that Read drew was that Europe was in less danger of succumbing to the disease than was America. For Europe 'has deep roots in tradition. America has only a gesture'.[1] Eliot's attitude is more akin to Read's than to that of his compatriot Munson. This expression of Read's opinion in the periodical with which Eliot had such close connexions, must have served to harden his faith in the European tradition as the external force by which the artist must let himself be guided. But his faith does not imply the unquestioning belief of the Augustans. Somewhere between that and violent rejection like Munson's lies Eliot's approach to tradition. We can say no more of the effect of his American birth than that while it did not lead to a rejection of European tradition, it led to a greater and more self-conscious enquiry into its nature than is customary with native Europeans.

As has been shown, he was dissatisfied with American literature because he found in it neither ordered progress nor coherent pattern. 'Tradition and the Individual Talent' elaborates his conception of the pattern of tradition. The pattern which tradition should compose is one in which the works of the past form, 'an ideal order . . . complete before the new work arrives'. With the addition of 'the really new' there is a modification of, 'The relations, proportions, values of each work of art toward the whole'; but no work is superseded, rejected, because of the arrival of the really new ('Tradition and the Individual Talent';

1. Review of 'The Esotericism of T. S. Eliot' by Herbert Read: *Criterion*, October, 1924.

Selected Essays, p. 16). It is complete in the sense that it contains within itself all that is necessary as a basis for change and for experiment. 'Complete' is not meant to imply that no addition is possible.

In this pattern there is no arbitrary arrangement of values, no detached object: the whole is coherent because all its parts are connected, interdependent. And so the really new is not, 'Exaggerated novelty, a novelty usually of a trifling kind, which conceals from the uncritical reader a fundamental commonplaceness.' Nor is it something, 'which attempts to do what has already been done perfectly' (*After Strange Gods*, pp. 23, 24). If it were the former it would have no place in the pattern of tradition, because it would bear no relation to anything already there. If it were the latter, it would add nothing new to the pattern, having the lifelessness of 'some pleasing archaeological reconstruction' ('Tradition and the Individual Talent': *Selected Essays*, p. 13). The really new uses methods based on traditional practices, adapted to the demands of the poet's material, to the demands of his art as they exist in his own particular time. It is, in other words, the logical descendant of what has gone before, as the metaphysical poets were 'the direct and normal development of the precedent age' ('The Metaphysical Poets': *Selected Essays*, p. 285).

Eliot's elaboration of this view of the metaphysicals enters into considerations that are irrelevant here. It is sufficient to indicate that what seemed their peculiar characteristic to later critics such as Johnson, was wit, by which 'the most heterogeneous ideas are linked by violence together'. Yet this is a development, a particular kind of the Elizabethan conceit. Their innovation, that is, was based on precedent, and on a poetry not long passed. At other times the effect of the immediately preceding literature may be to turn experiment from it. Experiment is none the less a result of it, and must in this case base itself on an earlier tradition. Thus Wordsworth found a greater kinship with the lyricism of the Elizabethans than with the formalism of the Augustans who more nearly preceded him. It was in fact his revolt from the Augustans that initiated his experimenting, and in this he is the product of what preceded him. Even in detail, too, some of his experimenting can be related to eighteenth-century verse. W. P. Ker, in his *Form and Style in Poetry*, has an interesting passage on this subject, which shows how eras apparently disparate in technique are in fact connected:

'. . . there is always something common, not individual, in the work of every artist . . . as when Gray writes his "Hymn to Adversity" not in the French pattern of most of his shorter odes, but in the stanza invented by himself, of octosyllabic verses with the Alexandrine at the end. Gray is not working in imitation of Milton, but with the same principles Milton had when he invented the stanza of his "Nativity Ode". Gray's "Hymn to Adversity" belongs to the Spenserian school in nearly the same degree as the verse of Milton's "Nativity Ode". When Wordsworth borrows that pattern of stanza for his "Ode to Duty" he is both following Gray and also following with understanding the principles on which Gray worked' (pp. 184–185).

. When we discover Eliot's view of the pattern in the history of poetical innovation, we will be able to analyse more exactly its quality of logical descent. Even now, though, it can be seen that it is its possession of this quality that gives unity to the variety in the mind of Europe. Nothing in that mind is a disconnected entity. For all their diversity, its components are connected by their belonging to a logical line of descent, whose changes and developments result from demands more constant than those of personality. It is these demands whose nature must be fully examined by the poet.

The following passage examines Eliot's conception of what the demands are. Its importance justifies lengthy quotation:

'If you look at the bad verse of any age you will find most of it lacking in the virtues of prose. When there is a period of good verse, it has often been preceded by a period in which the verse was bad because it was too poetic, too artificial: and it is very commonly followed by such another period. The development of blank verse in the hands of Shakespeare and some of his contemporaries was the work of adapting a medium which to begin with was almost intractably poetic, so that it could carry the burdens and exhibit the subtleties of prose. . . . The work of Donne, in a lesser form, was the same' (T. S. Eliot: Introductory Essay to *'London'* and *'The Vanity of Human Wishes'*). We may say, then, that the history of poetical innovation is largely concerned with the varying dependence of poetry on a 'poetical'

27

language, or on speech idiom. Donne's experiments added to the often lifeless conceits of the earlier school a vitality, and a greater awareness of colloquial idiom. Of this nature too was Wordsworth's experiment. Neither was without precedent in tradition, each used slightly different methods from those on which their experiment was based. Their aim was to lead verse from stiffness to suppleness, to closer relationship with 'a social idiom'. It is because of this that 'there is something integral about such greatness, and something significant in his (Wordsworth's) place in the pattern of history' (*Points of View*, p. 84). In contrast to this is the search of Milton, who experimented 'to see how elaborate . . . the music could be made without losing touch with colloquial speech altogether' (*Music of Poetry*, p. 24).

Eliot looks on the flux between the artificial and the prosaic as the basic characteristic of the pattern. Certainly much is involved in the relationship between poetry and the rhythm and idiom of ordinary speech. 'A living language analyses into idioms: idioms are the life organs of speech—words are molecules and letters atoms. . . . Idioms arise out of the contacts of daily life. They are the response of the human organism to the elements around it. They reflect the speed of life, the pressure of life, its very essence. . . . All the arts are built up from these primary elements, and their reality, their actuality, depends on this strict relation. To build up poetry with dead idioms is like living a life of dead habits and obsolete manners' (Herbert Read: *Collected Essays in Literary Criticism*, p. 50).

Constantly poetry becomes over-artificial, and constantly it is restored to a greater awareness of the common idiom. Always, too, experiment has been demanded by what has gone before, and its methods are based on traditional practices.. At different times the degree of change demanded will vary: 'It is a matter of the historical situation . . . it is the mark of the master to be able to make small changes which will be highly significant, as at another time to make radical changes, through which poetry will curve back again to its norm' (*Points of View*, p. 54). As will be shown in the third chapter, Eliot believes that his time was one in which poetry had again to be restored from the excess of artificiality and musical elaboration into which it had lapsed.[1]

1. This flux, considered the unifying principle, is illustrated here from

The whole, then, that is formed by the ideal order of 'the existing monuments', is based on the cycle of the suppleness restored by renewed awareness of colloquial speech, and the elaboration of that suppleness in verse which will gradually become over-artificial. Each experiment, in either direction, will alter the relations of the component parts towards the whole by its use in a new context of a dead author's methods. By showing, that is, that what had a significance to the pattern in terms of its first use has now an added meaning, because it is capable of being adapted to further experiment. We can now see that the effect on the pattern of tradition of the really new is analogous to the effect on the mind of Europe of the poet's mind. In each case a re-arrangement takes place, but nothing is superannuated. For too long—if we thought of tradition at all—we tended to associate it 'with the immovable: to think of it as something hostile to all change' (*After Strange Gods*, p. 18).

This is the distinction between Eliot and the Augustan poets. For them tradition was unchangeable, complete in all ways. For Eliot it is continually being added to: he looks on the poet as having an obligation to maintain tradition by creating work having its roots in what has gone before. It has been indicated that to do this he must let his mind be shaped by the mind of Europe, and he must base his innovation on methods to be found in the work of dead writers. Further, he may learn, by careful study of the development of tradition, when experiment is necessary, from the conditions which have previously demanded change. Usually, the flow of poetry away from the prosaic demanded that it should be once again restored to awareness of speech idiom, and speech rhythm. Because of this—and because of what Eliot means by 'extinction of personality'—he is able to say that 'not only the best, but the most individual parts of his

English literature. That the thesis has a wider application is shown by Eliot's remark that 'The vers libre of Jules Laforgue is free verse in much the same way that the later verse of Shakespeare, Webster, and Tourneur, is free verse: that is to say, it stretches, contracts and distorts the traditional French measure as later Elizabethan and Jacobean poetry stretches, contracts and distorts the blank verse measure.' Eliot's *The Use of Poetry and the Use of Criticism* is a development, in a different direction, of the same general theory, in that it is concerned to show how the critical ideas of any one period stand in a direct relationship to, are a logical development of, those of the preceding era.

(the poet's) work may be those in which the dead poets; his ancestors, assert their immortality most vigorously'('Tradition and the Individual Talent').

Tradition is not situated beyond reach in the past, something whose development is finished. There is a dedicatory note in his analysis of the poet's function. Merely to accept passively what already exists is not enough.[1] Tradition is a living body, the source of authority; but like all forms of life it is not immutable. As the poet, however, has the duty of altering tradition, he has the duty also of doing so in the proper manner. This requires in him 'the historical sense', which involves 'a perception, not only of the pastness of the past, but of its presence. . . . This historical sense, which is a sense of the timeless as well as the temporal and of the timeless and of the temporal together, is what makes a writer traditional. And it is at the same time what makes a writer acutely conscious of his place in time, of his own contemporaneity' ('Tradition and the Individual Talent': *Selected Essays*, p. 14). To be traditional, that is, the poet must realise that tradition is capable of informing his work, which is different from trying to re-create exactly outmoded poetical fashions. He must realise that each component of the artistic tradition has a significance not only for the time in which it was created but for his own time. He must, to ensure this, 'develop or procure the consciousness of the past' (ibid., p. 17), a process which involves something not usually considered as being specifically 'poetic'.

It involves wide reading—for by acquiring a knowledge of the mind of Europe the poet will develop the historical sense. As his reading extends he will come to see the pattern in tradition, and to recognise those parts of it which have the greatest relevance to his own time. And this means that he will become aware of the presence of the past, will realise that the poetry of a dead author may be read not solely because of some aesthetic, disembodied thrill that it communicates. Not solely because of this, but because it has a practical value in showing the living poet the means by which he may conquer his own difficulties. And as the past is, in this way, ever-present, the world in which the contemporary poet

1. 'Nor should we cling to traditions as a way of asserting our superiority over less favoured peoples.'—*After Strange Gods*, p. 19.

lives becomes a part of it. His study of tradition will have shown him

> *what has been lost*
> *And found, and lost again and again,*

and he will, because of this, feel more acutely what it is that his own time has lost and must find again. That is, he will become increasingly conscious of the conditions of his world, 'of his own contemporaneity'.

In order to gain the historical sense, the poet must of necessity subdue what may be more appealing desires. For as he must work to attain it, this must to some extent encroach upon what might well seem an easier task—the communication of impressions and feelings that are purely personal. But 'the question is, the first question, not what comes natural, or what comes easy to us, but what is right?' ('The Function of Criticism': *Selected Essays*, p. 28). The historical sense will enable the poet to speak authoritatively, to understand fully the particular problems and conditions of his time, to interpret and to communicate these. It is the possession of the historical sense which transforms all that has been said in this chapter from abstract theorising into proposals that can be put into practice. Unless the poet can establish in his consciousness the relationship between past and present his knowledge is mere pedantry. What he learns from the past is not something to be paraded as a means of proving his culture. When he realises that what he is writing is the product of traditional practices adapted to the conditions of his time, and that his adaptation is at once altering and maintaining the pattern of tradition, he will have the true conception of the timelessness of tradition.

The sense of community given by common submission to tradition, the poetic personality formed by contact between the poet's mind and the mind of Europe, to these must be added the poet's awareness of his functions. These are, to alter the pattern of tradition, to study the contemporary relations between poetry and the prose idiom, to conduct the experiments suggested by this study in conformity with the pattern. For the inner voice, modern classicism substitutes the historical sense, which is dependent on an objective authority. The poet has regained a certain modesty: from looking on himself as an unacknowledged legislator of the world he has turned to an awareness of obligations as well as of rights. Yet he is not a subservient creature, for it is he who maintains tradition and alters that which already exists, so that it is shown, by the alteration, to be alive. Having behind him an objective authority, he can hope to achieve in his creation, and to communicate, a synthesis of 'the apparent unrelatedness of things' (*A Garland for John Donne*) that forms his world. He has gained too, a renewed care for the technicalities of his art.

Of the various objections to this theory of poetry we may consider one of the more important, that of D. S. Savage ('The Orthodoxy of T. S. Eliot', in *The Personal Principle: Studies in Modern Poetry*). This condemnation attacks the extremely self-conscious nature of the theory. None of the dead authors who compose tradition found it necessary to make this very conscious effort to relate his work to what had gone before. They wrote as they felt they must, without thinking that their work might suffer, might lose its validity because of their lacking a studied attempt to integrate it with the pattern of tradition. If the contemporary poet is to alter this instinctive approach to art he will reduce it to something mechanical that must inevitably lack the 'enthusiasm', the disturbing incantatory quality that is the basis of true poetry.

That is the substance of Savage's objection: it assumes that poetry containing the quality of enthusiasm is true poetry. Yet this drugging incantatory quality cannot be ascribed to much that we are compelled to recognise as poetry—the work of Dryden or of Pope.[1] To say that poetry must provide a synthesis of reality, must take the ugliness and evil of the world and show that it has a meaning, that it is an essential part of some universal pattern—this is more capable of being applied to all kinds of poetry.

1. Tillotson's *On the Poetry of Pope* has a passage (pp. 119-121) on Pope's use of rhythm, in which the point is made that important as the effect of rhythm is, it must never make 'the sounds predominate over the sense,' as it often did with Tennyson. It is to this 'too ready magic' that Eliot's theory is opposed. Eliot is not unaware of the power of rhythm, which penetrates 'far below the conscious levels of thought and feeling': he stresses, however, that 'it works through meanings, certainly' (*Points of View*, p. 55). That is, there must remain a conscious element, and the rhythm must not obscure the meaning of the words. Matthiessen, dealing with this point in *The Auditory Imagination* ('The Achievement of T. S. Eliot'), minimises the importance of this conscious element when he refers to the effect of Eliot's rhythms as 'incantatory'.

And as Eliot's theory, with its insistence on order and design, is more likely to help the poet to see a pattern than to atrophy his ability to do so, one cannot well maintain that it must be destructive of poetic creation. Quite apart from this we may consider further the part played in a poem by enthusiasm. Coleridge, the spokesman for a school of poetry that laid great stress on the importance of enthusiasm, said that a poem could not be all poetry. The parts that are not poetry may be kept in harmony with the rest by possessing one essential quality of poetry, that of 'studied selection and artificial arrangement'. Even with those poets who laid most stress on the importance of enthusiasm, there had to be a conscious choice, at least in parts of their creation. This, apparently, did not destroy their faculty of enthusiasm. Emphasis on the necessity of conscious effort in Eliot's theory is not any more likely to destroy it.

We may say, then, that Eliot's theory need not necessarily destroy any inherent faculty of enthusiasm that the poet may possess. Should the poet feel that at least one kind of poetry—that depending for effect on an exquisite choice of words—may exist without such a force, his work is more likely to be helped than hindered by belief in Eliot's teaching. In neither case does adherence to the theory cause harm. The application of Eliot's doctrine is positively valuable for the creation of the quality common to all poetry—that it should produce from its material a final harmony. And in our time the importance of this quality, because of the weakening of faith in tradition, in any objective standards, was being minimised. The doctrine, that is, has a particular relevance to contemporary problems, is in fact the sole remaining hope for the construction of ordered art. This alone is sufficient to justify it, that it is essentially a product of its own time, and was evolved specifically to provide for the needs of that time.

We must remember that this theory was conceived by a poet who saw the basic failure of his time in its refusal to act—in any way, whether good or evil. Such a time could create nothing likely to satisfy man's eternal spiritual needs. It was a consistently evasive age, unwilling to submit to suffering. Eliot is in sympathy with the Baudelaire who said, 'la douleur est la noblesse unique', that suffering is the 'divin remède à nos impuretés'. The lesson of

The Waste Land is that man's worldly life is spiritual death, that there must be a renewal of asceticism before this can be remedied. 'The collocation of these two representatives of eastern and western asceticism (Buddha and St. Augustine) as the culmination of this part of the poem' is most certainly not an accident.[1] The people who inhabit the waste land are portrayed,

> not as lost
> *Violent souls, but only*
> *As the hollow men*
> *The stuffed men*

('The Hollow Men': *Collected Poems*, p. 87),

and the waste land itself is 'death's dream kingdom', for its people know nothing of supernatural experience, are spiritually dead.

Eliot's theory of poetry reacts against this all-pervading list-lessness. It stresses the importance of tradition, which is the history of man's artistic and spiritual enquiries. More than that, it demands of the poet that he should struggle to gain awareness of the mind of Europe, that he should sacrifice his personal whims to the compulsions of this external authority. Adherence to this doctrine requires that the poet should partake of the general subjection of self that must come before chaos may be resolved into order, and spiritual apathy become spiritual effort. Against the notion that poetic truth—which is the perception of an order composed by all the facets of life—may come unbidden in a flash of inspiration, Eliot sets the theory that it may be discovered only through effort. The superficial and facile mysticism which finds poetic truth in the uncontrolled operation on reality of strong personal emotion has as its criteria the strength of the emotion involved, the extent to which it offers an individual view of experience. This must serve only to emphasise man's division from man, to deepen rather than to bridge the separation between the elements composing the material of poetry. At another level it tends to minimise the importance of attention to the details of form, on the ground that the passion and stress of emotion must of their own accord integrate form and content.

Once again Eliot directs attention to the value of tradition which must, because of the pattern which it composes, form a

1. See Eliot's notes on *The Waste Land*.

part of the poet's experience. To experience it demands a conscious effort, valuable not only because it shows the poet more surely than uncontrolled emotion how best he may practise his art, but in itself as a discipline preliminary to the toil of creation. A toil because the writing of poetry demands 'the labour of sifting, combining, constructing, expunging, correcting, testing' ('The Function of Criticism': *Selected Essays*, p. 30). Tradition is the poetic authority because it contains the nature of poetic truth —order and design. By believing otherwise one pretends to see in the heterogeneous experiences which must be composed into order the starting point of the process. The true starting point is an understanding of the nature of the already existing pattern, and a willingness to find a community on the basis of that understanding. In this way poetry finds part of its material in something other than the disorder of life and the equal disorder of the emotions aroused by differing experience of it. That is, part of the poetic personality is formed by experience of something already ordered. As the imaginative world of Keats was real for him because it was accessible through the operation of the mind, so the experience of tradition is real for Eliot.

The organised labour of intellect rather than the fortuitous stimulation of emotion is the proper basis of poetry. In this intellectual bias, in belief that authority rather than liberty is the guide to truth, and in his regard for formal details, is Eliot's kinship with Augustan classicism. The operation of those beliefs in his poetry, has now to be examined.

Chapter Two
The New Classicism

ANY interpretation of poetic theory must be incomplete if it does not indicate the effect of the doctrine on the practice of poetry. It is not proposed to examine at this juncture the full scope of the relations between Eliot's special traditionalism, and his poetry. The relation between his practice and this element of his theory will be clarified in the examination of his early poems. At the moment we are concerned with those qualities of Eliot's poetry which are basically qualities of Augustan poetry too, although the forms in which they appear may differ. That is, to show that his poetry is classical as the term is usually interpreted, before showing that it possesses characteristics resulting from his theory that add to the scheme of Augustan classicism.

A characteristic of classicism that is relevant to this enquiry is its acceptance of an already existing poetic background, whose function is to provide the poem's incidental symbolism. 'The Rape of the Lock' is conceived within the framework of the classical epic, using its accepted symbols. Pope saw no reason for the creation of symbols peculiar to himself—as Shelley did in *Prometheus Unbound*—symbols whose full meaning could be appreciated only by their creator, although their necessary vagueness could produce a pleasing suggestion of profound significance and final order. Of the same nature is Eliot's acceptance of traditional literature as his poetic world. This can be seen most clearly in *The Waste Land*, where a blending of traditional European and

Eastern thought is the necessary background to his interpretation of the contemporary problem. The basic symbolism is taken from the Grail legend, and, particularly in the last section, Eliot introduces the journey symbol, which is a well-defined feature of European legend. The significances of this journey are defined by reference to traditional literature, as Pope defined a critical concept by reference to classical mythology:

> *When Ajax strives some rock's vast weight to throw,*
> *The line too labours, and the words move slow;*
> *Not so when swift Camilla scours the plain,*
> *Flies o'er the unbending corn and skims along the main.*[1]

We may examine a passage in detail to show more explicitly that Eliot's use of tradition is the same as Pope's use of the world of classical mythology: as a system providing a convenient symbolism which can be used to elucidate meaning, and to aid communication. The climax of 'The Burial of the Dead' is a blend of references to several traditions, the purpose of which is to reaffirm and illuminate what has gone before, by its relation of the poem's setting to these traditions. The city of this passage is not necessarily London alone—it is the same as 'the city over the mountains' of Section V, which is

> *Jerusalem Athens Alexandria*
> *Vienna London*
>
> (*Collected Poems*, p. 75.)

And this is because it is the same as the city of Baudelaire, to which our attention is drawn, a 'cité pleine de rêves' which is compounded of all 'les vieilles capitales' (Les Petites Vieilles).

To appreciate fully the significance of the reference we must have at the back of our minds all that Baudelaire meant by the modern city. For him it was enveloped usually in 'une atmosphère obscure', as Eliot's is seen 'Under the brown fog of a winter

---

1. That there is an even closer parallel between Eliot's usage and Pope's is suggested by a passage from Tillotson's *On the Poetry of Pope*. He states that Pope 'found that the particular composite effects he was aiming at, benefited from this increased area of consciousness. The reader has continually to be thinking of the parallel in Chaucer, Donne, Horace, or the epic poem, noting resemblance and difference.' All this section (pp. 144-148) is relevant.

dawn', and was peopled by creatures who 'n'ont jamais vécu'
(Le Crépuscule du Soir). Because of this death-like quality the
city is unreal, and this prepares the way for the next allusion, to
Dante's *Inferno*, the spiritual home of the city-dwellers as it is of
those,

> *who lived*
> *Without or praise or blame,*

who while on earth, 'never lived' (*Inferno*, Canto 3, lines 34–35,
60. Cary's translation). Having established by reference to
Baudelaire's city that the crowd flowing over London Bridge has
never truly lived, Eliot now indicates the reason. Because they
have avoided spiritual decision during their time on earth, the
people of the crowd are the same as the 'lunga tratta di gente' in
the *Inferno*,[1] who

> *of death*
> *No hope can entertain.*
>
> (*Ibid.*, ll. 44–45.)

That is, they are in a middle state, partaking fully of neither life
nor death. A contrast is implied as well, for Dante's shades, unlike
the city crowd, and like the Sibyl, accept the Christian paradox
that through death may come life, and 'wish to die' (Epigraph to
The Waste Land).

Stetson, who is now hailed in Eliot's poem, fulfils the same
function as the spirit singled out in the *Inferno* (after the line, 'Che
morte tanta n'avesse disfatta'). This spirit,

> *to base fear*
> *Abjured his high estate,*
>
> (*Ibid.*, ll. 56–57.)

pleasing neither God nor the enemies of God. Stetson is no one
person; he is a type, symbolising the crowd, universalised by his
association not with a recent war, but with Mylae, which as
Matthiessen has pointed out was a battle in the Punic war. The
corpse which Stetson has buried is to be identified with Dante's
'base fear', which we may take in this context as the part played

---

1. Not, it may be stressed, the same as those in Purgatory, for there, 'the
torment of flame is deliberately and consciously accepted by the penitent.'
(T. S. Eliot: 'Dante', *Selected Essays*, p. 255).

by Stetson 'in the ships at Mylae'. Stetson's failure at Mylae typifies man's eternal spiritual failure, and he has tried to destroy his consciousness of it by burial in his mind.

The lines:

> *Oh keep the Dog far hence that's friend to men,*
> *Or with his nails he'll dig it up again!*

are an adaptation of Webster's

> *But keep the wolf far thence that's foe to men,*
> *For with his nails he'll dig them up again.*

They have a compound function. Primarily they recall the atmosphere of Webster's Dirge, and the parallelism re-inforces the impression of Eliot's death-like city. But as the lines are altered this cannot be their only purpose. The Dog may be spiritual awareness or conscience, which Stetson makes no attempt to arouse, in the fear that it might force him to recognise his spiritual failings, to attempt to redeem himself—this none of the people of the waste land wishes to do, for it requires effort and positive action. The last line of the section,

> *You! hypocrite lecteur! mon semblable—mon frère!*

refers the condemnation of Stetson to all humanity and recalls to the reader the initial thesis that this city is the city of Baudelaire.[1]

Each step in the progress of the passage has been defined by its relation to an already formulated system, and by this juxtapositioning the meaning of the passage is communicated. Eliot's part has been the selecting and combining of various traditional symbols, which depend for their understanding mainly on their being recognised. This may be contrasted with interpreting the more arbitrary creations of a private symbolism. Despite the obvious differences between this more involved and more highly organised use of an existing poetic background, and that of the

1. In his analysis of this section Matthiessen does not make clear that the system of allusion comprehends Eliot's symbolism, the objective background to which the poem is related. In this more than in the projection of a poem into the person of another character is the 'objective correlative'—a creation such as Samson Agonistes for Milton, Prufrock or Gerontion for Eliot Matthiessen gives as examples of the objective correlative. It is the background created by allusion to literary tradition, however, that is the primary objective correlative in Eliot's poetry.

Augustans, the basic similarity remains. Eliot's use of allusion is not always for emphasis by parallelism. Frequently a contrast is implied; sometimes one allusion may contain at once a parallel and a contrast. Whatever the immediate purpose, the principle remains unaltered. By his technique of allusion and quotation Eliot indicates his acceptance of an objective symbolism, as the Augustans accepted that of the classical gods and goddesses, nymphs and satyrs. It may be objected that Eliot uses 'Dog' as a purely arbitrary symbol for spiritual awareness: certainly Eliot does not entirely repudiate the poet's right to create such symbols within limits. The point is that we are better able to interpret the symbolism of this arbitrarily selected figure because of what we have already learnt from the juxtapositioning of Eliot's poem and traditional literature.[1] Once it has been shown by the relationship between the two, what the corpse which Stetson buried is, it is comparatively easy to decide what would be most likely to disturb it.

We must stress too that Eliot in going to tradition for his symbols does not disturb what he uses. By relating the past to contemporary life in this way he not only charges his poetry with an added significance, but emphasises the continued virility of the past. When Shelley took Prometheus as the hero of his drama he did not mean by Prometheus what Aeschylus meant. The significance of Prometheus, and of all the other characters in the tragedy, is utterly and arbitrarily altered to suit Shelley's purpose, so that reference to Aeschylus will have no relevance to an understanding of Shelley's symbolism. The issue is not whether this is a good or a bad thing, but simply that Shelley's use of traditional figures is in no way similar to Eliot's. To seek symbols as Eliot does is to retain the essential suggestive quality of all symbolism, while limiting the suggestiveness to a clearly defined range. Eliot hints at precise concepts, whereas for the Romantics a symbol was a centre of unlimited expansion—something of this is said by Eliot in his essay on Swinburne (*The Sacred Wood*, p. 147). This is one advantage of Eliot's substitution of tradition for the classical mythology as the background which will provide imagery and symbolism. It can intensify the feeling, the content of the poem, retain the suggestiveness which does so much to

1. See also p. 83.

40

differentiate poetry from prose, and yet assure that the suggestiveness will be confined to the demands of the poem's purpose. It attempts to eliminate excessive blurring of the object, which tended to result from Romantic usage.

The Arab maiden in *Alastor* symbolises some element in the poet's life. The passage which describes her care of the poet is enveloped in an atmosphere of mystery. Enamoured of the poet, yet not daring to speak, she

> *Watched his nightly sleep,*
> *Sleepless herself, to gaze upon his lips*
> *Parted in slumber, whence the regular breath*
> *Of innocent dreams arose: then, when red morn*
> *Made paler the pale moon, to her cold home*
> *Wildered, and wan, and panting, she returned.*

When we unite the suggestion of mystery in this passage with the nature of the surroundings, 'where marble daemons watch', the significance of the Arab maiden can assume an increasing power, become lost in an unlimited suggestiveness, without ever being related to what she is meant to represent. The difference between this and the explicit suggestion of the Stetson image needs no emphasis.

Nor is there need to emphasise the gain in conciseness which results from this technique. This too is a characteristic of conventional classicism to which Eliot aspires, a reaction against the diffuseness of Romantic poetry, and especially of later Romantic poetry. Where Pope had tried to use as few words as possible, the Romantics tended to elaborate till little was left but the effect of elaboration. Eliot depends for the elaboration of detail on the associations roused in the reader's mind by an allusion to the background of tradition. Much of his description is by implication. Wishing, in 'Burbank with a Baedeker', to place the poem's action against a picture of past magnificence he refers obliquely to a well-known passage from *Antony and Cleopatra*—

> *Her shuttered barge*
> *Burned on the water all the day.*

In this way he leaves the associations which this reference summons up to form the necessary background to the contrasted affairs of Princess Volupine and her friends. These two impressions are directly linked by the fifth verse, in which Bleistein looks uncomprehendingly at a picture by Antonio Canaletto of an earlier Venice, the flame of whose glory has become

The smoky candle end of time.

Because of what had been previously aroused in the readers' mind, the impact of the contemporary decline to vulgarity is strengthened, for Bleistein is failing the beauty not only of 'the perspective of Canaletto' but of all the past. It is this verse which by forcibly juxtaposing all the recalled magnificence and the sordid present, fuses the poem into a unity, and lifts it above pastiche. The gain in conciseness is evident.

No school of English poetry has so consistently based its art upon satirical wit as the Augustan. With the decline of this school's power the astringent quality of its wit disappeared almost entirely from English verse. Eliot is the first to use it again to anything like the same extent, combining in his use the manner of Augustan wit with the purpose of metaphysical wit. The latter he has defined himself as levity intended to intensify the serious. Pope's apostrophe to his Muse—

> *Say what strange motive, Goddess, could compel*
> *A well-bred lord to assault a gentle belle?*
> *O say what stranger cause, yet unexplored,*
> *Could make a gentle belle reject a lord?*

is witty as these lines of Eliot are witty:

> *I shall not want Capital in Heaven*
> *For I shall meet Sir Alfred Mond.*
> *We two shall lie together lapt*
> *In a five per cent Exchequer Bond.*

But Eliot's have a purpose other than that of provoking amusement. They are part of his ironic reverie as his thoughts wander from the anecdotes of 'Pipit's experience', and by contrast they intensify his regret for wrecked illusions, that is expressed later—

> *But where is the penny world I bought*
> *To eat with Pipit behind the screen?*

> *The red-eyed scavengers are creeping*
> *From Kentish Town and Golder's Green.*
> ('A Cooking Egg': *Collected Poems*, p. 45.)

Although this wit is in manner the same as Pope's it is integrated with the different purposes of Eliot's poetry, and ceases to be an end in itself. That Eliot should think wit proper to poetry is, however, a result of his classical predilections. For wit requires brevity, careful phrasing and concern for clarity of thought and expression. We cannot imagine wit existing in 'the effort to construct a dream world, which alters English poetry so greatly in the nineteenth century' ('Andrew Marvell': *Selected Essays*, p. 301).

Apart from the purpose of Eliot's wit, its existence in his poetry indicates a view in life rather similar to that of Pope, who described man as, 'The glory, jest, and riddle of the world!' Each. has a certain casual irony, and Eliot's can be seen in those of his poems which are little more than light society verse. These are not intended to fulfil any deep purpose, although Eliot has spoken of his becoming accustomed to the habit of searching in these light verses for profundities that were certainly not part of the poem's design. When Eliot is not looking at the world with a moralist's concern he is inclined to adopt an attitude of ironical observation, which is basically a means of escape. It is this manner that he describes a Boston evening,

> *Wakening the appetites of life in some*
> *And to others bringing 'The Boston Evening Transcript'.*

This deflationary wit is that of Pope, and here it is indulged in purely for its own sake. It is when his mind turns from the ultra-civilised New England society to the jarring contrast between the past and the present of Europe that he begins to use his wit, practised in these early poems, as a more highly organised constituent of his poetry. Fundamentally, the connexion between Pope and Eliot on this issue is a matter not at all of verbal reminiscence, but of similarity of outlook. A similarity that can be best distinguished in certain of Eliot's early poems, which are not disturbed by the moral issues that later became his concern. Even in the later poems, when his wit has a different emphasis, it remains a descendant of Augustan satirical bias.

Finally may be mentioned Eliot's preoccupation with the formal problems of poetry, his desire for verbal precision. This precision demands conscious choice and experiment rather than a transcription of subconscious dictation. Its ideal is phrasing

> *where every word is at home*
> *Taking its place to support the others,*
> *The word neither diffident nor ostentatious,*
> *An easy commerce of the old and new,*
> *The common word exact without vulgarity*
> *The formal word precise but not pedantic*
> *The complete consort dancing together.*
>
> (*Little Gidding: Four Quartets*, pp. 42–43.)

The emphasis is on exactness and precision which must not give the impression of stiffness. It is the same idea as Pope's,

> *True ease in writing comes from art, not chance*
> *As those move easiest who have learned to dance,*

which employs the same image. The chief difference is that Eliot envisages a wider field of choice, for he admits 'the common word'. This is inevitable in view of his belief that poetry in his time demanded a closer connexion with popular speech than had existed in the late nineteenth and early twentieth centuries.

The first version of the second section of 'Ash Wednesday' affords an illustration of the way in which his search for precision makes for clarity by limiting suggestiveness. On its first publication as 'Salutation' (in the *Saturday Review of Literature*, 10th December, 1927, and *Criterion*, January, 1928), the text differed slightly from that in the collected poems. The thirty-first line of the final text, describing the Rose, reads

> *Exhausted and life-giving,*

whereas the early version is

> *Spattered and worshipped.*

As the Rose is a symbol used by Dante for Mary—

> *Here is the Rose,*
> *Wherein the Word Divine was made incarnate;—*
>
> (*Paradise*, Canto xxiii, lines 70–71: Cary's translation.)

44

we may conclude that this is its significance here. 'Exhausted and life-giving' must be considered in conjunction with the line, 'Calm and distressed': despite Mary's despair over the sins of man, she continues to offer hope and life to mankind. This idea does not bear collation with the line in the early version of the poem, which jars with the other descriptions of the Rose. The change is undeniably an improvement. Some lines further on in the early form of the poem, the words, 'with worm-eaten petals' are inserted between the lines

> The single Rose
> Is now the Garden.

This description alludes to the failings of the church on earth, which is now equated with the Rose. Such an extension of symbolism destroys the success of the first significance, and the line is deleted in the final version, to limit the suggestion to the Virgin.

Duncan Jones is probably correct in seeing the Rose as suggestive also of Christ, the Rose of Sharon, and of the blessed souls in Paradise, whom Dante describes in these lines:

> In fashion, as a snow-white rose, lay then
> Before my view the saintly multitude.
> (*Ibid.*, Canto xxxi, ll. 1-2.)

It is more difficult to agree with him when he says that the line 'may well have been left out because it limited the suggestions of the Rose' (Rajan: 'An Essay on "Ash Wednesday"' by E. E. Duncan Jones, p. 47). Surely the primary rose symbol refers exclusively to the blessedness and to the power to bless of spiritual beings. The line is omitted because it obscures this precision by relating the Rose to an object which has its existence on earth. Primarily the gain is in precision, brought about by careful selection and sifting. Similarly the omission of,

> For the end of remembering
> End of forgetting

which appears in the early version, eliminates an unnecessary repetition of,

> Rose of memory
> Rose of forgetfulness,

lines 29–30 in the final text. The same search for precision and consistency can be seen in the gradual moulding of 'The Hollow Men', which will be examined later.

These changes evidence an intellectual rather than an instinctive emotional approach to the construction of a poem's form. To this construction goes experiment based on deliberated analysis of what the poem has to communicate, and of the relationship between its parts necessary to form the whole which will communicate most precisely the meaning. Only repeated trial can produce the exact concatenation which will form a unity. That is, form and content are to be fused by the shaping spirit of the intellect, as well as of the imagination.

The structure of modern classical poetry is analogous to that of the eighteenth century. Each accepts an existing poetic framework, the rules of an objective authority, and makes a conscious effort to work within that framework. Satirical wit plays an important part in both, and with it goes a concern for the necessity of cultivating precision of form and word. This requires an intellectual rather than an emotional, instinctive approach to the task of selecting words, of relating them to each other and to the whole. Yet each of these similarities involves also a difference. The system to which Eliot relates his poetry has a greater scope than Augustan classical authority, and it becomes a more vital part of the poetry which depends on it. By its relationship with Eliot's poetry the traditional system acquires new significances, and becomes a living part of the poetic experiences transcribed in the poetry. Not only does tradition clarify the relation between symbol and object, reduce the need for elaboration, and add a dimension to the poem but it is itself altered by the relationship and so shown to be a vital force. This is a more intimate contact than existed between the eighteenth-century classicism and Greco-Roman literature, and it is a contact which can be common to all poets without inevitably resulting in uniformity.

The distinctive contribution of Eliot's theory is its insistence that twentieth century poetry did not appreciate the value of authority at a time when authority was most needed. Perhaps of equal importance is its assessment of the function of poetry, which had at various times been looked on as a legislative body and a religious institution. To replace these and similarly limiting conceptions Eliot offers the notion of the poet as an artist whose primary function is to maintain the pattern of tradition, within which is sufficient variety to offer a stable starting-point for any poetic creation. This notion does not spring from a desire to defend the existence of poetry—as the others seem to—but sees the function of poetry as the maintaining and re-designing of the historical artistic pattern. That is, it defines the function of poetry in terms which are within the acknowledged province of poetry. The only objection which can be brought against it is that it assumes without proof that art has a value in itself, which the other theories seemed to deny, if we can depend on the sincerity of their attempts to justify art by proving that it is something else.

The poet is 'involved with past and future'. With the future because he is assuring the continuance of tradition, and therefore of art; with the past because he must do this by exploring the past to discover a basis for his experimenting. His experiments will be an adaptation of what has preceded him, while remaining essentially the same. His search is to discover again what has been found before, and to adapt this to contemporary needs. His exploration depends on the working of his mind on the past, and as this exploration proceeds it will form a new mind and a new personality. The journey will end where it began, in the mind. But it will be now a mind whose structure is better understood—

> *We shall not cease from exploration*
> *And the end of all our exploring*
> *Will be to arrive where we started*
> *And know the place for the first time.*
> (*Little Gidding: Four Quartets*, p. 43.)

Chapter Three

Symbolism and the Unified Sensibility

THE Augustans helped Eliot to formulate his traditionalism. With their temperament and their attitude to the problem of writing poetry he has much in common. Those characteristics of his verse experiments which excited the most voluble early comment derive, however, from two schools widely separated from the Augustans: the Jacobeans and the French symbolists. The Jacobeans lived in a time which seemed in many ways to parallel our own; the French symbolists were the first to show any awareness of the poetry of the city. Both expressed their sensibility in methods having a great deal in common, and both were innovators in reintroducing to poetry the colloquial idiom.

It was Eliot in his essay on the metaphysical poets who first commented on the similarities between the English metaphysical and the French symbolist poets. And it is in *Prufrock and Other Observations* that the methods of these two schools are amalgamated, adapted and extended. The first simile in 'The Love Song of Alfred Prufrock'—

> Let us go then, you and I,
> When the evening is spread out against the sky
> Like a patient etherised upon a table;—

is a metaphysical conceit, an intellectual or 'wit' image, elaborated later in the poem:

> *And the afternoon, the evening, sleeps so peacefully!*
> *Smoothed by long fingers,*
> *Asleep . . . tired . . . or it malingers,*
> *Stretched on the floor, here beside you and me.*

These lines suggest that there is a kinship between Prufrock and the evening—peaceful, but artificially peaceful, and with an undertone of unhealthiness and unease—suggest even that the two are to be identified. This notion is intensified when the following lines from *East Coker* are considered. They reveal much of the significance that the idea holds for Eliot:

> *And you see behind every face the mental emptiness deepen*
> *Leaving only the growing terror of nothing to think about;*
> *Or when, under ether, the mind is conscious but conscious of nothing—*

Prufrock and the evening are 'conscious but conscious of nothing', and Prufrock certainly, rapt in a monotonous routine, pondering his 'overwhelming question', which if it exists at all in any coherent shape will certainly, we feel, never be asked, must experience the 'terror of nothing to think about'. All this is involved in the first simile and in its relations to the rest of the poem. It is not altogether successful, for synthesis fails to result from the yoking together of the disparate ideas—we can see the relationship between the evening and Prufrock, who *is* the etherised patient, but are not convinced that this is sufficient to justify their being linked so violently together. There is a similar failure in this line from another poem—

> *He laughed like an irresponsible foetus.*
>
> (*Collected Poems*, p. 31.)

Better is the comparison, in 'Prufrock', of the material 'streets', to the abstract 'arguments', for here the similarity is sufficient to suggest immediately the nature of the material. These images fall under both Johnson's definition of metaphysical wit—' a combination of dissimilar images, or discovery of occult resemblances in things apparently unlike'—and Edmund Wilson's analysis of symbolist technique—'The medley of images; the deliberately mixed metaphors; the combination of the grand and prosaic manners; the bold amalgamation of material with spiritual.'

More particularly may be mentioned the similarity in atmosphere between 'Prufrock' and these lines of Laforgue:

> *Ah! que la vie est quotidienne.*
and > *Tâchons de vivre monotone.*

There is the same preoccupation with trivial routine,

> *I have measured out my life with coffee spoons;*[1]

the same desire to escape from any spiritual experience of a higher order than monotony—

> *I should have been a pair of ragged claws*
> *Scuttling across the floors of silent seas.*

the same delicately ironic expression. Prufrock, wandering by the sea and thinking of trivialities—'Do I dare to eat a peach?'—is aware that the mermaids will not sing to him, yet there is none of the desire implied in Donne's,

> *Teach me to hear mermaids singing,*

to which Eliot's lines seem to allude.

'Prufrock' begins with a highly selective piece of scene-setting, in which is established the character of the surroundings and incidentally of Prufrock. As there is an identity between Prufrock and the evening, so there is between him and 'the restless nights in one-night cheap hotels', the 'streets that follow like a tedious argument'. Each is unstable, shifting. We learn that Prufrock is undecided and vaguely troubled:

> *And indeed there will be time*
> *To wonder, 'Do I dare?' and 'Do I dare?'*
>
> .   .   .   .
>
> *Do I dare*
> *Disturb the universe?*
> *In a minute there is time*
> *For decisions and revisions which a minute will reverse.*

1. A line such as this, with its swift transition from the grandiose 'I have measured out my life . . .' to the bathos of the finished statement, mingles 'the grand and prosaic manners', as Verlaine did in 'Le Faune', where the phrase,

> .   .   .   *cette heure dont la fuite*
> *Tournoie . . .*

is completed by, 'au son des tambourins.'

The feeling of these lines is intensified if, as seems possible, we are meant to recall Ford's,

> *Yet still a rumour of some novel fancy*
> *Untasted or untried, puts off the minute*
> *Of resolution, which should bid farewell*
> *To a vain world of weariness and sorrows. . . .*

If this is intended it is particularly interesting as showing Eliot's belief in the necessity of suffering, a bidding farewell to the 'novel fancies', of death even, as the essential precursor of spiritual rebirth. But this may be no more than the tendency that afflicts all of us in reading this allusive poetry, to see allusions that were not intended. In any case the aptness of Ford's lines is indisputable, and that they are among those that have impressed Eliot is shown by his quoting them in his essay on Ford: *Selected Essays*, p. 195.

Eliot's conception of Prufrock's attitude to these 'novel fancies' is perhaps best revealed by some consideration of the nature of Prufrock's 'overwhelming question'. It is justifiable to think of it as being the same as the question asked in *The Waste Land*: (*Collected Poems*, p. 66).

> *What shall we ever do?*

with its answer which answers nothing:

> *. . . The hot water at ten.*
> *And if it rains, a closed car at four.*

This answer pointedly avoids anything of true significance that is implied in the question: and so it is that Prufrock and the others accept boredom—it is from fear that worse may ensue from an attempt to probe too deeply.

This next re-expression of Prufrock's enervated indecision is again allusive, to create a contrast, as with the oblique reference to Donne:

> *Would it have been worth while,*
> *To have bitten off the matter with a smile,*
> *To have squeezed the universe into a ball*
> *To roll it toward some overwhelming question,*

The allusion is to Marvell's

> *Let us roll all our strength and all*
> *Our sweetness up into one ball,*
> *And tear our pleasures with rough strife,*
> *Thorough the iron gates of life.*

('Coy Mistress.')

The contrasted philosophy, as well as the similarity of the formal pattern, needs no emphasis. Prufrock never reaches a decision, never penetrates beyond 'the cups, the marmalade, the tea', to a conclusion either with the ladies in the poem or with his surroundings. The poem ends with a reiteration of the desire to escape to 'the chambers of the sea', beyond the complexities and troubles that may possibly be raised by human associations. Prufrock does not see in the water symbol the significance so often given it elsewhere in the poetry. For him it is only a sufficiently remote place of escape.

Prufrock typifies all the characters in Eliot's first volume of poems. He is essentially the same as Aunt Helen, who achieved significance only with death, as the readers of *The Boston Evening Transcript*, as Miss Nancy Ellicott with her futile modernity, as the 'damp souls of housemaids'. Exception has been taken to this last phrase for no very good reason. Although Eliot does not say so directly one is surely left with the impression that Prufrock and the lady in 'Portrait of a Lady' are equally afflicted with soul-dampness. Eliot is very far from attributing this exclusively to housemaids as a class: but they share in the universal condemnation. Only Mr. Apollinax, 'the resourceful man' as we are told in the epigraph, is free from the taint. He is reminiscent of 'Priapus in the shrubbery', god of the fertility cults, and is associated also with the life-giving water—

> *His laughter was submarine and profound*
> *Like the old man of the sea's*
> *Hidden under coral islands.*

Here the significance given generally to the water symbol in Eliot's poetry is elucidated by its being associated with fertility in the person of Mr. Apollinax.

The poem is concerned with the impact on the ultra-refined

52

society of Professor and Mrs. Channing-Cheetah of someone possessing vitality, whose talk still retains passion—a quality lacking in Eliot's other characters. He is remembered as rich in significant associations, while his hosts remain in the memory only as,

> . . . a slice of lemon and a bitten macaroon.

Eliot tends to draw out of an image all the suggestion possible, and this rapid association of ideas is well illustrated in 'Mr. Apollinax':

> I looked for the head of Mr. Apollinax rolling under a chair
> Or grinning over a screen
> With seaweed in its hair.

It is by the association of Apollinax with 'the worried bodies of drowned men', tugged by ocean currents, that this image is aroused. Its connection with the previous lines, though not overtly stated, is implicit, and this swift elaboration of the initial idea is equally a characteristic of metaphysical poetry.

Of the same nature as 'Prufrock' is 'Portrait of a Lady', which communicates the same 'slight sensation of being ill at ease'. It resembles, too, Ezra Pound's 'Portrait d'une Femme.' Pound's

> And bright ships left you this or that in fee.
> Ideas, old gossip, oddments of all things,
> Strange spars of knowledge and dimmed wares of price.
> Great minds have sought you—lacking someone else.
> You have been second always. Tragical?
> No. . . .

may be collated with the description of the 'bric-à-brac' in the lady's room in Eliot's poem, with her commonplace thoughts—

> Yet with these April Sunsets, that somehow recall
> My buried life and Paris in the Spring,

which impress as being no more than

> . . . things that other people have desired.
> (Collected Poems, p. 18.)

And also with Prufrock's denial of tragedy—

> No! I am not Prince Hamlet, nor was meant to be;
> Am an attendant lord. . . .

All these are poems of a society concerned exclusively with trivial refinement, second-hand experience and complete spiritual inaction, although Pound does not reject the worth of his material.

In both 'Prufrock' and the 'Portrait' Eliot stresses the same social characteristics. In 'Prufrock'—

> *There will be time, there will be time*
> *To prepare a face to meet the faces that you meet;—*

and in the other—

> *'I shall sit here serving tea to friends,'*
> *And I must borrow every changing shape*
> *To find expression . . . dance, dance*
> *Like a dancing bear,*
> *Cry like a parrot, chatter like an ape.*

In both it is the same trivial hypocrisy and dissimulation. Yet even in 'Portrait of a Lady' there is an advance, a glimpse of the way in which Eliot's moralising will lead him. 'The Love Song' portrays a man indecisive, incapable of the vigorous decision of Marvell, or the conscious effort of Donne. As yet, however, there is no hint of the most serious implications of such spiritual indifference. These lines do give such a hint:

> *Now that the lilacs are in bloom*
> *She has a bowl of lilacs in her room*
> *And twists one in her fingers while she talks.*
> *'Ah, my friend, you do not know, you do not know,*
> *What life is, you who hold it in your hands';*
> *(Slowly twisting the lilac stalks)*

Life, if it is lived as the lady and Prufrock live it will be destroyed by them as surely as the lilac stalks which are also in their hands. In the slow deliberation of the last line is the first hint of the death-in-life theme that is to occupy so much of Eliot's later poetry.

That the people of these early poems are in essence the same as the inhabitants of *The Waste Land* is shown by these lines from 'The Hollow Men':

> *Let me be no nearer*
> *In death's dream kingdom*
> *Let me also wear*
> *Such deliberate disguises*
> *Rat's coat, crowskin, . . .*

Again, the dissimulation, the suggestion by Eliot that the disguises adopted are animal-like. In this connexion we may recall a remark from Eliot's essay on Baudelaire: 'This means, I think, that Baudelaire has perceived that what distinguishes the relations of man and woman from the copulation of beasts is the knowledge of Good and Evil. . . .' In other words, without this perception, human beings are indistinguishable, spiritually, from animals,[1] and this is implied in the two poems already considered —particularly in 'Portrait of a Lady'. Primarily, however, they are preliminary sketches of the society of *The Waste Land*, without the full moral implications of the later poem.

Phrase repetitions in 'Portrait of a Lady'—and in 'Prufrock'— lend to the conversational rhythm a sense of the repetitive quality, the boredom, of the lady's life:

> *And how, how rare and strange it is, to find*
> *In a life composed so much, so much of odds and ends, . . .*
> *To find a friend who has these qualities,*

The same is found in her speech on page eighteen of the *Collected Poems*, beginning, 'I am always sure that you understand', and its last line re-occurs as she says goodbye towards the end of the poem. As well as sustaining the atmosphere this hesitant reiteration charges the conversational rhythm with a pattern that lifts it

1. The same idea is found in a later poem, 'Marina', in these lines:

> *Those*
> *Who suffer the ecstasy of animals, meaning*
> *Death.*

This poem, whose title directs our attention to the re-discovery theme in Shakespeare's *Pericles*, is concerned with spiritual rebirth. A contrast is implied between this play and Seneca's *Hercules*, from which the epigraph is taken, where the hero who has killed his children has suffered an irreparable loss, in that no re-discovery is possible. The influence of Baudelaire is discernable here too: . . . *let me*

> *Resign my life for this life, my speech for that unspoken,*
> *The awakened, lips parted, the hope, the new ships.*

The coupling of hope with the image of a ship recalls Baudelaire's making the ships in the harbour say, 'Quand partons-nous vers le bonheur?' As Eliot says in his essay on Baudelaire (*Selected Essays*, p. 390), this imagery has its origin in 'a dim recognition of the direction of beatitude'. The theme of Eliot's poem is greatly clarified by the knowledge that he is using the image of ships as Baudelaire did.

above exact reproduction of speech idiom. The device is taken from the work of the French poets—particularly Verlaine and Verhaeren. Two poems illustrate their use of the method, which is constant in Eliot's poetry. This quotation is from Verhaeren's, 'Le Vent':

> *L'avez-vous vu, le vent,*
> *Au carrefour des trois cents routes?*
> *L'avez-vous rencontré, le vent,*
> *Le vent des peurs et des déroutes,*
> *L'avez-vous vu, cette nuit là,*
> *Quand il jeta la lune à bas . . .*

The same characteristic is apparent in Verlaine's 'L'Amour par Terre':

> Le vent de l'autre nuit a jeté bas l'amour
> *Qui, dans le coin le plus mystérieux du parc,*
> *Souriait en bandant malignement son arc,*
> *Et dont l'aspect nous fit tant songer tout un jour!*
> Le vent de l'autre nuit l'a jeté bas! *Le marbre*
> *Au souffle du matin tournoie, épars.* C'est triste
> De voir le piédestal, *où le nom de l'artiste*
> *Se lit péniblement parmi l'ombre d'un arbre.*
> Oh! c'est triste de voir debout le Piédestal
> *Tout seul! Et des pensers mélancoliques vont*
> *Et viennent dans mon rêve où le chagrin profond*
> *Évoque un avenir solitaire et fatal.*
> Oh! c'est triste . . .

Eliot's adoption of this feature is not merely an uninspired stereotype of a device that happened to catch his fancy; he has adapted it to the different rhythm of his poetry, and integrated it with the poems' purposes. Its source is, however, in the work of these French poets, who have suggested so much else to him. The ending of 'Prufrock' as Edmund Wilson has pointed out, bears a marked resemblance, formally, to the conclusion of Laforgue's 'Légende':

> *Hier l'orchestre attaqua*
> *Sa dernière polka*
> *Oh! L'automne, l'automne!*
> *Les casinos*
> *Qu'on abandonne*
> *Remisent leurs pianos! . . .*

> *Phrases, verroteries,*
> *Caillots de souvenirs.*
> *Oh! comme elle est maigrie!*
> *Que vais-je devenir?*

> *Adieu! Les filles d'if dans les grisailles*
> *Ont l'air de pleureuses de funérailles*
> *Sous l'autan noir qui veut que tout s'en aille.*

The swift changes of tempo in Eliot's poetry can be traced, as
even this passage from Laforgue shows, to the metrical precedents
created by the French poets, as the frequently abrupt introductions
to his poems are based on the example of some of Donne's opening lines: they are the same in kind as Donne's, but without the
same vigour—as is of course suitable to Eliot's poetry.

Compare, for example, these opening lines: Donne's, 'For
God's sake hold your tongue and let me love,' and Eliot's, 'Let
us go then, you and I.' The relationship here is parallel to that
between Eliot's tempo changes and those of Corbière. In 'Burbank with a Baedeker', these lines,

> *The smoky candle end of time*

> *Declines. On the Rialto once.*
> *The rats are underneath the piles.*
> *The jew is underneath the lot.*
> *Money in furs. The boatman smiles,*

recall the staccato effect of Corbière's,

> *English spoken?—Espagnole? . . .*
> *Batignolle? . . .*
> *Arbore le pavillon*
> *Qui couvre ta marchandise.*
> *O marquise*
> *D'Amaégui! . . . Frétillon! . . .,*
>
> ('Après la Plui.')

although Eliot's effects are not so extreme.[1]

---

1. A closer parallel is that Eliot based his 'Mélange Adultère de Tout' on
Corbière's 'Épitaphe pour Jean . . . Corbière, Philosophe' (Subtitled, 'Épave
Mort-Né'), taking the title from the first line of Corbière's poem. It is interesting

Another aspect of French symbolist poetry is reproduced in Eliot's 'Rhapsody on a Windy Night', examined later in the chapter. The poems cited here illustrate its 'mode mineur', represented in Eliot's work most completely by 'Conversation Galante'. Its closest ancestor, apart from Verlaine's 'Colloque Sentimentale', is perhaps Laforgue's 'Autre Complainte de Lord Pierrot', also in the dialogue form, and with the same sophisticated weariness:—

> *Celle qui doit me mettre au courant de la Femme!*
> *Nous lui dirons d'abord, de mon air le moins froid:*
> *'La somme des angles d'un triangle, chère amie,*
>   *Est égale a deux droits'*
>
> *Et si ce cri lui part: 'Dieu de Dieu! que je t'aime!'*
> *—'Dieu reconnaîtra les siens.' Ou piquée au vif:*
> *—'Mes claviers ont du cœur, tu seras leur seul thème.'*
>   *Moi: 'Tout est relatif.'*
>
> *De tous ses yeux alors se sentant trop banal:*
> *'Ah! tu ne m'aimes pas; tant d'autres sont jaloux!'*
> *Et moi, d'un œil qui vers l'Inconscient s'emballe:*
>   *'Merci, pas mal; et vous?'*

It must be mentioned that Eliot's formal patterns owe a great deal to the Jacobean dramatists, as well as to the symbolist poets; there is in fact a combination of the two practices. The Jacobeans loosened the texture of the blank verse that had preceded them, and some of Eliot's poems reveal a further experimenting with a basic blank verse pattern—of which there is a suggestion in 'Prufrock' and 'Portrait of a Lady'. It contrasts with such syncopated rhyming lines as,

> *Oh, do not ask, 'What is it?'*
> *Let us go and make our visit.*

The regular pattern breaks down completely with lines as short as,

> *Do I dare,*

that in the French original is a playing with the meanings of life and death:—

> *Mort, mais pas guéri de la vie . . .*
> *Il mourut en s'attendant vivre*
> *Et vécut s'attendant mourir.*

and an interesting comment on Eliot's allusion to Marvell is that the last line of the four,

> *To roll it towards some overwhelming question,*

postpones the rhyme for the preceding line. All this enhances the effect of wandering indecision. A subtle use of the same deliberate disintegration occurs in 'Gerontion', where the regular structure dies away to the whining effect of:

> *. . . Vacant shuttles*
> *Weave the wind. I have no ghosts,*
> *An old man in a draughty house*
> *Under a windy knob.*

to be restored as, in a sudden access of energy, Gerontion tries to justify himself:

> *After such knowledge, what forgiveness? Think now*
> *History has many cunning passages, contrived corridors*
> *And issues . . .*

This alternation is sustained skillfully throughout the poem, and is an extension of the loosening apparent in the Jacobean blank verse.

This, then, is no mere playing with a pedantically exact reconstruction of traditional metres. The usage in each case is integrated with the need of the poem; symbolist technique is co-ordinated with an adaptation of the truncated blank verse of the Jacobeans to form a new structure. The passage in 'Prufrock' beginning, 'No! I am not Prince Hamlet . . .' reads like a parody—when what he says is considered—of the vigorous metre of this passage from 'Hamlet', Act V, Scene ii:

> *Sir, in my heart there was a kind of fighting*
> *That would not let me sleep . . .*
> *Up from my cabin,*
> *My sea-gown scarf'd about me, in the dark*
> *Grop'd I to find out them: had my desire:*
> *Finger'd their packet:*

And Prufrock's lines are followed immediately by the enervated,

> *I grow old . . . I grow old . . .*

This violent and deliberate contrast is purely in the symbolist tradition.

In the four 'Preludes', the Sweeney poems, and certain others among Eliot's early poems, can be discerned the background, the milieu, of *The Waste Land*. It owes much to Baudelaire, to Verlaine, and to the Jacobean dramatists. Firstly, Baudelaire, who 'gave new possibilities to poetry in a new stock of imagery of contemporary life . . . the use of imagery of the sordid life of a great metropolis, . . . the elevation of such imagery to the first intensity—presenting it as it is, and yet making it represent much more than itself' ('Baudelaire': *Selected Essays*, pp. 387–388). This description from 'Rhapsody on a Windy Night'—

> *Remark the cat which flattens itself in the gutter,*
> *Slips out its tongue*
> *And devours a morsel of rancid butter.—*

and,

> *The reminiscence comes*
> *Of sunless dry geraniums*
> *And dust in crevices. . . .*

recall Verlaine's

> *Toits qui dégouttent, murs suintants, pavé qui glisse,*
> *Bitume défoncé, ruisseaux comblant l'égout, . . .*

and the first two lines of the same poem ('La Bonne Chanson', xvi) with their reference to 'Les platanes déchus' lining the pavement. It is noteworthy that Verlaine and Eliot, seeking something peculiarly suggestive of the squalor of the modern city, seize the one on trees, the other on flowers, both reduced from freshness to the condition of their surroundings. Similarly Eliot's description:

> *Regard that woman*
> *Who hesitates towards you in the light of the door*
> *Which opens on her like a grin.*
> *You see the border of her dress*
> *Is torn and stained with sand,*
> *And you see the corner of her eye*
> *Twists like a crooked pin*

is akin to Baudelaire's,

> . . . *Monstres brisés, bossus*
> *Ou tordus.* . . .
> *Sous des jupons troués, et sous de froids tissus.*

This background of squalor is not, as MacNiece has suggested, a mere romantic décor. It is, as has been shown, intimately related to the people whom it surrounds. The fog, in 'Prufrock', in 'Portrait of a Lady', 'the brown waves of fog' in 'Morning at the Window'—predecessor of 'the brown fog of a winter dawn', 'the brown fog of a winter noon' in *The Waste Land*—is so consistent a feature in Eliot's scene that one is justified in seeing in it something more than décor. This dusk, of dawn and of noon, of morning and of afternoon, is the dusk of Dante's limbo with which Eliot equates the modern city. The passage of *The Waste Land* already examined suggests the way in which Eliot presents the setting as it is and yet makes it 'represent much more than itself'. The initial impulse comes from Baudelaire; its application is Eliot's alone.

Of the age of Donne and Webster Eliot has said, 'It seemed as if, at that time, the world was filled with broken fragments of systems', a description which applies equally to the chaos of the waste land, in which man knows only, ' a heap of broken images'. The relation between Eliot's poetry and Jacobean drama is that each has as its background a violent world, peopled by creatures unsure of their relations with each other, and with spiritual forces above them. Webster's is a world of doubt and uncertainty, symbolised by Julia's

> *I go, I know not whither,*

by Vittoria's,

> *My soul, like to a ship in a black storm,*
> *Is driven I know not whither.*

In the world of Prufrock is the same doubt, but of a different intensity; his time appears to him created

> . . *for a hundred indecisions*
> *And for a hundred visions and revisions.*

Similarly Gerontion is unsure of his spiritual bearings: he speaks
to 'Christ the Tiger'—

> *I that was near your heart was removed therefrom*
> *To lose beauty in terror, terror in inquisition.*

The bewilderment of Flamineo—

> *While we look up to Heaven we confound*
> *Knowledge with knowledge.—*

suggests the bewilderment expressed in these lines from *The
Waste Land:*

> *On Margate Sands*
> *I can connect*
> *Nothing with nothing.*

Despite these similarities there is a difference, a contrast implied
within the major parallelism. The characters of Webster's drama
are more aware of the existence of true spiritual experience than
are Prufrock and the others. Flamineo confounds 'knowledge with
knowledge', but it is the knowledge, the experience of the world,
with that of heaven: knowledge and experience of both is implied.
There is little such recognition in the inhabitants of Eliot's world.
It is to 'the number of half-alive, hungry for any form of spiritual
experience, or what offers itself as spiritual good or bad',[1] that
they belong.

The background of the Sweeney poems is a 'cavernous waste
shore', the sound of an epileptic's shriek, the plotting—in
'Sweeney Among the Nightingales'—of Rachael and 'the lady in
the cape' against 'the man with heavy eyes'. The atmosphere of
'Sweeney Agonistes' is best suggested by these lines at the close
of the play:

> *You dreamt you waked up at seven o'clock and it's foggy and it's damp*
> *and it's dawn and it's dark*
> *And you wait for a knock and the turning of a lock for you know the*
> *hangman's waiting for you*
> *And perhaps you're alive*
> *And perhaps you're dead*

1. *After Strange Gods*, p. 61

It is partly the unthinking violence of modern life that this play portrays—

> *Any man might do a girl in*
> *Any man has to, needs to, wants to*
> *Once in a lifetime, do a girl in.*
>
> *(Collected Poems, p. 130.)*

The importance of this aspect of the background of Eliot's poems has perhaps been minimised. It has more than a suggestion of the violence of the Jacobean drama. Eliot's own impressions of industrial civilisation combine with those of Baudelaire, Verlaine, Laforgue, while his background of indecision, incertitude and violence recalls that of 'the broken fragments and systems' in Jacobean drama. Impressions of the present are collated, compared and contrasted with a section of the past to form a vital part of his poetry. Symbolist technique is adapted to his purposes, and the work of individual symbolist poets helps to form his conception of the essentials of modern life. In these is the source of his atmosphere of boredom, futility and squalor, and his conception of the modern malady—the inability to be either damned or saved: '. . . damnation itself is an immediate form of salvation—of salvation from the ennui of modern life, because it at least gives some significance to living' ('Baudelaire,' in Eliot's *Selected Essays*). With this is compared the Jacobean drama, similar yet differing—equally violent but with significance implicit in its violence, being on the side of Good or of Evil and so leading to a life of meaning, because of either damnation or salvation.

From this examination of Eliot's poems we can make a tentative analysis of his method of communication. Certain characteristics can be grouped. The carefully selected juxtapositioning appears in various forms. The blending of vague descriptive phrases with words grammatically precise used in a vague sense—'restless *nights* in *one-night* cheap hotels', the eyes 'assured of *certain certainties*' in the Preludes suggesting that the certainties are in fact not clear-cut and assured. This contrast is the basis too of the metaphysical images, and of the placing together by allusion of Prufrock's ideas and those of Donne and Marvell. Nor is it entirely unrelated to the swift changing of scene and rapid progression of thought: in the passage from 'Mr. Apollinax' already examined, for example—or in this passage from 'Prufrock'—

63

I grow old . . . I grow old . . .
I shall wear the bottoms of my trousers rolled.

Shall I part my hair behind? Do I dare to eat a peach?
I shall wear white flannel trousers and walk upon the beach.
I have heard the mermaids singing each to each.

This suggestive juxtapositioning of past and present, of commonplace troubles with the singing of the mermaids, of ideas, phrases, and scenes, of the hinted sympathy for the lonely men in shirt sleeves with the desire to escape to the sea-floor—all these fuse to communicate to the reader Prufrock's dilemma, the utter impossibility of his ever solving it. It is by the same process that 'Portrait of a Lady' achieves its communication: repetition and analogy. 'An atmosphere of Juliet's tomb', '. . . a tobacco trance', 'My self-possession gutters; we are really in the dark'.

This music is successful with a 'dying fall'[1]
Now that we talk of dying—

Death, gloom, trance, a complete lack of vitality—the poem states little directly, but conveys exactly its atmosphere of futility and indecision. This is an adaptation of symbolist practice: Mallarmé communicated by allusion and suggested analogies. In one sonnet he considers the starry sky, looked on by many as showing man's nothingness. For him it is a phantom palace whose ebony and garlands are falsehoods. But he does not overtly compare the sky to a room so decorated. He simply describes such a room, 'conjuring up the splendid palace with its dead garlands'. (This example is taken from C. M. Bowra's, *The Heritage of Symbolism*, p. 10.)

1. Adapted in 'Prufrock' (written in Paris and Munich in 1911, one year after 'Portrait of a Lady') to,

I know the voices dying with a dying fall
Beneath the music from a farther room.

Also belonging to that year—and written in Paris—is 'Rhapsody on a Windy Night'. On the pervasive music, see Chapters One (i), and Four.

Eliot too communicates indirectly by means of metaphor and symbol, by a suggestive association of ideas. On the other hand his symbols and metaphors are not private and beyond the complete understanding of the outsider. His associations are with traditional literature and past eras, and it is by allusion to these that his symbolism is defined. Where Mallarmé was concerned with a very personal emotion or sensation, requiring its own special language and symbolism, Eliot tries to transmit an objective view of society, using an impersonal symbolism in order to accomplish this. Mallarmé, too, sought no contact between poetry and reality, and was perhaps over-scornful of the world of reality. Eliot has sustained better the correspondence between symbol and reality. Passages from past writings are taken as one symbol, the presentation of actuality as another. The value of the former is at times as a contrast, but more generally in its profounder significance, as showing the eternal needs of the spirit.

This juxtaposition of past and present is also Eliot's method of showing the temporary characteristics of the present time—which distinguish it from others—as part of a greater pattern, for it shows that they are in some degree related to what has gone before: it is not merely a valueless nostalgia for the glories of a non-existent past that motivates Eliot. Prufrock typifies a general state, not peculiar to himself but with an application to everyone —to the 'hypocrite lecteur', and to Eliot himself, as *The Waste Land* makes clear. This basic symbolism is reinforced by the other devices cited; the cumulative effect of the setting and its relations to the human beings, the contrast of words and ideas, the delicately phrased indecisions, repeated in their various manifestations. These achieve their full effect only when coupled with the allusions to the past. This is 'the conscious creation of the field of the present out of the past', of which Paul More speaks. (Quoted by T. S. Eliot: *The Sacred Wood*, p. 46.)

More in this than in 'Rhapsody on a Windy Night' can Eliot's debt to the symbolists be truly assessed. The latter is a conscious attempt to do in English what the symbolists had done in French —to mirror a mood by a selection of images which have in common subservience to that mood, and hence act as symbols for it. This symbolism—although equally subjective—is not of the same nature as the romantic symbolism considered in Chapter One.

Firstly, it is not its normal practice to select any one particular object as a symbol, but rather to bring together inter-related images of the kind described, which because of this act as symbols. Further, as with Eliot, it is by the very nature of this symbolism that communication is achieved, which is not generally so with romantic symbolism. It is for this reason that Eliot can accept a great deal of the French school's methods, while rejecting the romantic. These verses of Verlaine provide a good example of the technique:

> C'est l'extase langoureuse,
> C'est la fatigue amoureuse,
> C'est tous les frissons des bois
> Parmi l'étreinte des brises
> C'est, vers les ramures grises,
> Le chœur des petites voix.
> O le frêle et frais murmure
> Cela gazouille et susurre,
> Cela ressemble au cri doux
> Que l'herbe agitée expire . . .
> Tu dirais, sous l'eau qui vire,
> Le roulis sourd des cailloux.

('Romances sans Paroles'; *Ariettes Oubliées*, i.)

This is exactly what Eliot does in the Rhapsody. One can detect the connexion between these images in the third section—the twisted branch, 'eaten smooth and polished', the world's skeleton, the broken spring that is 'hard and curled'. In the following section these also are associated within the mood—the child's eye, with nothing behind it, the prying eyes behind the shutters, the prying crab in its pool. These lead naturally to the next section, in which the moon is described as winking 'a feeble eye', as having lost its memory and therefore as being also vacant. All these are summoned up by the dominant mood, and at once symbolise the mood and are fused into unity by being linked within and because of the mood.[1]

1. Strictly speaking, the poem does not 'mean' anything: it is purely the translation of a mood. A useful comment on it is made by Charles Williams (*Poetry at Present*: essay on T. S. Eliot, p. 163). 'It is a moonlit poem—but a modern moonlit poem, with all that those words connote. It would be unfair to say that what those words connote is Hell, but not entirely unfair.'

Similarly with 'La Figlia che Piange', which is vividly reminiscent of certain sections of Verlaine's 'La Bonne Chanson'. It is a lyric, set against a formal background, with a strong hint of the atmosphere of these verses:

> *En robe grise et verte avec des ruches,*
> *Un jour de juin que j'étais soucieux,*
> *Elle apparut souriante à mes yeux. . . .*
> ('La Bonne Chanson', iii.)
> *Et qu'il vous suffirait d'un geste,*
> *D'une parole ou d'un clin d'œil,*
> *Pour mettre tout mon être en deuil*
> *De son illusion céleste.*   (Ibid., xv.)
> *Pour ce portrait, son goût infaillible a choisi*
> *La pose la plus simple et la meilleure aussi:*   (Ibid., ix.)

The poetic stimulant is in each case a gesture observed by chance, in each is the same posing of the subject. The ending of Eliot's poem, briefly ironical, recalls—

> *Et la nuit seule entendit leurs paroles,*

the ending of Verlaine's 'Colloque Sentimentale', itself reminiscent of 'Conversation Galante'. But these parallels do not indicate the true nature of his debt to the symbolists. They do show that such a debt exists, but reveal nothing of the way in which Eliot, while adopting the symbolist method of communication, has endowed it with objectivity without destroying its delicacy.

The technique and the ideas of Eliot, combining the symbolist and Jacobean traditions, were a potent factor in abstracting his poetry from the failing romantic tradition. Such poetry demands close reading, extreme concentration, to enable the reader to follow its progression, and the significance of its methods. This was enough to remove it beyond the comprehension of a public nurtured by the soothing escapism of the Georgians, and to subject the poet to a discipline of combining and selecting that had for too long been absent from English poetry. It is mainly this that makes his poetry esoteric and obscure, and yet it is the only method that could satisfactorily contain the expression of what concerned Eliot: the mirroring of a complex and decadent civilisation that had abandoned the choice between two moral attitudes—for Good or for Evil—for preoccupation with a soul-killing monotony of meaningless routine.

In Eliot's return to these two traditions is the source of the method of his esoteric devices. It has still to be seen why such methods should have for him such a strong appeal. Partly it is for the reasons discussed in the first chapter. On the other hand they do not explain why it should be to these particular methods—the conceit, for example—that he turns. That is a matter of his intellectual and emotional predilections, and in order to formulate these, the following section examines his desire to rehabilitate in the poetic sensibility a quality lacking in all the Georgian and most of the earlier romantic verse. It is a quality making for cohesion in the various kinds of poetic experience, and becomes in Eliot's verse subtly allied to his traditionalism as well as to his esotericism. By it he is led to the influence of yet another poetic tradition and frame of mind: that of Dante.

(ii)

'It happened that at Dante's time thought was orderly and strong and beautiful . . .' ('Shakespeare and the Stoicism of Seneca': *Selected Essays*, p. 136). This remark formulates the distinction made by Eliot between Dante's mind, his poetry, and the mind and poetry of today. The coherent body of thought—the thought of St. Thomas—that formed Dante's background enabled him to regularise his experiences, to see them as something more than unrelated occurrences. It is with one particular aspect of this ability—peculiar to a certain kind of poetry—that we are here concerned. Dante's sonnets make 'brave attempts to fabricate something permanent and holy out of his personal animal feelings'[1] (ibid., p. 137), and with this we come closer to the characteristic to be isolated. In the 'animal feelings' Dante saw a spiritual significance, a relationship with a plane of being other

1. Or as Herbert Read expresses it in *Reason and Romanticism* (p. 45); 'Dante and Guido Cavalcanti . . . in perfect seriousness identified their love of women and their love of philosophy; and in singing of their love of women made an allegory that expressed their love of philosophy, . . . all experience whether intellectual or sensual or instinctive was regarded as equally and contemporaneously the subject matter of their poetry. The result was a desirable continuity or coherence. . . .'

than that on which they were experienced. Not only did he see that different levels of perception were united, but he translated into poetry his homogeneous receptivity. Particularly this affected the part played by thought in his poetry, for he experienced it as forcibly as he did any sensuous happening. Rather than elaborating a thinking process Dante resolved into sensuous imagery the impact of thought on his sensibility, for its effect was analogous to that of any other mode of experience: the one can be transcribed in terms of the other.

Because 'a good metaphor implies the intuitive perception of the similarity in dissimilars', it is in imagery that the unification of sensibility finds expression. Imagery transcribes one experience in terms of another. It reveals, for instance, the similarity between two visual, or between two aural experiences.

> The barge she sat in, like a burnish'd throne,
> Burn'd on the water;
>
> (Anthony and Cleopatra.)

or
> A shout from the whole multitude arose,
> That lingered in the air like dying rows
> Of abrupt thunder . . .
>
> (Endymion.)

But to go further than this is to limit the function of imagery. In the work of the French symbolist poets there is apparent a more complex desire to express one sense-perception in terms of another: an aural experience in visual terms. Thus we find Verlaine writing of 'le contour subtil des voix anciennes', or of 'les lueurs musiciennes' (Ariettes Oubliées, 11). In a tradition yet earlier we find Keats writing,

> In neighbourhood of fountains (by the noise
> Soft-showering in my ears), and, (by the touch
> Of scent), not far from roses . . .

These examples indicate that it is dangerous to fix limits to the range of imagery, beyond Aristotle's generalisation. So when the poet experiences thought with the impact of the sensuously perceived, his impulse is to communicate this in sensuous terms. Only in these terms, those closest to the experience of the normal mind, can its immediacy be suggested.[1] Exactly what kind of imagery is thereby produced must be considered. It is the defining characteristic of metaphysical poetry—though not entirely limited to the 'metaphysical poets'—and appears also in Dante. This is not to say that some poets think and others do not. It is rather a distinction between two different apprehensions of thought. Dante and the others had the quality 'of sensuous thought, or of thinking through the senses, or of the senses thinking, of which the exact formula remains to be defined' (*The Sacred Wood*, p. 23).

In numerous essays Eliot has made the attempt at definition: 'Tennyson and Browning are poets and they think; but they do not feel their thought as immediately as the odour of a rose. A thought to Donne was an experience: it modified his sensibility. When the poet's mind is perfectly equipped for its work it is constantly amalgamating disparate experience . . . in the mind of the poet these experiences are always forming new wholes' (T. S. Eliot: 'The Metaphysical Poets'). Remembering this judgment it is surprising to find Matthiessen saying, 'His (Donne's) probing analytic mind was keenly aware of the complexity of things. . . . The jagged brokenness of Donne's thought struck a responsive chord in our own age. . . . Eliot's own early enthusiasm for this element in Donne is now considerably modified in view of his own growing desire for order and coherence.' Desire for order and coherence is in no degree a new growth in Eliot's poetry. It has been his constant desire, too, to object to 'the simplification and separation of our mental faculties' (Matthiessen, p. 10: *The Achievement of T. S. Eliot*). The quotation from 'The Metaphysical Poets' shows that Eliot ascribes to Donne the ability to 'amalgamate disparate experiences', to escape the abstraction of thought from experience.[2] It is this that is the primary attraction

---

1. Obviously, simile and metaphor by their very nature provide the most effective method of showing that an intellectual experience can be related to the same values as any other. Being realisable in poetry in the same terms all experiences are seen as belonging to a coherent system of apprehension. This mingling in imagery of abstract and visual is illustrated in Shakespeare's powerful lines on Antony:

> his delights
> Were dolphin-like; they showed his back above
> The element they liv'd in. . . .

2. It was Dante's fortune to live at a time when such an amalgamation was

of Donne for Eliot. In his essay he goes on to say that 'in the seventeenth century a dissociation of sensibility set in from which we have never recovered'. From that period there has been no poetry so well equipped to show the unity in all experience, that all the impacts of the outer world can be brought within the limits of a coherent system.

The essence of this quality is the ability to feel thought, to experience it as just as much reality as 'the noise of the typewriter, or the smell of cooking'. For unless thought is so experienced, and so expressed in poetry, the attempt to reveal unity must fail. Here we have the explanation of Donne's attempts to fuse material with spiritual, to see similarities where apparently none existed:

> *My face in thine eye, thine in mine appears,*
> *And true plain hearts do in the faces rest;*
> *Where can we find two better hemispheres*
> *Without sharp north, without declining west?*

or

> *Whoever comes to shroud me, do not harm,*
> *Nor question much,*
> *That subtle wreath of hair, which crowns my arm;*
> *The mystery, the sign thou must not touch;*
> *For 'tis my outward soul . . .*

Donne worked quite deliberately and consciously towards this end; with Dante there is not so great a self-conscious basis. Perhaps for the very reason that they saw all belief and coherence crumble around them, the metaphysical poets offer the most sustained illustration of deliberately sought unification of sensibility. Perhaps, too, it is for this reason that their images often fail to convince, while Dante's always succeed. Dante's mind was genuinely affected in this way, while Donne and the others merely sought such a mind.

This is the fundamental reason, too, for Eliot's use of the conceit—to blend into unity experiences having no obvious connexion. To demonstrate, for example, that a connexion does exist between a certain kind of street—which is an experience—

made easier by the immediate presence of a generally accepted system of thought. Such uniformity is more sympathetic to the quality under discussion than an age of innumerable and often unsettled and enervated beliefs.

and a certain kind of thought—which is also an experience, and one communicating itself to the sensibility as immediately and as forcibly as does the street. This, from Cowley's 'Anacreon', is a similar attempt:

> Love was with thy life entwined
> Close as heat with fire is joined.

These images give some idea of the way in which thought thus experienced is to be expressed in poetry.

Cowley's metaphor suggests Dante's image of the 'simple flame', in this passage:

> Within its depths I saw ingathered, bound by love in one mass, the scattered leaves of the universe: substance and accidents and their relations, as though together fused, so that what I speak of is one simple flame.

> (*Paradise*, canto 33, ll. 80–85 Translated by Eliot in
> his Essay on Dante, *Selected Essays*, p. 267.)

Here the spiritual, the apprehended thought, is expressed in terms of the material; as Eliot points out, in a visual image—the simple flame. Thus the identity between thought and material reality is sustained. Another passage from Dante that employs exactly the same system is this:

> From the hands of him who loves her before she is there issues like a simple child that plays, with weeping and laughter, the simple soul, that knows nothing except that, come from the hands of a glad creator she turns willingly to everything that delights her. First she tastes the flavour of a trifling good; then is beguiled, and pursues it, if neither guide nor check withhold her. Therefore laws were needed as a curb.

> (*Purgatory*, 18, 86.)

The initial image couples material with spiritual, and it is of course to this passage that the first line of 'Animula' alludes:

> Issues from the hand of God, the simple soul.

The parallel between the two sections of Eliot's poem and the passage from Dante is evident. The world of the child, which concerns Eliot in the first part of the poem, is a world that has in a way order and coherence, for each experience, material or ideal, is equally felt. The child 'Confounds the actual and the fanciful,' and for it 'what the fairies' do has as much reality as 'what the servants say'. The simple soul that issues from the hand of time, however, has lost this unity and reached disorder. Guideless, confused by complexity and division—'the imperatives of "is" and "seems" '—it leaves behind

> . . . *disordered papers in a dusty room.*

This poem has affinities also with the work of Baudelaire. With this portrayal of the child's world:

> *Pour l'enfant, amoureux de cartes et d'estampes,*
> *L'univers est égal à son vaste appétit.*
> *Ah, que le monde est grand à la clarté des lampes!*
> *Aux yeux de souvenir que le monde est petit!*

The philosophical doctrine, of felt thought, and of the child's sensitivity that encourages it, concerns Baudelaire in this passage from 'Le Peintre de la Vie moderne':

> . . . *j'affirme que l'inspiration a quelque rapport avec le congestion, et que toute pensée sublime est accompagnée d'une secousse nerveuse, plus ou moins forte, qui retentit jusque dans le cervelet.*

It is this effect which produces in poetry a unification of sensibility, and it is the mind of the child that is sensitive enough to be equally affected by material and ideal experiences. Baudelaire continues:

> *L'homme de génie a les nerfs solides; l'enfant les a faibles. Chez l'un, la raison a pris une place considérable; chez l'autre, la sensibilité occupe presque tout l'être. Mais la génie n'est que l'enfance douée maintenant, pour s'exprimer, d'organes virils et de l'esprit analytique qui lui permet d'ordonner la somme de matériaux involontairement amassée.*

(Baudelaire; *Œuvres*, ed. Y-G Le Dantec, Vol. 2, p. 331.)

Here then, we have an exposition both of the nature of 'Felt thought' and of the results that it should produce in poetry. The poet, experiencing the creations of the mind with as great an immediacy, as great an impact, as he does material happenings—in the manner of a child—must in his poetry integrate the two kinds of experience in the way here suggested. Attempts at a unification of sensibility appear in Eliot's poetry in various forms, of which some have been mentioned. Its most elaborate manifestation is in 'Whispers of Immortality', a poem that would seem to owe its initiation to Donne's.

> *When my grave is broke up again*
> *Some second guest to entertain,*
> *—For graves have learn'd that woman-head,*
> *To be to more than one a-bed—*
> *And he that digs it, spies*
> *A bracelet of bright hair about the bone* . . .

'Whispers of Immortality' is not purely a protest against sexual vice, against an outlook which sees nothing beyond the 'pneumatic bliss' promised by Grishkin's charms.ᵛ That the poem is divided into two sections, each of four verses, suggests immediately that its basis is either a contrast or a parallelism. This is in fact so. The first verse is concerned with Webster's perception of the bone beneath the 'bracelet of bright hair'—Donne's line immediately suggests itself.[1] Implied in this is the immediacy of Grishkin's inevitable identification with the 'breastless creatures underground'. Parallelisms between the descriptions of physical characteristics in these two verses need no emphasis:

(a)   . . . *the skull beneath the skin;*
(b)   . . . *her Russian eye*
             Is underlined for emphasis;

(a)   . . . *breastless creatures under ground*
(b)   *Uncorseted, her friendly bust*
             Gives promise of pneumatic bliss.

Both sections are an elaboration of the ideas in their first verse. In the first section Webster's perception of death is symbolised by his seeing beneath the flesh to the skeleton, whose bones

---

1. A reiterated idea in Eliot's poetry. See the lines in a minor poem, 'Lines to a Duck in the Park':

> . . . *soon the enquiring worm shall try*
> *Our well-preserved complacency,*

adapted from the lines in Marvell's 'Coy Mistress':

> . . . *then worms shall try*
> *That long-preserved virginity* . . .

endure longer than the flesh that covered them. And around these bones clings thought, more lasting than either, associated with the less ephemeral of the two. Donne, whose similarity to Webster is now pointed out, suffered not the torments of the flesh but

> *. . . the anguish of the marrow*
> *The ague of the skeleton;*

Taken in conjunction with the preceding this can mean only that Donne and Webster felt intensely the effects of thought, and suffered spiritual anguish from their incertitude. They were, that is, concerned with matters more significant and more enduring than any that could arise from preoccupation with the purely material side of carnal attractions. The section devoted to Grishkin associates her entirely with experiences of the senses: 'subtle effluence of cat', 'A feline smell'.

Apparently, then, the poem contrasts the exclusively carnal, sensual, existence of Grishkin with the more intense mental existence of Donne and Webster. Yet there is not so complete a divorce between the two sections as this would suggest: there is also a parallel. The peculiar nature of the imagery in the first section is suggestive. Thought is described as

> *Tightening its lusts and luxuries.*

Donne experiences 'the fever of the bone , which is identified with thought. The experience of thought, that is, is described in sensuous terms just as much as is the sexual experience of Grishkin. Far from there being a complete dissociation of the differing experiences described in the two sections, it is in fact implied that they are in a way of the same nature, because experienced in the same way. The experience of thought is described in sensuous terms because it can be as immediately and as keenly apprehended as carnal experience. It is treated as physical reality, as being able to produce similar effects on the sensibility. The important point, implied in the imagery, is that thought is described as being felt just as material reality is felt. This is the real issue of the poem, and the manner of presentation—contrast between the affairs of the mind and those of the body—is chosen as the most effective of emphasising the similarity, because the effect must be startling and convincing in proportion to the apparent initial dissimilarity of the two subjects. This is one of Eliot's most successful poems, and by its success emphasises the insufficiency of the evening-patient, and of the foetus-laughter rapprochement.[1]

The outlook that seeks a unification of sensibility has further implications not so apparent in the work of the English poets as it is in Dante. 'The poet was inspired with an overmastering desire to link the present with the past and with the future, to blend all knowledge into one coherent system, and to bring the experiences of life into one harmonious whole.' (William W. Jackson, D.D., Introduction to his translation of the *Convivio*, p. 18).[2] The desire to link past, present, and future finds expression in some moderns too. Claudel, the French Catholic poet, 'mingles Christian images with pagan invocations, Latin names with biblicial names, and lends automatic rifles to the hordes of a European Attila. His reason is that the past remains ever-living in the present. . . . Among all the moments he cherishes those which are not precise hours: "That hour which is between Spring and Summer" in the *Cantate*, or "the hour which is not an hour: midday" in *L'Échange*' (René Lalou: *Contemporary French Literature*, pp. 255–256).

Claudel's preoccupation with imprecise times is suggestive of certain things in Eliot's poetry:

> *Midwinter spring is its own season*
> *Sempiternal though sodden towards sundown,*
> *Suspended in time. . . .*
> (*Little Gidding: Four Quartets*, p. 35.)

> *Because I do not hope to know again*
> *The infirm glory of the positive hour . . .*
> ('Ash Wednesday', I.)

The common inspiration may be in the poetry of Verlaine, who wrote in 'Les Ingénues':

> *Le soir tombait, un soir équivoque d'automne.*

---

1. In 'The Love Song of J. Alfred Prufrock' (opening lines) and 'Mr. Apollinax' respectively.

2. In the very plan of the *Divina Commedia* can be seen the desire. Dante joins with Vergil, the leader from the past, to explore the confines of the spiritual, which contains past, present, and future.

But with Verlaine this was a purely emotional response to vagueness: with Eliot there are philosophical implications. It was with Verlaine another expression of his instinctive love of the blurred, the indecisive, the nuance.

This is an aspect of Eliot's work that appears in many of his poems: partially it may be traced to the influence of Verlaine, possibly even of Claudel. Its basis, however, is Eliot's perception of the dissociation of sensibility, and its effects on poetry. In it we can see his dislike of clear-cut chronological divisions, on the ground that all experience, whether of the past or of the present, of the mind or of the senses, is united. Similarly, where Claudel dealt in anachronisms, we may see in Eliot's allusions to traditional literatures a more delicate and subtle manifestation of the same impulse, of the desire to show the past as having a relevance to the present, and therefore as being 'ever-living'. There is this reason too for his allusions. Any quotation incorporated in his poetry from an author who has had no more general influence on Eliot's work may have this dual function. It will have some specific part to play in the poem, and it will also show how a voice from the past can speak with vitality, can be still a present reality. It is thus a step towards unification of experience, for it shows that past experience, recorded in literature, is equally a present experience for the person reading it:

> . . . . : *the communication*
> *Of the dead is tongued with fire beyond the language of the living.*
> (*Little Gidding: Four Quartets*, p. 36.)

In this lies the relationship between Eliot's traditionalism and his attempts to secure again the unification of sensibility: each is an attempt to order experience and to attain a wide scope of coherence. That neither had been a feature of the generally accepted poetic style inevitably removed Eliot's work from the bounds of popular appreciation. I mention now this aspect of the unification of sensibility in order to elucidate the harmony between it and his traditionalism, in turn related to his esotericism. Dependence on tradition is necessary to Eliot for the reasons set forth in the first chapter. It must also be a part of poetry because in the experiencing of traditional literature we come into contact with a past inseparable from the present.

A consideration of the time theme is a great part of the matter of *Four Quartets*. A direct statement of the inter-relationship between the past, present, and future occurs at the beginning of *Burnt Norton*:

> *Time present and time past*
> *Are both perhaps present in time future,*
> *And time future contained in time past.*

And again in *The Family Reunion*:

> *How can we be concerned with the past*
> *And not with the future? Or with the future*
> *And not with the past?*

In the play however, its most compelling statement is in the form of an image of the kind discussed in this section:

> *There are hours when there seems to be no past or future,*
> *Only a present moment of pointed light . . .*[1]

The direct visual image crystallises here the elusive and uncertain 'present moment', the abstraction realised in concrete terms. By its very clarity it emphasises the uncertainty with which we know the present. In such lines as the above, this theme is stated explicitly as a philosophical doctrine and is implicit in Eliot's use of quotation within his poetry.

In this poetry the past, experienced through the mind, is made real by association with present experiences: the two blend to form a new whole. Goldsmith's song of loss of virtue is transposed to the modern context in *The Waste Land*:

> *When lovely woman stoops to folly and*
> *Paces about her room again, alone,*
> *She smoothes her hair with automatic hand,*
> *And puts a record on the gramophone.*

By this the past is recreated in the present and indirectly adds its

1. Also related to this kind of imaginative experience is Harry's,
> *Do you feel a kind of stirring underneath the air?*
> *Do you? Don't you? a communication, a scent*
> *Direct to the brain . . .*

Here the sensuous is conceived as having a direct repercussion on the brain: the reverse process, for the more usual conception is of the intellectual's reacting on the senses.

unvoiced commentary to the poetic imitation of the present scene, the cheap seduction of the typist, unvalued by either party.

In these considerations one is led beyond the fundamentals of the operation in poetry of unified sensibility. Nevertheless, the relationship is implicit within the scope of Eliot's desire for coherence, and for synthesis of the disordered impressions that must form a part of the poet's material. It is in this aspect of Eliot's work that we see 'the profounder possibilities in wit and in violently joined images' which are mentioned in his essay on Dryden.

Also related to this is the constant intrusion into the affairs of Eliot's characters of the background of reality: the 'narrow streets' in Prufrock, and the 'street piano, mechanical and tired' in 'Portrait of a Lady'. In *The Waste Land* and the preceding poems the prevailing impression is not of man considered divorced from his surroundings, nor of the surroundings divorced from their inhabitants. Always the two are in immediate contact, and this insistence on the inevitable background to the existence of man shows Eliot to have a mind that—instinctively philosophical—does not care to lose sight of the material reality that must to a considerable extent actuate man's life and nature, Eliot's fundamental concern. We are never allowed to forget that the people and the ideas in the poetry are to be seen in relation to their 'local habitation'. In the more abstract patterns of *Four Quartets*, there is a certain change of temper, and they are not so directly and unceasingly integrated with the modern city. Even here, however, Eliot does not entirely lose sight of the material setting. This is a stage of his development that will be considered later.

In revolution motivated by reaction Eliot turned to the modes of thought and expression considered in this chapter. Essentially esoteric in appeal, they reach their final expression in *The Waste Land*. After this, though much of the early ideas remains, there is clearly apparent a change of direction. This examination of the esotericism of the poetry has been based mainly on 'Prufrock and other Observations'. The poems of the 1920 volume, now to be considered, represent the next stage in the progress that culminates in *The Waste Land*. They help to illuminate not only what is to come, but also what has gone before, and being the part of Eliot's work least thoroughly discussed, repay detailed examination.

Chapter Four

Poetry and Beliefs

I N 'Prufrock and other Observations' to a limited extent, more apparently in *Poems 1920*, are dispersed the themes which are developed and organised to achieve their greatest impact in *The Waste Land*. Some of these anticipations have already been indicated. Before it can be properly seen how *The Waste Land* uses its material, however, it is necessary to examine the more tentative grouping of themes in the second volume of poems. This volume contains the seeds not only of *The Waste Land* but also of the transition poems leading to *Four Quartets*. An examination of it is therefore essential to detailed interpretation of *The Waste Land*, and to an understanding of Eliot's poetic development.

Perhaps the clearest allusion in 'Prufrock and other Observations' to the fertility motif is in 'Mr. Apollinax':

> *I thought of Fragilion, that shy figure among the birch trees,*
> *And of Priapus in the shrubbery*
> *Gaping at the lady in the swing.*

A parallel reference in *Poems 1920* occurs in 'Sweeney Erect', where Ariadne replaces Priapus:

> *Display me Aeolus above*
> > *Reviewing the insurgent gales*
> *Which tangle Ariadne's hair*
> > *And swell with haste the perjured sails.*

The intricately devised opening stanzas lead from a description of the Grecian islands to Greek mythology. The link is Aeolus, whose winds disturb the seas and Ariadne's hair. The reference to Ariadne is the first key to the poem's theme. She is the goddess of vegetation, personification of Spring and returning life, symbol of fertility. On this level of interpretation a contrast is immediately suggested with 'this withered root of knots of hair', associated with Sweeney and his bed-fellow. Theirs is a mating that has denied the aim of reproduction, a sterile coupling in a brothel. The contrast, then, is between this and the cycle of death and rebirth in the Ariadne fertility myth. Once this is seen the essence of the poem is revealed. Yet there is a further complexity in the classical allusions.

Ariadne, before her rebirth and marriage with Dionysus, is abandoned by Theseus and her love betrayed: as love is betrayed by Sweeney too, though in a different way. As additional emphasis, the winds that 'tangle Ariadne's hair' also 'swell with haste the perjured sails'. In Eliot's elaborately concise poetry there is no place for merely decorative phrasing, and as this last line must have a meaning, it is most likely that it refers to the sails of the ship bearing Isolde to the dying Tristan[1]: again a betrayal.[2] This is particularly interesting in its anticipation of the use made of this legend in *The Waste Land*. Time is telescoped to include at the same instant Sweeney, Ariadne, Tristan and Isolde, connected by what might seem to be the superficially descriptive opening stanzas.

What is suggested is not a bare and simple contrast. Always love has been betrayed and fertility denied; always the hope of rebirth is offered. But the rebirth demands sacrifice, suffering,

1. This is purely conjectural. There is nothing in the legends alluded to, nor in their organisation within the poem, to enable us to say with any assurance that this connection is in fact intended. It must be accounted a failure in the poem that, if this is the meaning of the line—and no other suggests itself—its unravelling has been left so haphazardly to chance association of ideas. Eliot's normal practice produces so closely-knit a pattern of mood and idea that elucidation presents no insurmountable difficulty. Here, however, the concise development is so rapid as to defeat its own purpose.

2. The epigraph is from a speech by Aspatia, the betrayed maiden, in Act II, scene ii of Beaumont and Fletcher's *The Maid's Tragedy*. In it she suggests a fitting background for her portrait.

and a life conditioned by principles far different from those to which 'the ladies of the corridor' call witness. In this way from the suffering of Philomel came rebirth and the 'inviolable voice' of the nightingale. (See *The Waste Land*, ll. 97–103.) There is no indication here, however, that the offer of rebirth is acceptable to the contemporary world. It accepts living death, and the only remedies produced by Doris are sal-volatile and neat brandy. This poem illustrates well the obliquity of Eliot's poetry, the layers of meaning that can lie behind a single line.

A comparison between the openings of 'Sweeney Erect' and 'L'Allegro', which have a certain similarity of pattern, emphasises the peculiarity of Eliot's method. All we need to know of the classical figures to whom Milton alludes is given within the poem. It is sufficient to know that Cerberus is associated with 'blackest midnight', that Venus is lovely, that Zephyr and Aurora can be fitly mentioned with 'frolic' and 'playing'. Milton's method, then, is quite direct. The classical figures, summoned to provide a suitable parentage for Euphrosyne, have their characteristics and functions straightforwardly allotted to them. The pattern is similar to that of 'Sweeney Erect': a picture of desolation, reinforced by classical memories is followed in Milton by a charming evocation of lightness and joy, in Eliot by a reminder that his desolate background contained the beauty and fertility of Ariadne—as Sweeney's does not. There the similarity ends. For the success of Eliot's method depends on the reader's recognising that Ariadne is not to be looked on as representing merely a picture of jolly, flower-bedecked Spring. No direct indication is given within the poem that this Ariadne has the deep religious significance that she had for her original devotees. Yet when what is implied in the relations between the figures of the opening stanzas and those of the body of the poem is considered, the reader must come to see that it is this aspect of the myth that is significant in the context.

This is not a contrast between a good and a bad technique, but between two entirely different methods in use at widely separated times. The poets of the decadent romantic school continued to use the direct expansive method with diminished technical skill, and on subjects already sadly overworked. Eliot's bare and restrained utterance forges by its reticence a more powerful relationship between the classical and the modern scene than could have resulted from an elaboration of the opening verses. A selective elaboration comes at the proper point, where knowledge cannot be assumed, to create in a few lines a vivid picture of the sordid:

> *This withered root of knots of hair*
> *Slitted below and gashed with eyes,*
> *This oval O cropped out with teeth.*[1]

The variation of the 'o' and 'i' sounds, the impact of 'gashed' and 'cropped' support most precisely the visual picture. Elaboration of the earlier part could serve only to unbalance the structure. Comparison between Milton's and Eliot's lines reveals very clearly the distinction between Eliot's methods and those of an earlier tradition.

Closely connected with *The Waste Land* is 'Sweeney among the Nightingales', again concerned with the fertility theme:

> *Gloomy Orion and the Dog*
> *Are veiled; and hushed the shrunken seas.*

Orion, seen at midnight, heralded the vintage season in the Egyptian calendar, but the natural order is destroyed by Sweeney and his associates. The waiter brings them 'hothouse grapes' to be torn by Rachel's 'murderous paws'. The function of Orion is negatived, and this is but one aspect of the distortion of fertility and the natural order. The verse quoted suggests what is perhaps the primary significance of the Dog symbol in 'The Burial of the Dead'. In this context the Dog is obviously Sirius, the Dog star, which for the Egyptians foretold the coming of the fertilising floods of the Nile. Stetson—and Sweeney—would not welcome this returned fertility, with its attendant disruption of the settled way. In *The Golden Bough* Frazer tells how Isis and Osiris were also connected in Egyptian mythology with the rising of the

---

1. A strong rhetorical force is infused in these lines. One may compare John of Gaunt's,

> *This royal throne of kings, this sceptred isle,*
> *This earth of majesty, this seat of Mars,*

Eliot's own comments on rhetoric make it quite clear that he does not think it necessarily a vice; see his essay 'Rhetoric and Poetic Drama', *Selected Essays*, p. 37.

waters. Effigies of the god, made of corn, were buried to symbolise the death of the corn god. From this burial ensued the new harvest: hence from the death of Osiris came the deliverance of the people. With this ritual should be compared the burial performed by Stetson, which can symbolise only the attempt to forget a spiritual failure. Not, as with Osiris, a bringing of life by the burial of the material body. From Stetson's ritual can come no resurrection. Frazer points out the similarity between the Osiris and Dionysus legends: so we return to the Ariadne allusion in 'Sweeney Erect'.

Egyptian ritual, described in Frazer's work, that has a relevance to 'Sweeney among the Nightingales' is the practice whereby images of Adonis and Aphrodite were displayed on couches, and beside them were placed ripe fruits of all kinds.[1] A debased version of this is represented by the fortuitous offering of,

> . . . *oranges*
> *Bananas figs and hothouse grapes;*

by the waiter. These allusions are an early use of the fertility myths as symbols of the poems' significance. Orion and the Dog are veiled; the fertilising floods are far distant, and the life-giving water is diminished in the 'shrunken seas'. The horned gate guarded by Sweeney is possibly that of *The Spanish Tragedy*, guarded by Pluto, king of the Underworld, 'Where dreams have passage in the silent night' (I, i, ll. 75–82). This is the atmosphere of the trance-like cities of *The Waste Land*.

The opening stanzas of this poem have the same function as those of 'Sweeney Erect'. They evoke an atmosphere—one of foreboding, and some impending disaster—and elucidate in their indirect way the fertility theme at the core of the poem. Here the loss of fertility is again associated with the idea of infidelity and betrayal. The major parallelism is to the story of Agamemnon. Aegistheus, who has seduced Clytaemnestra during Agamemnon's absence, plots with her to kill Agamemnon on his return. Agamemnon's dying words form the epigraph to Eliot's poem. In 'Sweeney' there is again a plot: that of Rachel and the lady in the cape against the man with heavy eyes. This is in keeping with the feeling of foreboding aroused in the opening verses, but the

1. *The Golden Bough*, Vol. 2; Chapter 4.

real betrayal lies deeper in the relations between the men and women in the poem. It is the same betrayal that occupies Eliot in 'Sweeney Erect': the degradation of love to an animal-like mechanical relationship. By this Sweeney too—and it is part of the condemnation that he does not realise it—has been 'struck a mortal blow within'. Of this there is more to be said. But first may be mentioned Eliot's inevitable association of the nightingale in some way with misfortune.

On its first publication in *Ara Vos Prec*, 'Sweeney among the Nightingales' bore this additional epigraph:

> *Why should I speak of the Nightingale? The Nightingale sings of adulterous wrong.*

Within the narrow limits of his verse-form Eliot achieves, at the culmination of this poem, the tremendous effect of:

> *The nightingales are singing near*
> *The Convent of the Sacred Heart.*
>
> *And sang within the bloody wood*
> *When Agamemnon cried aloud;*
> *And let their liquid siftings fall*
> *To stain the stiff dishonoured shroud.*

The nightingales sing at betrayal and death, at the decay of fertility, as they did when Agamemnon was killed. Harry in *The Family Reunion* says of the Eumenides:

> *In Italy, from behind the nightingales' thicket,*
> *The eyes stared at me and corrupted that song*

For Harry, the birds accompany the agents of retribution.

At the end of the Sweeney poem, it is the nightingales that link the betrayal of Agamemnon, of Sweeney's activities, and apparently of the Convent too, for there also fertility is denied. This association probably has its source, as has been suggested, in the original Philomel legend. This involves a betrayal, and gives a further meaning to the proximity of the nightingales to the brothel. They sang as retribution followed Harry, as the women of the brothel plotted, and the song itself was born of Philomel's suffering. This use of the nightingale is a deliberate break with the romantic conception of the bird as being associated entirely with beauty, and a vague feeling of nostalgia—desire to be elsewhere. Of this break the mention of the birds' 'liquid siftings'—excrement, and not the birds' song—is a detail. Similarly the 'golden grin' of verse eight is intended not to evoke a pleasurable upsurge of romantic feeling—Housman's 'hearts of gold'—but to describe the gleaming of gold-filled teeth. Frank Wilson in his book on Eliot produces from the lines a similar misinterpretation: 'There is a sinister suggestiveness, almost a furtive beauty, in the scene, for all is illuminated by the eerie light of impending disaster, just as the weird light in Grendel's mother's cavern shone upon her fight with Beowulf:

> *Branches of wistaria*
> *Circumscribe a golden grin'*

(Frank Wilson: *Six Essays on the Development of T. S. Eliot*, p. 18.) With these lines, however, a diversion can be offered. Looking on to the gardens of Merton College, Oxford, where Eliot spent a year of post-graduate study, is a window surrounded by wistaria. It is pleasant to think of the poet's seeing through this window, one day, the flash of teeth, and focusing the incident with sharp clarity and intensity, years later, in a poem. No doubt part of the fascination lies in the minute relevance of Eliot's biography to his poetry, in the infrequency with which we can divert ourselves with such imaginings.

It is difficult not to think that the close relationship between brothel, convent, and the death of Agamemnon implies that the convent also represents a distortion of values.[1] Withdrawal from the world is not an effective means of coping with the world's distress. Collingwood, in a perceptive note on this passage, sees the relationship between the three strands of the poem,[2] but he errs, I think, in supposing that Sweeney also sees the connexion

[1]. The Puritan traditions of Eliot's New England background had not at this time been replaced by his later religious preferences. Even his Anglo-Catholicism, as will be shown, bears the signs of his upbringing. It is fair to assume, then, that he speaks at least partially from his own experience when, in *Notes towards the Definition of Culture*, he discusses the Puritan attitude to the life of the religious celibate:

'. . . just as a culture which is only accessible to the few is now deprecated, so was the enclosed and contemplative life condemned by extreme Protestantism, and celibacy regarded with almost as much abhorrence as perversion' (p. 33).

[2]. R. Collingwood: *Principles of Art*, p. 310.

between them, in his drunken reverie: Sweeney never heard of
Agamemnon. Castigation of established religious practices is not
a novelty in these poems. Here, the implied condemnation of the
convent, and in 'The Hippopotamus' the more general gibes at

> . . . *the True Church,* . . . *below*
> *Wrapt in the old miasmal mist.*

This is not atheism, nor a condemnation of objective religious
values and morals. It is an expression of dissatisfaction with the
negative attitude to life which Eliot saw operative in the established religions almost as much as in the lives of the Sweeneys of
this world. On the one hand we have a negative attitude to evil,
on the other an equally negative attitude to good:

> *The hippo's feeble steps may err*
> *In compassing material ends,*
> *While the True Church need never stir*
> *To gather in its dividends.*

Such an attitude is a weakening, a vulgarisation of the churches'
task. Broadly speaking, it is particular instances of the general
process of vulgarisation that occupy Eliot in these poems.

In the Sweeney poems, the motivation is revulsion from the
unthinking abandonment of the characters to passionless sexual
pleasure. 'Burbank with a Baedeker' places side by side the art
of the past, the beauty of a bygone Venice, and their modern
inheritors—Burbank zealous with a Baedeker, Bleistein indifferent
with a cigar. In the contest for Princess Volupine it is of course
Bleistein and Klein who conquer. Burbank is Anthony, whom the
god Hercules had left, the composite 'Chicago Semite Viennese'
is Caesar. This revised version of Shakespeare's play is implied by
the two quotations from it in Eliot's poem. A further complexity
is suggested by the allusion to 'The Phoenix and the Turtle'.

> *Defunctive music under sea*
> *Passed seaward with the passing bell*
> *Slowly:* . . .

In Shakespeare's poem, where the word 'defunctive' was coined:

> *Let the priest in surplice white*
> *That defunctive music can*
> *Be the death-divining swan* . . .

Rarely used, and not just a stock archaism, 'defunctive' compels attention to the new phoenix and turtle. Its unfamiliarity, following on the colloquial 'They were together and he fell', diverts the consciousness from a simple recital of a modern seduction to expectation of another layer of meaning. The idiom of 'They were together and he fell' evokes the 'blues' of innumerable contemporary lyrics. 'Defunctive' comes from the restless experimenting with an as yet incompletely defined language that characterised the Elizabethan zest for words. The mind is thus prepared for the allusion that follows, with its direct juxtapositioning of the ancient and modern 'co-supremes and stars of love'.

The 'Easy commerce of the old and new' of which Eliot speaks in *Little Gidding* is illustrated here by the use of 'defunctive'. In this connexion we may remember too his remark in *The Music of Poetry* that 'it is only at certain points in a poem that word can be made to insinuate the whole history of a language and a civilisation' (p. 19). 'Burbank' depends for its effect on just such a fusion, and the achievement of this is greatly aided by the intrusion of 'defunctive' into the setting.

The death-like music that so fittingly accompanies Burbank's affaire looks back to,

> . . . *the ariettes*
> .*Of cracked cornets*

in 'Portrait of a Lady', forward to the typist's gramophone record whose

> . . . *music crept by me on the waters.*

Something of the significance of this recurring music—a vital element in *The Waste Land*—has been mentioned in Chapter One (1). While

> *Weeping, weeping multitudes*
> *Droop in a hundred A.B.C.'s*

the almost inevitable accompaniment is half-heard music, remotely perceived only as an additional factor in the general blur of sound. Music—of a kind—pervades all the activities of contemporary life, seeping through the disembodied conversation of mass eating centres, drifting from the wireless to accompany all the facets of experience. Constant Lambert's *Music Ho* gives this succinct summary of the situation: 'We board our buses to the strains of Beethoven and drink our beer to the accompaniment of Bach . . . classical music is vulgarised and diffused through every highway and byway. . . . The principal objections to music provided by the now almost universal loud speakers are its monotony and unsuitability . . . now no one can avoid listening to music, whether in town or country, in a motor car, train or restaurant, perched on a hilltop, or immersed in the river' (pp. 169–170). It is this inescapable and ultimately depressing background that Eliot deftly transposes to his poetry.

The 'weeping multitudes' in 'A Cooking Egg' weep over a vaguely discerned sense of loss of values. Their heaven, portrayed in this poem, contains impartially Sir Philip Sidney and Sir Alfred Mond. It was to Sir Alfred's commercial capabilities that the fortunes of the *English Review* were entrusted when Ford Madox Hueffer's lack of financial flair became too patently obvious. Modern idols are more clearly satirised, however, in the appearance of Madame Blavatsky. For it is to her that the multitudes would turn, open to any specious spiritual appeal.[1] She is the counterpart of the great popular fertility gods. Her legend shows

---

1. Formally parallel to these poems are the stanzas of Pound's 'H. S. Mauberly'. The theme is more blatantly stated:

> Faun's flesh is not for us,
> Nor the saint's vision;
> We have press for wafer,
> Franchise for circumcision.

and there is a less expert manipulation of detail. Pound's use of the quotation from Heraclitus:

> All things are a flowing
> Sage Heraclitus says:
> But a tawdry cheapness
> Shall outlast our days.

is not so wittily organised, does not strike home so profoundly as Eliot's,

> The lengthened shadow of a man
> Is history, said Emerson
> Who had not seen the silhouette
> Of Sweeney straddled in the sun.

The last two lines seem the modern counterpart of Shakespeare's heroic,

> . . . he doth bestride the narrow world
> Like a Colossus. . . .

many characteristics of their tradition, all in a more or less debased form: reincarnation, journeying preceding an initiation (in her case probably fictitious), trial and persecution, alleged resurrection after death. But with her the myth has lost its original force, and she is a suitable realisation of modern ideals. The old legends were sustained by their closeness to the elemental sources of life, the cycle of the seasons. Now this vitality has gone. Miss E. M. Butler gives this summary of Madame Blavatsky's powers: 'They (the occult phenomena produced by Madame Blavatsky) are of a disillusioning nature, for the link binding her to the medicine man of the past and of present-day primitive tribes is a woefully slender one, and her similarity with a parlour conjurer much more striking. . . . They were obviously performed for the purposes of mere display' (*The Myth of the Magus*; chapter on Mme. Blavatsky).

The poem divides into three sections, of which the first describes the trivia surrounding Pipit, with no suggestion that the poet finds any particular inadequacy in them. For Miss Nancy Ellicott's aunts traditional values were embodied in the figures on the glazen shelves of Matthew and Waldo, 'guardians of the faith'; for Pipit they are similarly embodied in the pictures on the mantelpiece of her dead relatives. In a 'Game of Chess',

> *Above the antique mantel was displayed*
> *As though a window gave upon the sylvan scene*
> *The change of Philomel, by the barbarous king*
> *So rudely forced;* . . .

Again, traditional values come to be looked on as a means of ornamentation, and nothing else. In 'A Cooking Egg', it is only with the third section, after the reverie involving

> . . . *Coriolanus*
> *And other heroes of that kidney,*

that the realisation comes that something is lacking in the surroundings, that the escapist world whose only traditional values are represented by the security of the decorative 'daguerrotypes and silhouettes' on the mantelpiece, is in fact entirely insufficient. So the dream world collapses:

> *Where are the eagles and the trumpets?*
> *Buried beneath some snow-deep Alps.*

The eagles and the trumpets represent a vanished vigour and vitality. The symbol recurs in 'Coriolan' II—

> *That is all we could see. But how many eagles! and how many*
> *trumpets!—*

which in its title also introduces the figure of Coriolanus, the lost leader. The figure of Coriolanus has taken a strong grasp on Eliot's imagination, and is found again at the end of *The Waste Land*, when

> *. . . aetherial rumours*
> *Revive for a moment a broken Coriolanus.*

An early poem, 'Ode', appearing among the collected editions only in *Ara Vos Prec*, takes its epigraph from Coriolanus's,

> *My name is Caius Marcius, who hath done*
> *To thee particularly, and to all the Volsces*
> *Great hurt and mischief;*
>
> > (*Coriolanus*, IV, v.)

It is an obscure poem, but its subject, coupled with the allusion to the banished Coriolanus, has a relevance to the childless women in 'A Game of Chess' (*The Waste Land*, II). The ode deals with the resentment of the 'Succuba eviscerate', bride and bridegroom, over their sexual experience—the bridegroom regretting not the 'deep damnation' but 'the cheap extinction of his taking-off'—hearing in the morning the singing in the orchard of children not their own. Coriolanus, the lost leader, betrayed by both aristocracy and mob, adds his condemnation through the epigraph. In *The Waste Land*, as will be shown, a further dimension is added to the symbol, combining the ideas of the lost father and the lost leader.

These two poems—'Burbank', and 'A Cooking Egg'—explore the modern consciousness in relation to temporal and spiritual affairs. With the more obviously disgusting vulgarisation of the Sweeney poems there enters an atmosphere of barely repressed violence, and a profounder repugnance than in the ligher irony of the other poems. In them recurs the animal theme referred to in a previous chapter.

Rachel, in 'Sweeney among the Nightingales', takes the grapes not with hands but with 'murderous paws', and the description of 'the silent man in mocha brown' is deliberately written so that it might apply equally well to an ape:

> *The silent vertebrate in brown*
> *Contracts and concentrates, withdraws;*
> *Rachel nee Rabinovitch*
> *Tears at the grapes with murderous paws.*

In 'Sweeney Erect', Sweeney rises with a 'gesture of orang-outang'. A quotation from the *Confessions* of St. Augustine, the influence of which is so strongly apparent in *The Waste Land* and much of the later poetry, casts further light on this theme—apparently suggested originally to Eliot by Baudelaire. In the final book of the *Confessions* (Symons's edition, p. 244), where the nature of temptation is recapitulated, Augustine refers to 2 Corinthians v. This is the relevant quotation:

'We are confident, I say, and willing rather to be absent from the body, and to be present with the Lord.'

With this may be considered the epigraph to 'Sweeney Agonistes', from St. John of the Cross:

'Hence the soul cannot be possessed of divine union until it has divested itself of the love of created beings.'

The poems of the 1920 volume are concerned with the most obvious manifestation of inability to be absent from the body—sexual indulgence which loses sight of any higher relationship between men and women, reducing it to the level of the beasts. On one level it is a protest against this vulgarisation, and the revulsion felt by Eliot's reticent nature, that motivate these poems. Firstly in *The Waste Land*, this is brought within the framework of Augustinian thought, and condemned because it must, by its insistence on an aimless pleasure in physical relationship, put still further away the withdrawal from obsession with the body and created beings which is the necessary precursor of spiritual union with God. In this connexion *Poems 1920* reveal part not only of *The Waste Land's* purpose, but also that of such a poem as 'Ash

Wednesday', where the body is represented as being quite literally destroyed—see Psalm 51, verse 8, for the idea:

> Make me to hear joy and gladness; that the bones which thou hast broken may rejoice.

With the destruction of the body in Eliot's poem, the bones do rejoice:

> Under a juniper tree the bones sang, scattered and shining
> We are glad to be scattered, we did little good to each other,
> Under a tree in the cool of the day, with the blessing of the sand,
> Forgetting themselves and each other, united
> In the quiet of the desert.

('Ash Wednesday', II: *Collected Poems*, p. 96.)

Here, however, we enter the firm ground of positive belief that is found in Eliot's later poetry. Before this his poetry is generally of a satiric and negative sort. Some consideration may now be offered, before the hardening of Eliot's beliefs intrudes, of the problem of poetry and belief. The problem, that is, of determining the dependence of the reader's enjoyment of poetry on the extent to which he shares the beliefs embodied in the poetry. This must be a part of any examination of Eliot's work, for he is a religious poet, and it is in such poetry that the question is most acutely posed.

In Milton, for example, Eliot himself has found that a barrier to enjoyment is raised. 'As a man he (Milton) is antipathetic. Either from the moralist's point of view, or from the theologian's point of view, or from that of the political philosopher. . . . Milton is unsatisfactory.'[1] With this many people will be in profound disagreement: much, in any case, depends on the views of the moralist, the theologian, and the political philosopher. For it is more likely that there exists, in such specific matters of opinion, not an abstract 'Theologian's viewpoint', but the viewpoints of many individual theologians. One can find little reason to suppose that Milton's beliefs would prove obnoxious to many non-conformist tempers. Eliot's strictures on Milton, we feel, condemn him on artistic grounds entirely because Eliot is instinctively opposed to Milton's opinions: the judgment is not objective.

With Eliot's comments on Dante the reverse process operates.

1. T. S. Eliot: 'A Note on the Verse of John Milton.'

Writing of 'in la sua volentate e nostra pace', he says that 'it has more beauty for me now, when my own experience has deepened its meaning, than it had when I first read it'. We may reasonably suspect that Eliot is to some extent deluding himself here, and that he does not experience an intensified beauty, but that an entirely new pleasure of a different order is added. It appears to me that we must distinguish two different planes of enjoyment. The aesthetic pleasure, which must involve comprehension of the poet's ideas: before we can claim a full aesthetic enjoyment of any poem we must understand what the poem says. If we accept the poet's belief, it is not that this pleasure is intensified, but that pleasure of an entirely different kind is added to it. The pleasure of seeing stated, in a form aesthetically pleasing, a view of life to which one can attach one's sympathies, one's entire acceptance. This new pleasure can be as well obtained, on its own, from a philosophical study. But being presented in poetry, the two excitements are placed side by side, and it may well seem that the one is merely an intensification of the other.

Again, the poet may create in us a mood that enables us to accept the validity of his views within the unit of his poem, whatever our opinion may generally be. Or, at least, we can recognise that a particular poem is the perfect formal realisation of an intellectual concept. The pleasure that arises from this need not be diminished by our withdrawal of sympathy from the philosophy. Belief and disbelief become irrelevant. It is hardly to be sustained that the agnostic will derive greater aesthetic pleasure from Prospero's 'our little life is rounded with a sleep', than the man who believes in some form of survival after death.

Eliot, in his examination of the problem (*Selected Essays*, pp. 269–271) remarks, 'I cannot, in practice, wholly separate my poetic appreciation from my personal beliefs.' This ignores any difference between poetic, philosophical, and moral appreciation, implying that the latter must necessarily affect poetic appreciation. They are not unrelated to it, yet there is a distinct poetical appreciation owing nothing to the others. To it the other appeals may be added. Some proof of self-contained poetic worth is offered by the fact that we are not encouraged by acceptance of an author's beliefs to claim his work as artistically good—there are of course the exceptions of fanaticism

Concluding his observations on the subject, Eliot says: 'there is a distinct pleasure in enjoying poetry as poetry when one does not share the beliefs, analogous to the pleasure of "mastering" other men's philosophical principles.' This is of course quite true, but it is a pleasure additional to that derived from experience of the artistic competence of the poem, and it is exactly the same pleasure that is derived from poetry with the beliefs of which we are in accord. To conclude, then, we may say that in reading poetry we experience pleasure on two different planes. The pleasure we derive from the beliefs—accepted or rejected—is entirely distinct from that we derive from the indefinable poetry in which they are embodied. But that we cannot define it does not mean that it does not exist.

Those of Eliot's poems so far considered are concerned, briefly, with the depicting of a civilisation content with grossly debased moral standards. Such a description would find acceptance among men of widely different opinions, each with his own idea of the most effective cure. With the general statement, however, that there was something to be cured, and that the sickness was at the roots of the normal man's morality, there would be a wide measure of agreement. For this reason, especially when given the intellectual and imaginative concentration of the individual poems, no barrier is raised to appreciation of them. And in so far as they are a consideration of the dangers that must always attend humanity, this is not merely a temporary phenomenon. Their appeal is not solely that they seem to speak with a peculiar urgency at the present time. The later poems, more positive in belief, do not enjoy this immunity, and considerably irritate certain political mentalities. Such objections are treated in a following section.

The Gautier, or 'Bay State Hymn Book' stanzas[1] of the 1920 poems are not suited to the complete expression of what concerned Eliot. They have their power, especially in Eliot's use of them, but one is conscious that they impose a restraint which,

1. See Ezra Pound's remarks in *Polite Essays* (p. 14), where he states that he and Eliot imposed this form with the deliberate intention of giving effect to their decision 'that the dilution of vers libres . . . had gone too far, and that some counter-current must be set going'. Such was the limited specific aim of Eliot's work in this medium.

while not to be dismissed as worthless, cramps almost as much as it disciplines the full operation of the poetic sensibility. Their use is strictly limited. With the greater variation of *The Waste Land* a fuller statement becomes possible.

To summarise, then, we find in these poems the requirements for the transmission of both levels of enjoyment. They are sufficiently close to the experience of anyone likely to read them to avoid an automatic exclusion of sympathy with their views. They afford a statement of those views that has sufficient poetic power to arouse a positive interest. With *The Waste Land*, now to be considered, the philosophy is more positive, but still sufficiently related to a widespread feeling to preclude objection. Its central theme—the necessity for control and leadership of the spirit—anticipates much in the later poetry. It must be said, however, that had this not been but one of the many facets of this remarkable poem, had it been more overtly the central issue, then the attacks on Eliot's Christian poetry, considered in Chapter Six, would have been directed also on *The Waste Land*.

Chapter Five

The Turning World

WHAT must strike the reader most forcibly about *Poems 1920* and *The Waste Land* is their insistence on the setting. Temporal human affairs are presented directly within this setting, while their spiritual significance is left implicit, in the imagery and in the allusions to past literature. These poems present Eliot's vision of 'the turning world', a symbol first used in 'Coriolan' II. The characteristics of mechanical civilisation and urban squalor provide the necessary starting point for Eliot's investigation of the distress peculiar to the modern soul. The poetry is never concerned solely with the presentation of a picture of 'the turning world': the spiritual undertones are always present. But what most distinguishes the early from the later poetry is that in the former the streets, the houses, the music, the routine affairs of the people overlay the spiritual considerations and are essential to their communication.

In the final section of *The Waste Land* can be seen the first divergence from direct insistence on the surroundings. The method is still allusive—as it always is—but it operates now away from the contemporary setting. Composed, as will be shown, in the figure of Coriolanus, the Fisher King, and the lost father, is the notion of a focus towards which the instability and flux of material affairs should converge. From such convergence they will be endowed with a meaning which they must lack if there is no stable centre. This concept is symbolised—also in 'Coriolan' II—

as 'the still centre'. From his vision of the world, which forms the foreground of this poetry, Eliot moves to contemplation of the true reality, contained in God, the still point. This process continues to the *Four Quartets*, where it is the social reality that is largely left implied, and direct contemplation of spiritual affairs occupies the foreground. But this is to anticipate.

Much of the poetry between *The Waste Land* and *Four Quartets* continues to stress the social reality. However, it is in *Poems 1920* and *The Waste Land* that we find the fullest account of the physical characteristics of 'the turning world'.

The Waste Land has been so many times analysed and dissected that some relief is found in a return to the refreshingly forthright comments made on the poem when it first appeared. The uniform characteristic of these is that none of them looked on it as a poem at all. It was considered, at best, as a series of slightly related separate poems. So assured was this attitude that *The Times Literary Supplement* was able to dimiss casually 'some references to vegetation ceremonies', not unimportant to the structure of the poem. The following comments on various aspects of the poem, as they are concerned with some of the fundamentals of the poetry, provide a useful starting point.

On the unity of the poem

New Statesman and Nation, 4th November, 1922, p. 140. 'Affable Hawk' notes that in the first issue of *Criterion* appear 'several separate poems entitled *The Waste Land*.'

Scrutinies, II. Alec Brown, in an essay entitled 'The Lyric Impulse in T. S. Eliot', decides that '*The Waste Land*, for all the suggestion made by calling it a poem, is but a set of shorter poems . . . tacked together.'

American Poetry since 1900 (Louis Untermeyer): '. . . it is doubtful whether *The Waste Land* is anything but a set of separate poems . . . a piece of literary carpentry, scholarly joiner's work; the flotsam and jetsam of desiccated culture . . . a pompous parade of erudition.'

On the system of allusion

Generally one notes the common antithesis indicated between the true poet who looks directly on life and the pseudo-poet who looks on it through the spectacles of books.

New Statesman and Nation, 3rd November, 1923, p. 117. Review of the poem by F. L. Lucas. As an introductory comment he notes that Alexandrian poetry finds 'in literature an inspiration that life gives no more', with the implication that this is to be deplored. The generalisation is unconvincing. Neither Pope nor Eliot ignores life, even the life of which literature is not a part.

Untermeyer, op. cit.: 'It is an anthology of assimilations—a poetry, as Mary C. Colum pointed out, "of interest to critics and people professionally interested in literature; it appeals to their sophisticated consciousness, whereas great literature appeals either to our subconscious or superconscious minds—that is to something that either transcends our experience or is profoundly buried in our experience". Eliot's poetry does neither; it appeals only to our acquired knowledge.' One may question the assumption that only our experience of literature is to be described as 'acquired knowledge', and that it cannot appeal to those parts of our minds open to other transcribed experiences.

Times Literary Supplement, 20th September, 1923: 'parodying without taste or skill'—adding that, 'of this the example from Goldsmith is not the most astonishing'.

New Statesman; F. L. Lucas: '. . . the parodies are cheap and the imitations inferior.'

Untermeyer, op. cit.: Describes the allusions as 'weak burlesque'.

On the poet who might have been

On this issue we find Lucas and Brown united in considering Eliot a romanticist manqué, scattering occasional pearls among his litter. With this is coupled regret over the urban influence in Eliot's poetry, and nostalgia for a vanished rural impetus. Eliot, says Brown, is 'almost morbidly attracted' by the sordidness of city life. This critic looks in Eliot's work for passages he considers lyric, describes this as the outcome of Eliot's innate—and deliberately stifled—lyric impulse, and condemns the rest almost in its entirety. Lucas similarly: 'The first of the five sections opens in spring with one of the snatches of poetry that occur scattered about the poem.' Implied in this is refusal to look on the poem as a whole. He goes on to object to the 'young man carbuncular' as 'a typical instance of that squalor which seems perpetually to obsess Mr. Eliot with mixed fascination and repulsion . . . suburban sordidness'.

On the symbolism

Lucas's is the final word: Speaking of the necessity for a knowledge of *From Ritual to Romance* he says, 'Miss Weston is clearly a theosophist, and Mr. Eliot's poem might be a theosophical tract. The sick king and the waste land symbolise, we gather, the sick soul and the desolation of this material life.' Having gathered this correctly, Lucas seems perverse in looking on the poem as giving any suggestion of being a theosophical tract. The symbols are quite obviously used for their poetic value, with no suggestion that they have so specific and limited a meaning as Lucas suggests. That Lucas is not merely speaking ironically in saying this is indicated by his opinion that Eliot has 'sacrificed his artistic powers on the altar of some fantastic mumbo-jumbo'. Morosely he concludes, 'Perhaps this unhappy composition should have been left to sink itself.'

Whatever may be our opinion of the worth of these early criticisms it is undeniable that they deal with matters that must arise in any serious consideration of the poem. Despite the exhaustiveness of the commentaries by Leavis, Matthiessen, and Brooks, it will be necessary to give some account of the poem, as a basis on which speculation may rest. The following analysis is considerably indebted to the work of these critics. The conclusion, however, is somewhat different, and there are differences of detail.

Of greatest importance are the questions of the poem's unity, of the success of the system of allusion, and of the beliefs embodied in the work. This last is particularly interesting, for the general view of the poem is that it offers no evidence of positive belief, even that it has effected 'a complete severance between . . poetry and all beliefs'—an interpretation which Eliot has professed himself unable to understand (*Selected Essays*: 'Dante', p. 269). The poem is not, as Day Lewis sees it, a social document. Nor is it an Act of Parliament setting forth exact instructions for the removal of evil conditions. But it does reveal a poetic treatment of certain aspects of a civilisation, placing them in the perspective of time.

Miss Weston's *From Ritual to Romance* is by now so well known as to require little comment. The Fisher King of the Grail legend having lost his virility through sexual mutilation or illness, his lands become waste and desolate, the power of propagation generally suspended. These ills are considered the direct result of the king's disability. On the success of the Quester in his task of journeying to the Grail chapel, there undergoing trials and ascertaining the office of the Grail and the significance of its symbols, depends the return of fertility to the land. Further, Weston distinguishes two parts of the legend, the esoteric and exoteric. The former concerns the significance of the Grail symbols. The latter gives the popular, folk-lore elements: the suffering king, the waste land, the task that lies before the Quester. It is this that Eliot uses. One can detect here the feeling for the spiritual condition of the large masses of humanity that prompts his introduction of Madame Blavatsky in 'A Cooking Egg'. Finally it must be noted that Eliot's use of Miss Weston's study involves an extension of the symbolism, found also in some of the legends, to cover not only physical but spiritual decay.

In the exoteric aspect of the legend, interest—as far as any hope of regeneration is concerned—must centre on the Quester's journey to the Grail chapel. Each of the five sections of *The Waste Land* introduces a journey undertaken by the inhabitants, generally a journey of no spiritual import, part of a social routine. Only in sections IV and V—'Death by Water' (the voyage of the Phoenician sailor) and 'What the Thunder Said'—does the travelling assume any wider scope. The first three sections of the poem deal with what we may call the social realities of the waste land: with what its people see and do. This picture is illuminated by occasional flashes of insight on the part of some of the speakers, by the introduction of Tiresias, who comments on the action, and by the hidden commentary of the allusions to past literatures.

In the fifth part the emphasis changes and we are shown behind the social coverings to see directly the disease of the land and its people. It has entirely the atmosphere of nightmare, but this apparent fantasy probes beyond the earlier social reality to the basic issues of the poem. We remain conscious of the preceding background, but are aware now that it was partly responsible for concealing from the people the true nature of their position.

To show how this comes about, and to consider it in greater detail, each of the sections must now be examined.

'The Burial of the Dead'

'From the middle of June the land of Egypt is but half-alive, waiting for the new Nile' (*The Golden Bough*, Vol. 2: *Attis, Adonis, Osiris*, chapter 3, p. 31). This is the state of Eliot's waste land. The coming of April with its refreshing rain is resented, as Stetson resents the idea of disturbance later in this section. The line

> *Bin gar keine Russin, stamm' aus Litauen echt Deutsch,*

places the speaker in the same category as the 'Chicago Semite Viennese' of 'Burbank with a Baedeker', as the Jew in 'Gerontion',

> *Spawned in some estaminet in Antwerp,*
> *Blistered in Brussels, patched and peeled in London,*

as 'Mistah Kurtz', type of the hollow men—the epigraph to that poem tells us that Mistah Kurtz is dead. Conrad's description of him in *The Heart of Darkness* is:

'His mother was half-English, his father was half-French. All Europe contributed to his making.'

We are reminded of Eliot's contention in *After Strange Gods* that the struggle of our time is to establish a vital connexion between the individual and the race. These déraciné cosmopolitans represent for him the last stage in the loss of connexion with a national life. And being so deprived of tradition and national culture they become susceptible to undue awareness of self, and to the temptation to cut adrift from any external authority, spiritual or temporal. In them is exemplified the disease of the waste land—refusal to surrender one's desires to an external directing force.[1]

The speaker's thoughts then drift to memories of her childhood—[2]

1. For a different opinion see Alec Brown's *The Lyric Impulse in T. S. Eliot*, where he concludes that Eliot's treatment of the Jew in 'Gerontion' indicates racial prejudice and nothing more. This attitude to poetry is discussed in chapter 6.

2. The sex of the speaker is revealed by the German phrase in line 12. Each of the first three sections of the poem introduces a man and a woman, dissecting

> *And when we were children, staying at the arch-duke's,*
> *My cousin's, he took me out on a sled. . . .*

This tells us that she is separated not only from the life of a nation, but also from that other natural unit, the family, for her memories involve neither father nor mother, only a holiday at a cousin's. The importance of the family unit Eliot has stressed in his *Notes towards the Definition of Culture.* To take this reading here is not mere unsupported ingenuity, for the same theme is part of the subject of the next section, where it is more fully elaborated.

The journey symbol is briefly introduced in the remark, 'I read, much of the night, and go south in the winter. . . .' Ivy, in *The Family Reunion*, expresses the same desire when she says, 'Were I in Amy's position I would go south in the winter . . .', equally attracted by the shiftless travelling of the social seasons. Absorption in such interests cloaks the true conditions, glimpsed in the following words, one of the flashes of insight granted to the people:

> *What are the roots that clutch, what branches grow*
> *Out of this stony rubbish? Son of man,*
> *You cannot say, or guess, for you know only*
> *A heap of broken images, where the sun beats,*
> *And the dead tree gives no shelter, the cricket no relief . . .*
> *I will show you fear in a handful of dust.*

The complete revelation of the 'fear in a handful of dust' is postponed to the last section, but even at this stage the nightmare has intruded.

To the recounting of the love between the speaker, who is the Hyacinth girl—Hyacinth was one of the fertility gods—and her silent companion, quotations from Wagner's 'Tristan and Isolde' add their comment. The first is from the sailor's song in Act I, an ironic motif later used to accompany Isolde's,

> *Degenerate race, unworthy your fathers.*

the barrenness of their experience of love. Here the presence of the man is implied by the woman's speaking to him of their meeting in the Hyacinth garden, ll, 35–36, where she breaks from her reverie into direct speech. She is evidently one of the earlier generation of displaced persons, an heir to the political confusion created after the first world war by the carving from Russian territory of a few tiny republics.

It is far from being what Brooks calls it in his analysis of *The Waste Land*—'a song of happy love'. The second allusion, a description of the sea as waste and empty when Tristan asks if Isolde's ship is in sight, has the implication of the same allusion in 'Sweeney Erect'. This, from *Tristan and Isolde*, by A. L. Cleather and Basil Crump, is illuminating:

'. . . as Tristan anxiously inquires whether the steersman can be trusted to guide her safely into port and is not a treacherous ally of Melot, who may perchance betray him, the Betrayal motive . . . reappears.'

We are probably meant to recall this when the description of the typist's seduction is coupled with the evening hour that 'brings the sailor home from sea'.

The predictions of Madame Sosostris, the society fortune teller, are important to the development of the poem. The precise original significance of the Tarot symbols has little relevance to Eliot's design, but it is a measure of the waste land's decline that these cards, once used to foretell an event of primary importance—the rising of the Nile's waters—are now used in connexion with the tawdry, worn, coinage of the modern fortune teller's clichés.[1] The Wheel, the one-eyed merchant, the Hanged Man, 'Death by water', 'crowds of people, walking round in a ring', all recur in the following sections.

The Wheel and death by water are found again in section IV, where the wheel symbolises the attempts of humans to direct unaided their own destiny:

1. A theme that recurs quite frequently in Eliot's poetry—in Doris's manipulations of the cards in 'Sweeney Agonistes', or more explicitly in this passage from 'The Dry Salvages':

> To communicate with Mars, converse with spirits,
> To report the behaviour of the sea monster,
> Describe the horoscope, haruspicate or scry,
> Observe disease in signatures, evoke
> Biography from the wrinkles of the palm
> And tragedy from fingers; release omens
> By sortilege, or tea leaves, riddle the inevitable
> With playing cards . . .
>   . . . ; all these are usual
> Pastimes and drugs, and features of the press.

> Gentile or Jew
> O you who turn the wheel and look to windward,
> Consider Phlebas, who was once handsome and tall as you.

And, at the end of the poem, in response to the thunder's crying for submission to control, we find that only other hands can safely control the wheel:

> Damyata: The boat responded
> Gaily, to the hand expert with sail and oar
> The sea was calm, your heart would have responded
> Gaily, when invited, beating obedient
> To controlling hands

The one-eyed merchant reappears in 'The Fire Sermon' as Mr. Eugenides, the Smyrna merchant, who later, as the Phoenician sailor, is drowned and forgets 'the profit and the loss' of his transactions. The contrast is between the peace and spiritual gain of Phlebas, on his body's destruction by the life-giving water, and the petty considerations of those who still inhabit the waste land. The crowds of people appear in the Stetson passage, which has already been discussed. It introduces the vast crowd of living dead, and extends the scope of the passage from the first lone speaker to cover all the people of the land.

'A Game of Chess'

The luxury surrounding the lady of the first part of this section fulfils the function of the decorative bric-à-brac in 'A Cooking Egg' and 'Cousin Nancy'. Tradition has become a collection of 'pieces', and the sense of decay is crystallised here, as it is in the Canaletto in 'Burbank', in a picture:

> Above the antique mantel was displayed
> As though a window gave upon the sylvan scene
> The change of Philomel by the barbarous king
> So rudely forced.

The description of the lady's accumulation of scents and jewels recalls, perhaps unintentionally, the parallel scene in Pope's the 'Rape of the Lock', where Belinda's toilet is described. But the relationship between the sexes here is not the harmless play of the

'Rape of the Lock'. Nor is it the passionate belief of Cleopatra—clearly alluded to in the opening lines—in the integrity of personal love, to which she is willing to sacrifice power and empire. It is that of Middleton's play, where a game of chess is played to distract attention from a seduction. So, when one of the characters here says, 'We shall play a game of chess', this is a euphemistic statement of their intention to turn again to the over-familiar routine of their physical relationships.

Their journey is once again a purposeless wandering, devoid of meaning, that preludes withdrawal to pleasure:

> *I shall rush out as I am, and walk the street*
> *With my hair down, so. What shall we do tomorrow?*
> *What shall we ever do?*
> > *The hot water at ten.*
> *And if it rains, a closed car at four.*

This union of the sexes is not in any degree actuated by a desire for children—the comment of the Cockney woman at the close of the section is relevant to the situation here as well as to her own friend's:

> *You are a proper fool, I said.*
> *Well, if Albert won't leave you alone, there it is, I said,*
> *What you get married for if you don't want children?*

We are shown two couples who desire to avoid propagation, to escape parentage. This is the same distortion of the sexual relationship that we find in the Sweeney poems. In *The Waste Land* however, the theme is developed, and the reason for the distortion, it is implied, is that these are the children of lost parents. Various allusions make this quite clear. The sylvan scene of line 98 is that of *Paradise Lost*, IV, 40, where Satan is described as a cormorant sitting on the tree of life, awaiting Adam and Eve. This summons to our minds the idea of original sin, and the fall of Adam and Eve, so many times re-enacted in the waste land. As well as this, though, there is the suggestion of the Satan who has denied God and so lost his spiritual father. The quotation from *The Tempest*, at line 125, 'Those are pearls that were his eyes', is from the song by Ariel that reminds Ferdinand of his drowned father. The father of the speaker in *The Waste Land* is similarly lost. At the end of the section Ophelia's words,

Good night, ladies, good night, sweet ladies, good night, good night,

recall that both Ophelia and Hamlet have lost their fathers, and from this stems the tragedy that overtakes them.

To these Kenneth Stevens, in the *Durham University Review* (December, 1948), adds others. In the dialogue between the man and the woman in the early part of the section—from

Speak to me. Why do you never speak. Speak.

to

You know nothing? Do you see nothing? Do you remember Nothing?—

he sees allusions to the dialogue between Lear and Cordelia at the beginning of the play, when Cordelia too answers 'Nothing', and through this loses her father and begins the tragedy. Also to Hamlet's scene with Gertrude when the ghost of his father appears in Gertrude's bedroom. Hamlet asks,

Do you see nothing there?

and Gertrude answers,

Nothing at all.

The probability that these allusions are intentional is not very high, and certainly Stevens is over-fanciful in suggesting that the Gertrude-Hamlet relationship is another aspect of the distortion of love motif. The love treated by Eliot is of a different kind altogether. In any case there is sufficient in the allusions of which we can be certain to elucidate the double strand in this section. Firstly, the unworthy nature of the physical relationships between the sexes—reinforced by the reference to Philomel—and secondly the notion of the lost father. This seems to blend with the figure of the maimed Fisher King, from whose sickness come the ills of the land. In the final section these are composed into the person of the lost leader, Coriolanus, under whose guidance the people may by their own efforts regain health.

The last part of the section is straightforward, and depicts the same situation existing in a different stratum of society. The effect of this passage is dramatic, and depends for a great part of its effect on the double meaning of the pub-owner's cry, repeated throughout the dialogue:

HURRY UP PLEASE IT'S TIME,

with its particular urgency at the very end. This is the time that must be redeemed before the land and its people can be restored.

'*The Fire Sermon*'

Here beside the deserted river—in the Grail legends the chapel was often situated beside water—is not even a sordid

> *. . . testimony of summer nights. The nymphs are departed.*
> *And their friends, the loitering heirs of city directors;*
> *Departed, have left no addresses.*

The journey is again one without aim, and one that can yield no hope. The person who fishes 'in the dull canal' is Ferdinand Prince of Naples,

> *Musing upon the king my brother's wreck*
> *And on the king my father's death before him.*

The ceremony of fishing is connected with fertility ritual. In the Māhāyana scriptures Buddha is referred to as the Fisherman who draws fish from the ocean, and is so represented in figures and pictures. 'The fish was sacred to those deities who were supposed to lead men from the shadows of death to life' (Weston quotes this from 'The Open Court' in p. 120 of her book). The allusion here is intentional, for it is the Buddha's Fire Sermon that combines with the reference to Augustine to close the section. Eliot is saying that the fishing is in the wrong hands, as the wheel in section IV is also in the wrong hands. The situation is presented again at the close of the poem where we are told that the question,

> *Shall I at least set my lands in order?*

must be decided. Presumably, that is, the affairs of each individual's life must be regulated before salvation can be expected. There is no short-cut, for it cannot be attained by attempts to construct

> *Systems so perfect that no one will need to be good.*
> (Choruses from *The Rock: Collected Poems*, p. 170.)

These lines provide a complicated illustration of the method of allusion:

> *But at my back from time to time I hear*
> *The sound of horns and motors, which shall bring*
> *Sweeney to Mrs. Porter in the Spring.*

We are meant to recall, firstly, Marvell's

> *But at my back I always hear*
> *Time's winged chariot hurrying near.*
> *And yonder all before us lie*
> *Deserts of vast eternity.*

and Day's

> *When of a sudden, listening, you shall hear*
> *A noise of horns and hunting, which shall bring*
> *Actaeon to Diana in the spring,*
> *When all shall see her naked skin. . . .*

Implied is the double idea of the fall of love from the Greek ideal, where it was looked on as a god, and the preoccupation of mankind with commonplace amusements which divert their minds from realisation of their insignificance in the face of eternity. This idea was in Marvell's mind even when he wrote an ode to his Coy Mistress. The Coy Mistress of modern times can arouse no such associations.

The method by which Eliot communicates this is in essence that of Pope when he wrote in the 'Epistle to Augustus':

> *Oh! could I mount on the Aeonian wing,*
> *Your arms, your Action, your repose to sing!*

The bathos of Pope's lines is completed by his intention that the reader should be misled by recollection of Pomfret's line in 'Cruelty and Lust':

> *Your sword, your Conduct, and your Cause attend.*

This is presumably one of Eliot's pointless and tasteless parodies, noticed by the early reviewers. It is certainly not without point, and the question of taste hardly arises.

Immediately after this, the reference to Mrs. Porter and her daughter who

> *. . . wash their feet in soda water,*

is associated with the singing of the children, which accompanies the ceremony of feet-washing in the Grail legend. This precedes the restoration of the Fisher King to health. Inevitably, too, it suggests the Christian ceremony of baptism. A comment by R. G. Collingwood on the basis of love in our civilisation is apposite as a summary of this section:

'. . . these things (*i.e.* the erotic nature of much advertising and newspaper illustration) reveal a society in which sexual passion has so far decayed as to have become no longer a god, as for the Greeks, or a devil, as for the early Christians, but a toy: a society where the instinctive desire to propagate has been weakened . . .' (*Principles of Art*, p. 85).

An echo from the previous section of the bird song and the account of Philomel's betrayal rounds off the meaning of the passage.

The seduction of the typist introduces Tiresias, representative of both sexes, who sees the consummation of the clerk's desires. The eighteenth-century attitude to 'lovely woman's' folly, even if only conventional, was, it is suggested, better than the indifference with which this couple regard their action. Tiresias looks on a scene that typifies all the sexual relationships in the poem, and so what he sees is 'the substance of the poem'. All the more so because the music that he hears repeats one of the leading themes —that of the lost father:

> *Sitting upon a bank*
> *Weeping again the king my father's wreck,*
> *This music crept by me upon the waters,*

And the father here, not only the leader of a family, is also the leader of a country, being once again Ferdinand's father, the king. As before, at the conclusion of the glimpse of the waste land's mechanical pleasure, it is impressed upon us that what these people lack is guidance from without.

The music leads the poem's action to one of the few manifestations of virility in the waste land, in lower Thames Street, abode of the fishmen, those who continue to give allegiance to the source of life. They live by the river, and by the church. Still by the river, 'Down Greenwich Reach', we come to the Isle of Dogs, where spiritual force is retained and the Dog is not, as before, bidden to 'keep far hence'.

This manifestation of virility is transitory, however, and with the song of the three Thames daughters who, like Wagner's Rhine daughters, have been violated, comes the treatment of the river as it appears now, dirty and sordid. That the following lines, switching to the scene on the Thames as Elizabeth travels in magnificent procession, are partially a contrast to the contemporary squalor is indubitable. Brooks goes astray, however, in saying that their function is that of the Cleopatra allusion, allotted in this section to the Marvell reference. The contrast here is purely between surface appearances. Fundamentally Elizabeth is the same as the childless lovers of all the earlier sections. She toys with the idea of marriage and remains childless—Eliot refers to this specifically in his note on the passage. The exact parallel to Elizabeth in the modern scene is the woman in the first part of 'A Game of Chess', also surrounded by luxury. The distinction is not between a gloriously colourful past and a drab present on any but the visual plane. Cleopatra provides a genuine contrast to both in that her love was not indifferent and sterile. She followed a way of life that was misdirected, but her choice of that way was positive. In an essay in 'Revelation' (ed. J. Baillie and H. Martin) Eliot's comment on D. H. Lawrence's search for an element in any religion that would go deeper than a simple code of morals, is equally a comment on his attitude to Cleopatra here:

'If, (I think he would have said) you find you can only accept an "evil" religion, then for God's sake do, for that is far nearer the truth than not having any. For what the evil religion has in common with the good is more important than the differences; and it is more important really to feel terror than to sing comminatory psalms.'

Each of the Thames daughters speaks in turn to recount the circumstance of her seduction. The broken quotations from St. Augustine and the Fire Sermon summarise the lesson of the section—that the sin of the actors is in the sterile burning of their lust. Buddha enunciates it thus:

The eye, O Bikkhus, is burning: visible things are burning; . . .
With what fire is it burning?
I declare unto you that it is burning with the fire of lust. . . .

So it has been in all ages. Human beings have at all times been open to, and have succumbed to, the same temptations. Tiresias observes nothing unknown to him from past experiences when he sees the typist:

> *And I Tiresias have foresuffered all*
> *Enacted on this same divan or bed;*
> *I who have sat by Thebes below the wall*
> *And walked among the lowest of the dead.*

While this is true there is some distinction made between past and present, for human beings at different times err differently. Cleopatra followed the wrong god, but did so wholeheartedly, and so invested her life with some meaning. She was not one of the living dead. We find the matter elucidated in one of the choruses from *The Rock*. The subject is the death of Christ:

> *Then it seemed as if men must proceed from light to light, in the light*
>   *of the Word,*
> *Through the Passion and the Sacrifice saved in spite of their negative*
>   *being;*
> *Bestial as always before, carnal, self-seeking as always before, selfish*
>   *and purblind as ever before,*
> *Yet always struggling, . . .*
> *But it seems that something has happened that has never happened before:*
>   *though we know not just when, or why, or how, or where.*
> *Men have left GOD not for other gods, they say, but for no god; and*
>   *this has never happened before. . . .*

It is the peculiarly negative attitude of the modern world to its life that differentiates it from earlier epochs. That and the sterility that is general to it. Again in 'Revelation', we find further discussion of this subject, in relation to the nature of secularism:

'. . . I do not mean by secularism primarily the various distractions from the Christian life, the various temptations to live on a purely animal level, which occasion so much distress to the faithful. I am not concerned with the cinema, or the press, or the wireless, or the degrading influences of a mechanised civilization. These are serious enough, but they constitute a minor problem. They represent merely the contemporary form—though it may be a form more powerful and oppressive than any before—of the permanent force of the world against which the spirit must always struggle' (p. 26).

The burning of lust, the sterility of love, the physical and spiritual drought, can be quenched only by the coming of the life-giving water, though this may mean, paradoxically, as it does in the fourth section, physical death by water. That is, a death that can lead to renewed spiritual life:

> this Birth was
> Hard and bitter agony for us, like Death, our death. . . .
> I should be glad of another death.
>
> ('Journey of the Magi.')

'What the Thunder said'

This section concentrates the essentials of the scenes enacted in the previous journeys, summarising their desolation. The social covering is stripped away, and, bereft of distractions, the people are shown in the deep horror of their self-created desert. The scene reveals what the modern journey amounts to when transposed into the terms of the orginal journey to the Grail chapel. It is a journey that cannot, as things are, be completed, and where the thirst cannot be relieved:

> Here is no water but only rock
> Rock and no water and the sandy road.

It has not been remarked that although the crux of this final section is whether the waste land is finally relieved by the coming of rain, the poem begins with a rain shower:

> Summer surprised us, coming over the Starnbergersee
> With a shower of rain;

Obviously, then, we are not now at the place in which we began, but in a land remote from the social reality of the first three sections. Only with line 423 do we make some return to the original setting. The frightening nature of the surroundings is built up to the point where the vague hordes swarm over the land, 'stumbling in cracked earth'—without a central guiding force. It is to be noted that the chapel is never reached; there is a break from the description of the travellers to the appearance of the chapel, and the two are never brought together. The chapel is empty, 'only the wind's home', as it must inevitably be from the insistence throughout on the lost father and the lost leader. The rain is certainly there—

> *Then a damp gust*
> *Bringing rain. . . .—*

but it never falls. The teaching of the poem is extremely austere, but although it is neither easy nor indulgent, we are made to see that hope remains. The rain will fall when its coming has been paid for by sacrifice: no sacrifice is made within the scope of the poem, so there is no rain at the end.

The lesson of the thunder shows what form the sacrifice must take. It involves sacrifice of self. 'The horrible tower' of Dante, in which Count Ugilino de Gherardeschi met his death, becomes here the prison of obsession with the individual personality. From this results the living death of the people. As it is expressed in the epigraph to *Burnt Norton*:

> *Although the Word is common to all, most people live as if they had*
> *each a private wisdom of his own.*

Demanded is entrance into community with the rest of one's people—implied by the background of the speaker in 'The Burial of the Dead'. And not only this, though it is a part of the design, but also common submission to the control of God. Only with this can the 'broken Coriolanus' be revived to lead the people from the wilderness, and re-establish the deserted chapel.

The dispute between critics who discuss whether the poem does or does not exhibit progression is founded on a misconception. The poem does not exhibit any progression, but this is not to be taken in the sense which Leavis gives it—that the poem ends without hope in exactly the same state as that of its beginning.[1] There is no question of progression, in the usual sense, at all. We end where we began, but reach that point by devious routes:

> *. . . the end of all our exploring*
> *Will be to arrive where we started*
> *And know the place for the first time.*

From Eliot's exploration of the waste land we see, as we could not see before, to the depths of its being. The new insight and

1. See *New Bearings*, by F. R. Leavis. Essay on T. S. Eliot.

understanding offer a hope of release from the prevailing desiccation. The leadership once contained in the chapel, now deserted, can, given certain conditions, be rehabilitated. The ultimate source of salvation has not been utterly destroyed, for although the rain remains potential, it is a potential that can be realised.

Some further support for this view is given in the allusion to *The Spanish Tragedy*:

> *Why then Ile fit you. Hieronymo's mad againe.*

These words are spoken by Hieronymo, the father who has lost his son, as he fits his actors with the parts they are to have in the play that will avenge his son's death. To this end Hieronymo eventually sacrifices his own life. Similarly in the waste land each must fulfil his true function to the extent of sacrifice and even death, before salvation may be won. The poem can not, then, be summarised in Forster's words. His view is rather similar to that of Leavis:

'It is about the fertilising waters that arrived too late. It is a poem of horror. The earth is barren, the sea salt, the fertilising thunderstorm broke too late'[1] (*Abinger Harvest*, by E. M. Forster, p. 91).

The Waste Land unfolds gradually the meaning of the symbols in each section: they are entirely interdependent. The first section presents one uprooted from his race and family, then the masses of his peers. Unconsciously the fortune teller summarises the future action—as Doris and Dusty do in 'Sweeney Agonistes'. 'A Game of Chess' reiterates and develops the symbols of unfruitful lust and the lost father. Further development in section three shows that while these are not purely modern phenomena, the modern sin is one more difficult to uproot, being not a positive election for evil, but a general lethargy. 'Death by Water' confronts us again with the merchant, now transfigured by his 'seachange'. To him the water has brought relief from temporal

1. A more recent statement of the same opinion is to be found in *T. S. Eliot*, a symposium compiled by Richard March and Tambimuttu:

'*The Waste Land* is a poem as static as is *Ulysses* or *Finnegans Wake*: in the end nothing has happened, and, as Pierre Leyris so rightly says: "King Metiegne still sins behind the gasworks".'

Claude Edmonde Magny: 'A Double Note on T. S. Eliot and James Joyce', *op. cit.*, pp. 208–217.

distractions. We are asked to consider his fate and pass immediately to the scene of horror, the land where refreshing water can be had at the cost of sacrifice which no one is prepared to make. To find Eliot's source for this echoing construction we have not far to look. Writing on Donne's sermons he has remarked:

'The method—the analogy and the repetition—is the same as that once used by a greater master of the sermon than either Donne or Andrews or Latimer: it is the method of the Fire Sermon preached by the Buddha.' (*Athenaeum*, 28th November, 1919, p. 1252).

The beliefs of this poem are entirely consonant with all Eliot's work. It is ascetic and unbending; it seems to offer only torment as a means to salvation. But beneath this can be seen a deep pity for a lost people, in which the poet includes himself. We must perceive,

> *The notion of some infinitely gentle*
> *Infinitely suffering thing*

in the 'Murmur of maternal lamentation' accompanying the progress of the 'hooded hordes'. The benediction at the close—
' "The peace which passeth understanding" is our equivalent of the word'—reaffirms the possibility of final gladness.

The total impression left by the poem, though, emphasises not the ultimate gain but the hardship that must of necessity precede this—

> *I say: take no thought of the harvest,*
> *But only of the proper sowing.*
> (Choruses from *The Rock: Collected Poems*, p. 159.)

It is the culmination of all Eliot's early thought, and in it we see clearly what was implicit in the social perplexities of the other poems. Particularly is it the final statement of the poems in the 1920 volume. The themes that troubled Eliot there are here inter-related, and a considerable step taken towards his affirmation of the Christian faith. One can see in the insistence on subordination of self to external control, in the desire for leadership, a mind deeply sympathetic to some authoritarian religion. This Eliot has since found in Anglo-Catholicism. His search for authority in literary matters is duplicated here in his search for authority in spiritual affairs. As yet, however, there is not complete acceptance. There are only the signs that it might well come to a mind so sharply aware of the uncomfortable truths of religion, so profoundly stirred by moral problems, so unwilling to believe that humanity can, by its own unaided efforts, overcome the 'traces du péché originel'.

In the 1920 poems these beliefs did not obtrude even to the limited extent that they do here. Enough of the Christian tradition has become engrained in western civilisation for there to be in most minds some residuum of sympathy for the beliefs embodied in this poem. So lax a bond will not serve to draw anyone to Eliot's work, but its existence precludes an aversion that would conceal the power of the poetry. A poetry embodying the beliefs of some traditional system is less likely to obstruct communication of the poetic pleasure, than a poetry concerned with constructing a private and personal myth from emotional reactions to the objects of reality.

By Eliot's placing his picture of the turning world in the perspective of history and traditional faiths, the forms and objects of that world draw life from their framework of myth. To the elucidation of this meaning direct presentation of the contemporary scene is necessary as it is not necessary to the later poetry. For the purposes of this study the chief interest of the remaining poetry is the gradually stronger anticipations of the later interests and methods. From the beginning Eliot has been essentially a moralist. In the majority of the remaining poems he is, equally a moralist, now unequivocally a Christian moralist. 'The Hollow Men' is generally regarded as representing the nadir of Eliot's despair, but it will be considered here as one of the transition poems leading to the *Four Quartets*. In the final analysis, it offers perhaps less hope of regeneration than *The Waste Land*, but there are signs, particularly in the symbolism, that the poet is turning from Dante's *Inferno* to his *Paradiso*. It is in this turning that can be discerned the direction that the later poetry was in fact to take.

Chapter Six

The Humanist Criticism

T HE importance to Eliot's early poetry of the contemporary scene cannot be over-emphasised. The alignment of past and present, of reality and myth,[1] is his way of 'controlling, ordering, of giving a shape and a significance to the immense panorama of futility and anarchy which is contemporary history'.[2] In this sense past and present are of equal importance. The people and their actions in 'the turning world', though, occupy the foreground and have the more immediate mastery over the imagination. The introduction of urban imagery and habits is essential to Eliot's oblique elucidation of the pattern that imperceptibly orders human affairs:

> *Even now in sordid particulars*
> *The eternal design may appear.*[3]

What distinguishes this from the later poetry is the strength of the former's dependence on evocation of the 'sordid particulars'. From the relationship between them and echoes from the past

1. Throughout, 'myth' is not intended to convey simply the idea of a fabulous story. What is meant, rather—except where the context indicates that it refers to a primitive religion—is a system of symbolism taken from a coherent philosophy. Thus a poetry which uses the Christian myth is one making use of the Christian symbols and ideas, without any implication that the validity of the religion is in doubt.

2. T. S. Eliot on James Joyce in *The Dial*, which had just awarded him its annual poetry prize for *The Waste Land*.

3. *Murder in the Cathedral*, p. 57.

results the communication of the poem's meaning and the composition of its final harmony. We are made to see, with Eliot, into spiritual matters through the details of contemporary social reality.

The later poetry moves gradually towards direct contemplation of 'the still point', and of the details of 'the eternal design'. Urban imagery ceases to be the predominant factor, and its place is taken by a revised symbolism. This shift of emphasis can be traced in the poems written between 1924 (first draft of 'The Hollow Men') and 1932 ('Difficulties of a Statesman'). They formulate the symbolism and interests of the *Quartets* much as 'Prufrock' and *Poems 1920* did those of *The Waste Land*.

Something of the earlier manner remains. The allusions, the abrupt contrasts and transitions,[1] the elliptical expression, the phrase repetitions, continue to excite the necessary mental agility. To the stuttering, conversational repetition is added a liturgical quality. The contrasts and transitions are engineered to provoke awareness of a precise religious faith.[2]

Eliot's conversion to Anglo-Catholicism has served to define the antipathy of the liberal and humanist critics to his beliefs.[3]

---

1. Similar, for example, to Prufrock's

> *I have measured out my life with coffee spoons,*

is this from 'The Dry Salvages':

> It seems, as one becomes older,
> That the past has another pattern, and ceases to be a mere sequence—
> Or even development . . .
> The moments of happiness—not the sense of well-being,
> Fruition, fulfilment, security or affection,
> Or even a very good dinner, but the sudden illumination—

2. Though Eliot's early poetry shows a strongly Puritan sensibility, the heritage of his New England upbringing, there is no attachment to any particular Church. In the later Anglican poems the same Puritan strain is evident, and the struggle between the two opposing forces, which accounts for much of Eliot's spiritual perplexity, will be discussed in the examination of the *Quartets*. (See also Chapter Five, p. 116.)

3. 'Humanist' is used here to describe all those beliefs which owe at least part of their being to the rationalism of Victorian times, and includes, therefore, the humanism of Irving Babbitt and the Marxism of Professor Laski: Babbitt was a sensitive literary critic, while Laski is not a literary critic at all. Common to both these philosophies, however, and to their allied beliefs, is a rejection of Christianity as such, though they may contain within themselves some homage to the more obviously attractive aspects of Christian morality. It is however,

Before analysing the evolution of the terms in which this faith is transcribed in the later poetry, attention may be paid to the attacks of his humanist critics. If their assertions be true, that Eliot's poetry is a betrayal of the function of art, and of the hopes of humanity, then the form in which the betrayal is enunciated becomes of slight interest. It is desirable, therefore, to assure oneself that the art with which one deals does not in fact function so unworthily.

Some remarks of David Daiches reveal the basis of the humanist, and particularly the socialist, antipathy to Eliot's work. In his comparison between Huxley, 'the thwarted romantic', and Eliot 'the thwarted classicist', Daiches protests against Eliot's joining the Anglican Church. It is, he says, an avoidance of 'the issue, which is not personal compensation but the alteration of the environment which has produced the need for that compensation —the evolution and stabilisation of a standard in which society can believe and with reference to which its activities can be given purpose and meaning and value'. This Edwin Muir calls the political view of literature, in his *Essays on Literature and Society*.[1] His short essay goes a considerable way towards exposing the fallacies of Daiches' view-point. It concentrates not on whether

with the egalitarian philosophies particularly that Eliot disagrees, so it is from that quarter that he is himself most severely criticised. With the more austere doctrine of Babbitt he is not entirely out of sympathy, finding it a valuable corrective to any tendency towards ossification in Christian dogma—see *Selected Essays*, p. 437. He insists that humanism is not to be set up as 'a view of life that will work by itself'. Though on a higher plane than humanitarianism, it is in constant danger of descending to the same level:

' . . . the humanitarian has suppressed the properly human, and is left with the animal; the humanist has suppressed the divine and is left with a human element which may quickly descend again to the animal from which he has sought to raise it.' (*Selected Essays*, p. 435.)

Egalitarianism is the kind of sentimental humanitarianism whose criticisms of Eliot's work are the subject of this examination. Holding—as Babbitt did— that there is nothing 'anterior, exterior, or superior' to the individual, they continue to the entirely sensual level, assuming that when the material needs of mankind have been entirely satisfied, nothing further will remain to be done. Man's chief end is for these new levellers the development of his personality, a personality whose appetites seem to seek no further nourishment than is suggested by the dictates of 'mere rationalism'. (*Selected Essays*, p. 439.) It is with these, then, that we are chiefly concerned.

1. Edwin Muir: *Essays on Literature and Society*, pp. 135–143.

Daiches' beliefs are themselves correct, but on his right so cursorily to dismiss Eliot's. 'Mr. Daiches thinks that Mr. Eliot's religion is merely an avoidance of the issue, and a compensation for his real duty;'—that is, to alter his environment. That Daiches should find this position tenable requires the assumption 'that Mr. Eliot's religion is not real religion, and ultimately, perhaps, that religion itself is unreal—the opium of the masses . . .' 'Mr. Daiches,' concludes Muir, 'is at liberty to say that Mr. Eliot is wrong, but not that his opinions do not exist.'

Humanist belief, then, may be considered in two aspects—the worth of its tenets, and its attitude to art not embodying those tenets. To the latter it adopts what is in essence the Platonist position:

'This being the case, ought we to confine ourselves to super-intending our poets, and compelling them to impress on their productions the likeness of a good moral character, on pain of not composing among us; . . . (*Republic*, p. 95, 'Golden Treasury').

'. . . we shall henceforth be justified in refusing to admit him (the poet) into a state that would fain enjoy a good constitution, because he excites and feeds and strengthens this worthless part of the soul, and thus destroys the rational part; . . . Exactly so' (ibid., p. 350).

The new Platonists consider that they have found a function that will render the artist socially useful. But to the artist who does not conform there can remain, one is inescapably driven to conclude, one fate—exclusion from the state. This decision does not obtrude in Daiches' remarks, but is certainly implicit in Professor Laski's examination of Eliot's poetry. Both Daiches and Laski condemn Eliot for his beliefs. Laski's fuller treatment of the subject, in his book *Faith, Reason, and Civilization* provides more detailed ground for discussion.

Not only because of his beliefs, but because 'he neither sought nor desired to make his music heard by ordinary people, (speaking) to an élite the real pride of which lay in its deliberate cultivation of remoteness from the ordinary people',[1] Eliot's poetry, in Laski's view, stands condemned. Bidden, then, to speak to the ordinary people, the poet is permitted to

1. H. J. Laski: *Faith, Reason and Civilization*, p. 105.

communicate to them only certain things. 'When the poet ceases to be Shelley's "unacknowledged legislator of the world" it is because he has ceased to find meaning in the world . . . it is rather the echo of his own voice than the message he has to proclaim that is of importance to him . . . he thus deliberately turns his back upon the supreme issue of whether it is in our power to elevate the standards of value and taste throughout our society . . . great literature cannot be either a means of escape merely from the tragic burden of life, nor can it seek to provide the artist with no more than a means of self-realisation. . . . Great artists can only be free when they call the world to freedom.'[1] On page 138, finally, Eliot is placed among those who, because they stand aloof from what Laski sees as the problems of their time—though in truth it is rather that they do not adopt what Laski thinks is the right attitude to those problems—'desert the main task to which they are called . . . of giving their fellow citizens counsel on the vital issues they have to solve'.

It is interesting that Laski should look on the poet as being specifically Shelley's legislator. To suggest that the attraction of Shelley's Godwinism prompted the choice is not unfair. Yet Shelley's poetry is still read despite rather than because of his Godwinism, a fact which should lead one to suspect that poetry depends for its power on something other than political science. Surprisingly enough, Dr. Johnson also looked on the poet as a 'legislator of mankind', though not one concerned with temporal, impermanent desires, conceived in politico-social terms. His 'legislator of mankind' was 'to estimate the happiness and misery of every condition; observe the power of all the passions in all their combinations, and trace the changes of the human mind as they are modified by various institutions and accidental influences of climate or custom, from the sprightliness of infancy to the despondence of decrepitude. He must divest himself of the prejudices of his age and country; he must consider right and wrong in their abstracted and invariable state: he must disregard present laws and opinions, and rise to general and transcendental truths, which will always be the same: . . .' (*Rasselas*, end of Chapter XI). And these things must not be thought of simply in terms of the material, for as Johnson says elsewhere in the same work,

1. H. J. Laski: *Faith, Reason and Civilization*, p. 109.

man surely has some desires 'distinct from sense which must be gratified before he can be happy' (Chapter I).

Johnson, then, looks on the poet's task as, basically, descriptive. The poet as legislator, unconcerned with 'present laws', systematises the laws by which man does act, and not, in the first instance, those by which he should. There is of course more to it than that. The selectivity of the poet's description, his making contiguous the texture of his own age and 'general and transcendental truths', are ultimately a positive criticism, not merely a description, of the mind and customs of his time. Further than this it is unwise to go. The poet's criticism is not a matter for which one can, *a priori*, define rules. It is, however, quite evident that to expect the poet to criticise purely in the dominant political mood is to deprive him instantly of what should be his greatest attribute, that he should 'divest himself of the prejudices of his age and country', while remaining sensitive enough to embody in his poetry the 'accidental influences of climate and custom'. The poet, that is, is not an advocate of change, but one who describes and interprets the pattern of his time. He is concerned, as Eliot is, with contemporary issues not *per se*, but in relation to past events and spiritual realities.

> The world turns and the world changes,
> But one thing does not change.
> In all of my years, one thing does not change.
> However you disguise it, this thing does not change:
> The perpetual struggle of Good and Evil.

(Choruses from *The Rock: Collected Poems*, p. 159.)

Incontestably Johnson's analysis applies to more past writers than does Laski's. In particular Eliot, as has been shown, is peculiarly sensitive to the characteristics of his time and has, by the light of his own principles, made his comment on them. It is no part of his business as a poet to draw up a social programme that will remedy the defects. What is called for, in fact, by the socialist professor at the poet's breakfast table, is an entirely new art, owing nothing to traditional canons, and suffering in Laski's analysis from insufficient definition. 'The ordinary people' are sufficiently well-known not to require definition. They are those least interested in art, and least qualified to discriminate between the subtlest and the crudest playing on their sensibilities. With the masses as arbiters then, the subject-matter of poetry, its 'message' and not its artistic power, must be the criterion. From such beginnings would be evolved an art designed to do nothing more than restate social aspirations, versifying plans considered by the masses to be in their own best interests. This theorising has been given practical application in the U.S.S.R.,[1] with the additional refinement of creating committees to 'interpret' the people's wishes, and protect them against 'bourgeois deviationist tendencies' in art.

Further, Laski fails to explain why the elevation of standards of value and taste should be one of the supreme issues for the poet rather than, say, the critic; and why, should he manage to further this end, it should result in his work's expressing the tragic burden of life. In practice, Eliot's work did much to raise his medium from the depths of poetastry to which it had been reduced by the Georgian versifiers. The effects of this are the subject of an earlier chapter. Paramount among them was the reintroduction of a spirit that did not seek to exclude from poetry 'the tragic burden of life'. To suggest that Eliot's poetry seeks to avoid tragedy reveals only ignorance of his work. Ultimately it is the humanist themselves who seek to escape it, by their naive faith that it can be eliminated by legislation.

There is a disturbing facility in Professor Laski's enthusiasm for this eventual earthly freedom, in the legislation for which the poet also, presumably, must partake. One's confidence in Laski's ability to decide what poetry actually does, quite apart from his idea of what it should do, is considerably shaken by the absurdity of his assertion that Eliot's poetry is written that he may hear 'the echo of his own voice'. Eliot has never looked with favour on the

1. It is from the cultural activities of this country alone that can be inferred what one might call the apotheosis of Laski's views. Inferred, for example, from such things as Eliot's recent inclusion in the Soviet bestiary as a Fascist jackal, during the Wroclaw Congress of Intellectuals. It may well have been this that prompted Eliot's comment on Russian Communism, one of the few outspoken remarks on contemporary politics that Eliot has permitted himself. He was quoted as describing the Cultural and Scientific Congress held in New York in March 1949 as 'the new Stalinist peace conference . . . an attempt to demoralise intellectual and moral integrity everywhere.' This opinion he expressed in a cable to a rival group—Americans for Intellectual Freedom.

notion that poetry is a transcription of the poet's personality. The community on which he depends, however, to adjust the balance between the privacy of personal impulses and objectivity is artistic and not social: it is the community of traditional literatures, and not the collective social desires of a particular level of society. In his critical writings Eliot shows himself to be out of sympathy with egalitarianism.[1] Had his critics confined their strictures to those works they would have been on surer ground.

So much, then, for the humanist attitude to traditional art. There remain to be considered the social structure and dependent culture offered as a substitute by scientific humanism. It should be remembered that 'scientific' is used nowadays to describe a system, of thought or action, that achieves the utmost efficiency in producing material trivia. While humanism is not concerned with trivia, the freedom which it envisages is formulated in non-spiritual terms, within the new myth of simple faith in material progress and the divinity of social amelioration. No longer is any spiritual longing of humanity to occupy the poet's attention, for the fulfilment of such longings is involved in the attainment of social comfort and security. It is a prospect rather flat and prosaic to confine the wanderings of the human soul and intellect so entirely to the mundane. With this insistence on the poet's social duty, and the denial that anything else should interest him, the humanist position becomes further clarified.

They are motivated by a flaccid and sentimental goodwill, which must be satisfied of the results of its benevolence, and therefore convinces itself that the final result may be obtained

1. Most recently in *Notes towards the Definition of Culture*. The irony of the following passage particularly displeased the writer of the review mentioned below:

'The Mute Inglorious Milton Dogma.

'The Equality of Opportunity dogma, which is associated with the belief that superiority is always superiority of intellect, that some infallible method can be designed for the detection of intellect, and that a system can be devised that will infallibly nourish it, derives emotional reinforcement from the belief in the mute inglorious Milton . . . (which) . . . assumes that . . . not merely ability but genius is being wasted for lack of education; . . . The proposition that we have lost a number of Miltons and Cromwells through our tardiness in providing a comprehensive state system of education, cannot be either proved or disproved: it has a strong attraction for many ardent reforming spirits.' (pp. 102–103.)

within the immediate scope of human experience. To believe that a profounder reconciliation between man and his sins may be obtained 'among the stars', requires an exercise of faith too great for humanist egoism: reward and punishment must be clearly evidenced before them. This is the limited pity that dissects 'Mr. Eliot's Cold Heart'.[1] Eliot is seen as possessing no pity for mankind. Certainly he weeps no blatant tears over their earthly misfortunes, but this is because he does not see that perfection in social conditions would carry with it the fullest and most satisfactory life. It is a justifiable opinion that the affairs of man will not necessarily become endowed with meaning 'when every theatre has been replaced by 100 cinemas . . . when every horse has been replaced by 100 cheap motor cars . . . when applied science has done everything possible with the materials on this earth to make life as interesting as possible',[2] and when enjoyment of these is accessible to all. Eliot's real pity is obscured by his lack of interest in what he thinks merely subsidiary: that is, in those things which the humanist thinks all-important.

These are, the full development of the personality (discovery of mute inglorious Miltons), harmonious relations between man and man, based on composite 'objective' systems of morality. Such systems, compounded from the works of widely diverse artists and thinkers, are fairly represented by the bits-and-pieces philosophy of Norman Foerster. He hoped to model his behaviour on:

'Greek sculpture, Homer, Sophocles, Plato, Aristotle, Vergil, Horace, Jesus, Paul, Augustine, Francis of Assisi, Buddha, Confucius, Shakespeare, Milton, and Goethe' (see T. S. Eliot *Selected Essays*, p. 449).

To expect that this would provide a coherent philosophy is a tribute to rationalist optimism, if not to its rationality. The list repeats the common error of confusing literature with morality and the formulation of precise schemes of living.

While poetry may be written in a direct relationship to some coherent, traditional system of thought, its primary purpose is

1. Title of a review of *Notes towards the Definition of Culture*, in *The Plain View*, a humanist quarterly, April 1949, pp. 36–47.
2. T. S. Eliot, *Selected Essays*, p. 421.

not to inculcate acceptance of that system. Poetry requires a background of myth to provide common ground between artist and audience. This it may seek even by appeal to the recesses of racial memory. Collective memory has its foundations in instinctive human responses to the seasonal cycle, the primary symbols of death and rebirth.[1] The most primitive religions not only sought from their gods satisfaction of their material needs alone, but also believed that by their god's death was ensured a new spiritual life. Living close to the earth, though, material reward they did expect, so in Western civilization the primitive instincts find their most spiritual embodiment in Christianity. Christian teaching promises no earthly reward, and to live by it demands the exercise of faith, for it is not a system fabricated by humans to answer pleasingly their own instinctive responses. Poetry, then, takes Christianity as its background not to formulate a morality, but because it is one of the ways by which the questions with which poetry concerns itself, the repeated attempts of mankind to perceive order in the material scene, may be related to something beyond the material. This is why, while poetry is not religion, it is not unconnected with religion.

With the advance of efficiency in applied science, and the resultant tantalising glimpses of a reconciliation between man and his surroundings, thinkers, by a kind of philosophical atavism, return to the position of the most primitive religions and expect from the god of science reward here on earth, with no thought now of any spiritual renewal. Denied, therefore, are those

---

1. As in *The Waste Land*, for example. The same thing is found, to some extent, in the later *Family Reunion*, a play, as Edith Fry puts it, 'with a background . . . of theories of the subconscious'. In some of the lyrics is recapitulated the association of spring not simply with renewed life, but with a renewal that depends on suffering and sacrifice. So to the appeal to subconscious responses is added a more exacting philosophy:

> *Spring is an issue of blood*
> *A season of sacrifice*
> *And the wail of a new full tide*
> *Returning to the ghosts of the dead*
> *Those whom the winter drowned.*
> *Return to the land in the spring?*
> *Do the dead wish to return?*

See essay by Edith Fry in *The British Annual of Literature*, Vol. 5, pp. 8-15.

spiritual longings of mankind which cannot be answered by canalisation into purely material channels. This is a natural result of the remoteness achieved by love of humanity rather than of men. Eliot's sympathy extends beyond human suffering on earth to the problems of man's relation with God, and the tragedy of their unsatisfactory nature. Foreseen is a reconciliation between man and God, not between man and his surroundings—

> *another intensity*
> *For a further union, a deeper communion*
> *Through the dark-cold and the empty desolation.*
>
> (*East Coker*, p. 23.)

It is difficult to see the cold heart as the dominating characteristic of a poet who, rejecting 'The worshippers of the machine', cries that

> *The only wisdom we can hope to acquire*
> *Is the wisdom of humility: humility is endless.*
>
> (*East Coker*, p. 18.)

Acceptance of humility makes all the more difficult belief that man can attain a state of bliss on earth by manipulation of the earth's resources. In the sight of Professor Laski Christ becomes a first-century socialist, making 'a deliberate appeal to the poor and the humble and the despised',[1] his whole teaching confined to the sermon on the mount. With this circumscribed view it is not surprising that Laski should come to look on the kingdom of heaven as being realisable on earth, to object to what he calls the 'aloofness' of Eliot's religion, in contrast to the 'massive simplicity' of its founders' teaching. Yet different ages require different poetic idioms, and this, not ideological considerations, is the reason for the complexity of Eliot's restatement.

In point of fact the reason for this dislike of Eliot is that he should attach his faith to Christianity at all. It is on the whole a system of belief that has fallen into disrepute with the humanists, except in so far as they may select from its morality. Daiches quotes with approval C. Day Lewis's pronouncement that 'for the past 100 years this Christian background (to literature) has been disintegrating, till now nothing remains of it but a few faded

---

1. *Faith, Reason, and Civilization,* p. 109.

tatters . . .' (Daiches, *New Literary Values*, p. 140). Believing this
the humanists seek a new literary myth in the various materialistic
philosophies which have in common a faith that man can be
satisfied by a peace encompassed by understanding. Anything
that passes the understanding, cannot be fully envisaged on earth,
is unreal and a compensation for true needs. Whatever may be
thought of this as a political programme it is certain that no
poetic myth can be established on so narrow a foundation. Nor is
it any argument against attempts to rehabilitate the Christian
background, so that it may once again provide a poetic myth—
assuming that such rehabilitation is necessary.

When Professor Laski says that 'great artists can only be free
when they call the world to freedom', it is to his own peculiar
conception that he refers, and for this that the poet must legislate.
The egalitarian society may be attainable, but equality does not
necessarily imply freedom. What has happened is that the cast of
mind that preferred liberty to equality has been replaced by one
that prefers equality, while continuing to pay lip service to the
older ideal. One result of this is the concern of Laski to sub-
stantiate his case by reference to writers of the past. The concern
is insincere.[1] The culture represented by the writers of the past
could have no kinship with the culture stemming from the new
order of society, and as it is this which Laski reveres he can have
no real sympathy for traditional culture, nor desire to see it
perpetuated.

The extreme socialist antipathy to Eliot's poetry is basically an
antipathy to all traditional art, entirely political at its source. Even
in the less extreme humanist philosophies[2] is evident the same

1. Part of the argument of *Notes towards the Definition of Culture*. The choice
is between culture as we know it today, and equality: 'Culture itself is regarded
either as a negligible by-product which can be left to itself, or as a department
of life to be organised in accordance with the particular scheme we favour.'
(p. 89.) It is easy to decide which of these alternatives is favoured by Laski,
intelligent enough to see that the powerful influence of art must not be allowed
to run counter to the imposed system.

2. To be seen, for example, in the conception of art as morality, as it is considered by Norman Foerster. While in itself this is quite innocuous, by placing
the emphasis wrongly it initiates the advance to the position where opinions
expressed in works of art are thought all-important. It is ironic that the
political theories most likely to adopt this attitude are entirely opposed to the
milder humanist philosophies.

tendency to judge an art by the opinions it seems to express. In fact humanist thought has so permeated society that there is generally felt to be something shameful in not sharing to some extent its 'liberal' philosophy. As E. M. Forster has said in *The Listener*[1] Eliot, despite his many-sidedness, is not a liberal. This is fairly evident: he has, for one thing, committed himself to the opinion that he sees nothing wrong in principle with the idea of having a list of prohibited books.[2] Because of prevailing prejudices some critics have convinced themselves of the necessity of explaining away what seem non-liberal views in his poetry, and seizing with joy on passages indicating non-authoritarian sympathies. Anne Ridler is at pains to clarify her dislike of 'the damp souls of housemaids', while suggesting that it might, with elaboration, have been transformed into a politically innocuous sentiment:

'Do I find this cheap because of a snobbish feeling that housemaids are not fair game? I think it is rather because the poet has not sufficiently proved the connexion between "damp" and their souls, as a class.'[3]

This introduction into poetic criticism of the social conscience, the suggestion that the passing phrases of poetry require proof, are disquieting developments. Being less extreme, however, these manifestations of the political view of literature have greater value, and, elucidating Eliot's opinions merely to disagree with them, not to reject them as entirely unreal, help in the exposition of Eliot's thought.

M. C. Bradbrook's comment on 'Coriolan'[4] is useful material for those who would seek to prove that Eliot is on the side of the liberal angels. As well as this, however, it illuminates what might have been part of Eliot's intention:

'. . . in general, Eliot's destructive criticism has also anticipated the more general verdict, even as in the poems "Triumphal March" and "Difficulties of a Statesman" (1932) he anticipated the spirit of Nazi Germany and the spirit of Munich with prophetic accuracy.'

1. *The Listener*, 20th January, 1949, p. 111.
2. *The Use of Poetry and the Use of Criticism*, p. 136.
3. *T. S. Eliot*, ed. B. Rajan. 'A Question of Speech', by A. Ridler, p. 117.
4. Ibid., *Eliot's Critical Method*, by M. C. Bradbrook, p. 119.

Apparent here is the extreme form of the desire to correlate poetry with contemporary social phenomena. Poetry inevitably bears some relationship to the society in which it is written, but this criticism goes further, to assume that poetry that might have been written with an explicit contemporary analogy in the poet's mind must have been so written. Eliot may have written these two poems with the notion of suggesting the frightening potentiality of political leader-worship—to be realised in Germany—and the not infrequent inability of democratic government to deal with it. There is little in 'Triumphal March', however, to suggest that it is intended as a warning against the danger of accepting an absolute ruler—rather the reverse.

It is the first of a proposed series of poems under the general title 'Coriolan'. The title immediately reminds us of Eliot's use of Coriolanus to symbolise the lost leader—the reminiscence of Roman victory ceremonial is thus explained:

> *Now they go up to the temple. Then the sacrifice.*
> *Now come the virgins bearing urns, urns containing*
> *Dust*
> *Dust . . .*

In 'A Cooking Egg' the absence of Coriolanus was associated with drabness, with absence of colour and vitality:

> *Where are the eagles and the trumpets?*

Now these have been re-discovered:

> *And the flags. And the trumpets. And so many eagles.*
> *How many? Count them. . . .*

This contrast may be applied also to the tedious formulae of committee meetings in 'Difficulties of a Statesman'. The emphasis on the glory associated with the crowd's hero is continued in the passage which describes the leader himself, strongly reminiscent of Heine's adulatory account of his seeing Napoleon march by. These are the relevant passages:

> *There he is now, look:*
> *There is no interrogation in his eyes*
> *Or in the hands, quiet over the horse's neck,*
> *And the eyes watchful, waiting, perceiving, indifferent.*

'. . . and those lips were smiling, and the eye too was smiling. It was an eye clear as the sky; it could read all the hearts of men: it saw all things in this world at a glance, while the others see them only one after the other, and see only shadows.'

There is the same difference between the perceiving of Heine's Emperor and that of his followers as there is between that of Eliot's leader and the 'press of people':

The natural waking life of our Ego is a perceiving,

but it is not the keener perception of the horseman.

The poem adopts a favourable attitude to attempts to restore strong leadership, to revive the 'broken Coriolanus'. The leader here may be one who keeps his eyes fixed on God, 'the still point of the turning world', as Frank Wilson holds.[1] Or he may be himself the still point. Turning for the moment to 'Difficulties of a Statesman', we find it concerned with the delays and triviality of democratically instituted committees, and once again with the necessity for religious discipline. There is a repetition of the symbolism in the first poem—the still moment, the haven represented by the dove, here sought, not, as in 'Triumphal March', attained:

> *May we not be some time, almost now, together,*
> *If the mactations, immolations, oblations, impetrations,*
> *Are now observed*
> *May we not be*
> *O hidden*
> *Hidden in the stillness of noon, in the silent croaking night.*

The anxiety and uncertainty of the speaker contrast with the assured community of the crowd which watches the leader pass— a crowd that is not idealised by Eliot, but whose mass forms a common ego through their localisation of interest in the leader. In his presence they become a community, their concerns subordinated to his power, focused at the still centre. This community depends to a considerable extent on the religious faith implicit in the ceremonial devolving upon the leader, a faith which, the speaker in the second poem feels, could produce the same result in his society.

It is not improbable then, that the leader is not any one earthly leader, but a transfigured version of the composite Coriolanus in

1. *Six Essays on the Development of T. S. Eliot*, by Frank Wilson, p. 45.

The Waste Land—not improbable that he represents even the law of God:

> The Word of the LORD came unto me saying: . . .
> I have given you speech for endless palaver,
> I have given you my Law, and you set up commissions,[1]

(Choruses from *The Rock: Collected Poems*, p. 165.)

This impression is intensified by the sharply deepened meaning of the closing lines, from the banal opening question to the final triumphal cry:

>   *Please, will you*
> Give us a light?
> Light
> Light
> Et les soldats faisaient la haie? ILS LA FAISAIENT.

The insistence on 'light', associated constantly by Eliot with the spiritual centre of life, confirms the possibility that the central character of the poem is more than a political figure. Most obviously the symbol is related to the common idea of Christ as the light of the world—an example of the way in which poetry can reanimate the weariest image. Eliot's use of it suggests that he owes something also to Dante's conception of the 'simple flame'. This passage from *Burnt Norton* illustrates clearly Eliot's vision of the still point:

> The release from action and suffering, release from the inner
> And the outer compulsion, yet surrounded
> By a grace of sense, a white light still and moving, . . .
>   . . . After the kingfisher's wing
> Has answered light to light, and is silent, the light is still
> At the still point of the turning world.

1. In *Coriolanus*, V. 2, the soldier speaks to Mercius of Coriolanus:
> The worthy fellow is our general: he is the rock,
> The oak not to be wind-shaken.

Something of this image seems to have been adopted by Eliot in his description of the spiritual leader in *The Rock*:
> I perceive approaching
> The Rock . . .
> The Witness. The Critic. The Stranger
> The God-shaken, in whom truth is inborn.

This offers further support for the argument that Coriolanus has become in Eliot's mind considerably more than a political leader.

The bearing of the Coriolan symbolism on the *Quartets* will be
further examined in the following section. Even from this much,
however, it is clear that a great deal more is implied in 'Triumphal
March' than an episode from the history of political leader-
worship.

The poem operates at many levels of experience: the suddenly
created unanimity of a crowd that watches a ceremonial procession, particularly a procession that gives a material form to some
shared attribute, such as nationality or religious faith; the desire
for a durable centre of stability and community; the intrusion into
a profoundly moving experience of trivial personal distractions.
Even if it is related to some definite happening—Montgomery
Belgion suggests the London Victory March of 1919—the recurring dissolution of scene, and the spiritual significance of the
symbolism, are assurances that Eliot did intend the work to have
the undertones that have been outlined.

Frank Wilson finds that 'Coriolan' is marred by a 'trailing and
diffuse verse pattern'. On the verge of the plays and *Quartets*, the
poems do reveal very clearly the fumbling for imagery and symbolism that is consummated in the later work. For this reason the
symbolism is, for Eliot, curiously undefined. The verse, though,
is not so much an attempt to formulate a new mode for future
use—the *Quartets* use generally the blank verse base of 'Prufrock'
and the other early poems—as an entirely individual exercise,
manipulated with considerable accuracy. To take one instance,
from 'Triumphal March': the wavering liturgical quality of

> *O hidden under the dove's wing, hidden in the turtle's breast,*
> *Under the palmtree at noon, under the running water*
> *At the still point of the turning world,*

is most skilfully blended into the staccato, almost martial quality
of

> *Now they go up to the temple. Then the sacrifice,*

with its precisely onamatopoeic climax,

> *Stone, bronze, stone, steel, stone, oakleaves, horses' heels.*

The passage beginning, '5,800,000 rifles and carbines' is certainly
unsuccessful, but it is not a failure inherent in Eliot's handling of
the medium he has chosen.

If these two poems are to be taken as proving anything about Eliot's political views, it is clear that they reveal non-liberal sympathies. Whether the quality of leadership evoked in 'Coriolan' be temporal or spiritual, Eliot obviously places no great faith in the strength or ability of those who are to be led. Bradbrook's remarks are valuable in that they reduce to the most easily understood terms the subject of the poems, although she misinterprets Eliot's attitude. Yet the limitations imposed by such political interpretation are defined by the obscurity which it blankets over the full scope of the work, designed to speak to and for considerably more than political man. Extreme humanist philosophy looks forward to a new art which will speak with the voice of the state. The less extreme forms, by looking on man as little more than a social animal, and on art as something that must respect his dignity and provide him with a morality, prepare the way for this final prostitution. Eliot, once described as a 'drunken helot', is the most powerful living defender of artistic orthodoxy. Only one political view could accept the hypothesis that his art is basically worthless.

Chapter Seven
Poésie du Départ

I. THE PERSONAL ELEMENT

THE title 'Poésie du Départ' is perhaps somewhat misleading, for it is applied usually to a specific aspect of French symbolist poetry, the vague nostalgic regret associated with voyages and departures, a regret that is at the same time exhilarating. The poetry to which it refers here, however, illustrates that deeper meaning of which, Eliot says, Baudelaire had some fleeting conception in parts of his work —notably *Mon Cœur Mis à Nu*. The phrase implies in this context Eliot's departure from the beliefs of his earlier poems to full acceptance of the Christian faith. In 'Marina' the departure makes use of Baudelaire's symbol (see p. 55), but this is a secondary matter, for the departure is more obviously concerned with a particular spiritual concept. That Eliot should divert his sympathies from the urban element in Baudelaire's poetry to his glimpses of beatitude, is symptomatic of the change in Eliot himself. It is paralleled in his turning from Dante's *Inferno* and *Purgatory* to his *Paradiso*, which is of more lasting value to Eliot's poetry. The parallel is not entirely valid, but we can see the links forged by Eliot between, firstly, Baudelaire's city and Dante's Limbo, then between Dante's *Paradiso* and Baudelaire's glimpses of the divine, less assured and less sustained though they were. Eliot does not abandon his early masters. But he continues to admire them for reasons different from those which first attracted him to them.

Something has already been said of the imagery in 'Ash Wednesday', and the importance to appreciation of the poem of the
borrowings from Dante. Eliot is indebted to Dante's exaltation
of the virgin for the imagery associated with Mary in 'Ash Wednesday'. To Dante she was the rose—as to Chaucer a 'freshe
flour', and to the church generally the Rosa Mystica. In 'Ash
Wednesday' she has for Eliot the same significance exactly that
she had for the two earlier poets. She is 'exhausted and life-giving';
Chaucer invoked her:

> *O verray light of eyen that been blinde*
> *O verray lust of labour and distresse.* . . .
> . . . *for God of his goodnesse*
> *Foryiveth noon, but it like unto thee.*

The conception is of Mary's saving grace, and it is in her power
that the hope of salvation is seen in 'Ash Wednesday'. ·

Even earlier, however, the beginnings of this faith can be seen—
in 'The Hollow Men', often looked on as the nadir of Eliot's
despair. True enough, it is closely related to *The Waste Land*, in
mood and in imagery, seeming finally but a more pessimistic
restatement of that poem's conclusion. The 'prayers to broken
stone' remind us of the 'heap of broken images'. The 'tumid
river' recalls the Thames, sweating oil and tar, in *The Waste Land*.
The actors are certainly the same, the empty half-alive creatures,
the hollow men. As against this, however, the imagery of the
urban scenes has entirely disappeared. Although the poem is set
throughout in the milieu of the final section of *The Waste Land*,
the imagery that replaces the urban setting offers more hope of a
clearly envisaged path to redemption.

In an early form the poem was entitled 'Doris's Dream Songs'.
Doris appears in 'Sweeney Erect' and in 'Sweeney Agonistes', and
is indisputably a typical spokesman for the mass of Sweeney's
peers. At this stage it would seem to have been planned purely as
an elaboration of one of the flashes of insight granted to the people
of the waste land, uttered by one of them in dream. Alterations in
its structure slightly modify this plan, and how this comes about
can be seen from its evolution from three drafts that appeared at
different times.

'Doris's Dream Songs' is the first, from the *Chapbook* for 1924

It consists of section II of 'The Hollow Men', a minor poem entitled 'The wind sprang up at four o'clock' (*Collected Poems*, p. 144) and section III of 'The Hollow Men'—in that order. Set in the milieu of part V of *The Waste Land*—'death's dream kingdom' —it reveals the speaker's desire to avoid spiritual decision:

> *Let me also wear*
> *Such deliberate disguises. . . .*

The second poem, in which the speaker describes herself as 'swinging between life and death', returns quite obviously to the 'hooded hordes' of *The Waste Land*. The concluding poem leaves Doris with only 'the supplication of a dead man's hand', fearfully wondering if death will resolve the perplexities of life—

> *Is it like this*
> *In death's other kingdom?*

The exact significance of the 'Eyes I dare not meet in dreams' is vague here.

Next, in the *Criterion* of January, 1925, the design is altered by the omission of the title. The three poems comprise section II of 'The Hollow Men' again, the minor poem 'Eyes that last I saw in tears' (*Collected Poems*, p. 143), and section IV of 'The Hollow Men'. From the first poem we move this time to elaboration of the significance that the 'eyes' have for the poet. They seem, certainly, to represent some sustaining force—'eyes of decision'. Also they seem to the speaker to have lost a pity that once they possessed:

> *Here in death's dream kingdom . . .*
>
> .   .   .   .
>
> *I see the eyes but not the tears*
> *This is my affliction.*

The third of these three poems offers the solution. The hollow men, 'gathered on this beach of the tumid river', are described as:

> *Sightless, unless*
> *The eyes reappear*
> *As the perpetual star*
> *Multifoliate rose.*

With the 'multifoliate rose' we are immediately brought to Dante's vision of the virgin and the saints in heaven:

> *All, as I name them, down from leaf to leaf*
> *Are in gradation throned on the rose . . .*
> *Adown the breathing tresses of the flower.*
> (*Paradiso*, xxxii, ll. 10–13.)

Further passages illuminate yet more clearly the symbolism. The eyes in this passage are Mary's:

> *The eyes, that heaven with love and awe regards*
> *Fixed on the suitor, witnessed, how benign*
> *She looks on pious prayers: . . .*
> (*Paradiso*, xxxiii, 39–41.)

In canto xxiii, when Dante gazes on the virgin, she appears to him as a star:

> *. . . ; when at the name*
> *Of that fair flower, whom duly I invoke*
> *Both morn and eve, my soul with all her might*
> *Collected, on the goodliest ardour fixed.*
> *And, as the bright dimensions of the star*
> *In heaven excelling, as once here on earth,*
> *Were in my eyeballs livelily portrayed:*
> *Lo! from within the sky a cresset fell. . . .*

In the brightness of this star can be seen the force of Mary's absence from the 'dying stars' in this third poem. Here the significance of the eyes is, by reference to Dante, made apparent. Without it one might guess that the eyes did, by their hinted strength, symbolise a promised hope. The correlation with Dante's words, showing the eyes to be Mary's, places their meaning beyond doubt.

'The Hollow Men' is first used as a title in the *Dial* of March, 1925. It begins with the first section of the final version, which elucidates directly the nature of the speakers, their spiritual dryness and emptiness, the fact that they are not even,

> *lost*
> *Violent souls.*

139

On the basis follow the second and fourth sections of the final version. From inability to consecrate their souls 'with all their might' to spiritual devotion results the instability of their vision: capacity for spiritual experience has become atrophied. Even in this form the poem must have seemed inconclusive to Eliot, and its ultimate form includes a section which specifies the barrier between the hollow men and salvation:

1. *Dial* I
2. *Chapbook* I, *Criterion* I, *Dial* II
3. *Chapbook* III
4. *Criterion* III, *Dial* III
5. Additional section.

The quatrains which open and close the new section are spoken by the hollow men. In them is formulated their aimlessness, and the despair to which they give way:

> *Here we go round the prickly pear*
>
> *This is the way the world ends*
> *Not with a bang but a whimper.*

The bulk of the section, though, is from another source, and tells the hollow men what it is that interrupts their vision:

> *Between the idea*
> *And the reality*
> *Between the motion*
> *And the act*
> *Falls the Shadow*
> > *For Thine is the Kingdom*
>
> *Between the conception*
> *And the creation*
> *Between the emotion*
> *And the response*
> *Falls the Shadow*
> > *Life is very long*

The Shadow is the 'attachment to self and to things and to persons', of which Eliot speaks in *Little Gidding*.[1] Particularly to self, to the gratification of personal impulses which was presented in *The Waste Land* as the barrier between man and God. With the hollow men, though, it is not even a full-blooded attachment, but rather an indifferent acceptance of the easy way. By this they behave 'as the wind behaves', blindly and without purposed aim. They experience the ideas, and motions, the conceptions and the emotions, but between them and their fulfilment lie indifference and surrender without thought or struggle to the least spiritual of desires.

The poem ends with little sign of hope, but the change of symbolism reveals that a way to salvation has been perceived. The hollow men's affirmation, 'For Thine is the Kingdom', fades into the complaint, 'Life is very long', but at least the affirmation has been made. There remains the struggle to overcome the baser compulsions of the personality before the way can be entered. This struggle we find mirrored in 'Ash Wednesday' and in the Ariel poems. In 'The Hollow Men' it seems that the burden of gaining entrance into the kingdom will prove too much. Ultimately it is the slight signs of faith in the body of the poem that bear fruit.

Excluding 'Sweeney Agonistes' (*Criterion*, October, 1926, January, 1927), 'Salutation', part II of 'Ash Wednesday', is Eliot's next published work. It appeared in the *Saturday Review of Literature* for 10th December, 1927. The general theme of this poem is, as has been indicated, the destruction of the body and the resulting clarity of spiritual vision, prayer being offered to Mary for her power of intercession. The first part of the completed series of six poems was published as 'Perch' io non spero' in spring, 1928, and though later in date than 'Salutation' recounts an earlier stage in the spiritual progress with which 'Ash Wednesday' deals. Briefly, it recreates the mood which, rejecting the delusory pleasures of life, is yet unable to achieve full spiritual regeneration.

---

1. The desired alternative,

> *Detachment from self and from things and from persons,*

is an Augustinean ideal. As Ottley puts it in his *Studies in the 'Confessions' of St. Augustine*, 'Detachment from earth and its concerns is exalted as the supreme duty. In Augustine's view, all external conditions are indifferent as compared with the soul's inward relation to God.' (p. 52.)

The 'I' of the poem has hope

> *Because I do not hope to know again*
> *The infirm glory of the positive hour,*

because, finding material pleasures joyless, he must make himself
worthy to receive spiritual peace. The things of the world which
Eliot has rejected are presented in a manner startlingly different
from that of the Sweeney poems. There sin was presented in its
most obvious and least attractive form; here it is symbolised in
natural scenes of considerable charm. In the first section the 'infirm
glory' is associated with a place 'where trees flower and springs
flow', whose seductive delights are described with greater
elaboration at different points throughout the poem. Now to
reject this apparently blameless loveliness evidently requires
greater resolve than to avoid such wrong-doing as Sweeney's.
The denial of the world's attractions, in this spiritual preparation,
is to be complete.

We are reminded of the dissolution of Eliot's childhood 'penny
world', powerless against the intrusion of 'the red-eyed scavengers'
because it was a frail unsustained fancy. Eliot's attitude to worldly
beauty—apart from the matter of choice between it and the
purely spiritual—can be partly clarified here. The childhood loss
of 'A Cooking Egg', whatever it was exactly, has profoundly
affected Eliot's outlook, for he seems to seek always some sustaining force without which beauty itself is powerless and evanescent.
In the last analysis all the attractions of the world are fleeting, but
for the outwardly pleasing to appeal to Eliot it must have some
toughened quality. The lilies of the field would have no claim on
his attention had they no quality other than that of not toiling and
not spinning. This sentiment will be considered in more detail
later, for it is not without relevance to the sensibility behind these
transition poems.

It would seem that after 'Salutation' had been written, the plan
of the series formed in Eliot's mind, and he returned to an earlier,
remembered mood for his preparatory experience. The Lady in
'Salutation' who withdraws to honour 'the Virgin in meditation',
is a figure analogous to Dante's Beatrice, spiritually lesser than
Mary, yet at the end of the poem seeming to become Mary. This
point is fully dealt with in Duncan Jones's commentary on the

poem,[1] though the essay fails to stress sufficiently the full significance of the bones, considering them 'not the death of the body but a spiritual dissolution, a dying to self. . . .' This is part of the meaning, but there is implied too a physical death—a dying to the affairs of the flesh. That this has been achieved is evident from the assertion that the lower loves have been successfully denied, and the higher spiritual love accepted:

> *The single Rose*
> *Is now the Garden*
> *Where all loves end . . .*
>
> . . . . . .
> *Where all love ends.*

The assurance of vision in this poem is clearly an advance on the spasmodic insight of 'The Hollow Men'. Here the 'multifoliate rose' has assumed control. This is not, however, the final stage of 'Ash Wednesday', for the following poem reverts to the struggle against the distractions of the world.

On his ascent of the stairs Eliot is aware of the world's 'pleasant vices', symbolised here as in section I:[2]

> *At the first turning of the third stair*
> *Was a slotted window bellied like the fig's fruit*
> *And beyond the hawthorn blossom and a pasture scene*
> *The broadbacked figure drest in blue and green*
> *Enchanted the maytime with an antique flute.*
> *Blown hair is sweet, brown hair over the mouth blown,*
> *Lilac and brown hair;*
> *Distraction, . . .*

By contrast in section IV, the pure vision of an enchanting silence which is partly the silence of death—'the gilded hearse' and 'the

---

1. E. E. Duncan Jones: 'Ash Wednesday', an essay in *T. S. Eliot*, ed. B. Rajan, p. 44.

2. Though the emphasis is on the beauty, the world's distractions are symbolised also in their ugliness. More in the mood of the Sweeney poems is the description of the figure

> *At the first turning of the second stair.*

The point is that both the beauty and the ugliness are in the end superficial:

'But the essential advantage for a poet is not to have a beautiful world with which to deal: it is to be able to see beneath both beauty and ugliness; to see the boredom, and the horror, and the glory.' (*Points of View*, p. 87.)

yews' make this clear—the world's perplexing diversions have been banished. The silent sister before whom the garden god's 'flute is breathless', recalls Mallarmé's saint who becomes 'Musicienne de silence'.[1] Mallarmé's theory of the silence that is more beautiful than music is recapitulated in Eliot's suggestion of the silence which outvies the sweetest earthly music. The idea is repeated in the next poem:

> *Against the World the unstilled world still whirled*
> *About the centre of the silent Word . . .*
> *Where shall the word be found, where will the word*
> *Resound? Not here, there is not enough silence . . .*
>
> . . . .
>
> *No time to rejoice for those who walk among noise and deny the voice.*

This is an attempt to relate to the world of reality the ethereal vision of the previous poem, whose stability lasted only while the dream itself endured; an attempt, that is, to 'redeem the dream'. After the bliss of the vision must come the repeated attempt to reject the snares of the world:[2] section IV ends, 'And after this our exile.'

What exactly this self-willed exile means to Eliot is communicated in a peculiarly revealing manner in the last poem of 'Ash Wednesday'. The imagery that evokes the assiduous distractions of the world is transposed from the general to the particular, and haunts many of the later poems. 'Marina' localises Baudelaire's generalised image of the voyage to a return to New England— symbolic of the wider scope of the spiritual journey. We know

> *What seas what shores what grey rocks and what islands*

set the scene at the beginning of the poem. The quail and the

---

1. See the *Heritage of Symbolism* by C. M. Bowra, p. 11. Parallels occur frequently in Eliot's poetry. In *Burnt Norton* for example, the bird's call which acts as a summons to the rose-garden comes in response to 'The unheard music hidden in the shrubbery'. The implications of this music are elucidated in the final section of the same poem.

2. In *Points of View*, p. 100, writing of 'automatic writing as the model of literary composition', Eliot goes on to say this, relevant here:

'No masterpiece can be produced whole by such means: but neither does even the higher form of religious inspiration suffice for the religious life; even the most exalted mystic must return to the world, and use his reason to employ the results of his experience in daily life.'

water-thrush of 'Cape Ann', the 'light-in-leaves' of 'New Hampshire' live in these surroundings as they do in those of 'Ash Wednesday' VI. The return to the scene of his native country adds to Eliot's stock of imagery some of the flowers prolific in New England. These flowers, particularly the golden-rod, bloom profusely there, despite the infertile soil:

> And the lost heart stiffens and rejoices
> In the lost lilac and the lost sea voices
> And the weak spirit quickens to rebel
> For the bent golden-rod and the lost sea smell
> Quickens to recover
> The cry of quail and the whirling plover
> And the blind eye creates
> The empty forms between the ivory gates
> And smell renews the salt savour of the sandy earth.

Here Eliot is saying that the stronger part of his nature rejoices in the loss of the lilacs and the sea voices, for they are the false dreams of the ivory gates, the distractions of the world.

The selection of detail in this New England imagery accentuates Eliot's unredeemed core of Puritan feeling. The ending of 'Cape Ann', trivial though it may seem, is entirely consistent with Eliot's dissatisfaction with the merely pretty, the satisfactorily complete picturesque:

> But resign this land at the end, resign it
> To its true owner, the tough one, the sea gull.

This insistence on the necessity for a resilient tenacious quality without which the peace and the loveliness cannot endure, prevents Eliot's religious faith from lapsing into spiritual relaxation or passive acceptance of bliss. The lost heart 'stiffens', and resolve must be continually renewed; the beauty of the New England scenery has been attained through struggle against 'the sandy earth'. We may recall, in this connexion, his definition of wit as 'a tough reasonableness beneath the slight lyric grace' (*Selected Essays*, p. 293). For such an outlook external guidance is not by itself enough. Always there is the tendency to reason, to question one's assumptions: Eliot does not rest satisfied with the vision of 'Ash Wednesday' IV, but returns to the struggle in the world that lies about him. Perhaps recognising this in himself, he says in the first part of 'Ash Wednesday':

> *And I pray that I may forget*
> *These matters that with myself I too much discuss*
> *Too much explain.*

The uncompromising coastline of Eliot's home is recreated in these poems as it is in 'The Dry Salvages', the small group of rocks off Cape Ann, Massachusetts, which may well be the rocks of 'Marina'.

A distinct conflict is discernible, then, in Eliot's use of the New England background. In 'Marina' the spiritual home-coming is symbolised in the suggestion of a return to New England; in 'Ash Wednesday' the former is directly opposed to the latter. The fact that Eliot should instinctively make use of this imagery at all is an indication that the influences of his New England upbringing have not been entirely conquered. The emphasis which his descriptions lay on the harsh and the tenacious expose the Puritan feeling that man's attainment of spiritual peace, as much as his creation of earthly beauty, must depend on his own power to struggle against circumstance. Subconsciously the imagery reveals the Puritan-sentiment that pervades his Anglicanism. As well as this there is an attempt, undoubtedly partly conscious, to correlate the symbols and impressions drawn from his earliest memories with his need for a new imagery to express his new-found faith.

The symbolism of the early poems is clear-cut and almost algebraic, patterned exactly from a literary background. Anglicanism, more mystical than Puritanism, calls for a less precise utterance. Eliot does not abandon his use of traditional writings, but there intrudes also a complexus of more personal symbols. In 'Marina' occurs the association of water with the turning world and the still point:

> *Whispers and small laughter between leaves and hurrying feet*
> *Under sleep, where all the waters meet.*

And in 'Triumphal March':

> *Under the palmtree at noon, under the running water*
> *At the still point of the turning world. O hidden.*

In *The Dry Salvages*, where the idea is more elaborately worked out in the symbols of the river, the life of man, and the sea, the life of all time, some conception is given of the impact on Eliot's youth of the constant nearness of the sea:

> *His rhythm was present in the nursery bedroom,*[1]
> *In the rank ailanthus of the April dooryard,*
> *In the smell of grapes on the autumn table,*
> *And the evening circle in the winter gaslight.*

The waters represent superficially a scene of turmoil and desolation—both the river and the sea. Beneath the turbulence, though, a pattern is discernible—'under the running water', 'all the waters meet'—and at this point the final stability is represented by a white radiance of light. Apprehension of this pattern comes to the individual only in flashes at 'the unattended moment'. These glimpses of the whole are symbolised in *The Dry Salvages* as 'the winter lightning' and 'the water fall', passing signs of the greater light and water.

This symbolism is very different from that of *The Waste Land*, being not so completely defined by reference to past authors, dependent for its elucidation mainly on associations within the poem, as is the imagery of 'Rhapsody on a Windy Night'. The inter-related stages of 'Ash Wednesday' VI are to be resolved by reference to the basic contrast between the sea which, observed from the land, becomes subsidiary to man's insignificant affairs, and the sea which assumes its true importance when man is isolated in it. The ascendant impression in the opening lines is of movement—'turn', 'Wavering', 'transit', 'dreamcrossed'. This is then transferred to the image of a journey from the land, far out to sea, where the distractions of earth become of no account:

> *From the wide window towards the granite shore*
> *The white sails still fly seaward, seaward flying*
> *Unbroken wings.*

1. Not necessarily to be read as precise autobiography. Eliot, though born in St. Louis, is of New England stock, and his impressions of the New England background may be ancestral and racial, reinforced by personal experience while he lived in New England—at Harvard University for example.

There, where the 'wavering between the profit and the loss' is put behind is found 'a place of solitude' and stillness:

> *Teach us to sit still*
> *Even among these rocks.*

It is fitly associated, as in *The Dry Salvages*, with Mary—'spirit of the river, spirit of the sea'—and recalls the 'granite islands' of 'Marina', towards which the ship sails. This closely-knit progression of imagery reverts to the symbolist manner of the 'Rhapsody on a Windy Night'. The ramifications of the symbolism are complicated. Already associated with the basic symbols of the still point and the turning world are water and light, silence and the Law of God, each with its own complexities.

To summarise, then, we find Eliot's religious struggles reflected in his unsuccessful attempt to forsake the memories of his childhood, and the Puritan tendency to demand rational proof for mystical revelation reflected in his evoking the barren and durable aspects of his native surroundings, in preference to their more immediately appealing characteristics. In contrast, the lucid, 'rational' imagery of the early poems is replaced by a symbolism that depends more on the transfigured impressions of his youth, though it continues to find sustenance in traditional writings. Still implicit, not so overtly as in the early poems, is the literary background, now of Dante and Baudelaire, and in 'Marina', of the epigraph and the title.

The personal element is almost invariably buttressed by literary reminiscence: the 'ivory gates' clarify the function of the 'bent golden-rod' and other personally significant images. Yet the associations of this and the other passages are not so obscurely private as to be meaningless, without the internal comment, to the outsider. It is not at all necessary to know that Eliot is here evoking the scenes of his homeland: in this particular instance the reader is required only to see that the passage is an echo of the earlier symbol of worldly beauty. To recognise it as springing from personal experience adds to our knowledge of Eliot's mind, but not to our appreciation of his poetry.

Eliot's later poetry shows an attempt to blend the two traditions to which he is heir—that of his English ancestry, and that of his American life. Awareness of these components initiates two of the

Quartets—The Dry Salvages and *East Coker*, the latter of which is also the name of the English village from which Andrew Eliot emigrated in 1627—as well as stimulating their selection of image and symbol. This desire, and the form which it takes in the poetry, can be read as Eliot's own response to his belief, as expressed in *After Strange Gods'* (p. 48), that 'the struggle of our time . . . (is) . . . to re-establish a vital connexion between the individual and the race: the struggle, in a word, against Liberalism'. The individual is related to the race, his earthly community, as a factor in the progression to the community of Heaven. The personal element in Eliot's symbolism, then, reveals a mind that seeks community on all planes, whether it be that of family, of race, or of the Church. It is not held that this is entirely, or indeed at all, conscious. It does, however, suggest that the selection of imagery in these poems answers a deep-rooted desire in Eliot's nature. *After Strange Gods*, published in 1934, is to some extent a summary of the ideas inherent in 'Ash Wednesday', 'Marina', 'Coriolan', and the New England 'Landscapes'. It might be said that in *After Strange Gods* Eliot is concerned, at least in part, 'to defend the kind of poetry he is writing' (*The Music of Poetry*, p. 8). One can reasonably suppose that the personal element discussed here is connected with the different planes on which operates Eliot's desire for a community in which the individual may find support.

II. TRANSPOSITION OF THE FERTILITY MYTHS

In John Lehmann's words, 'the problem the poet is faced with, who wishes to establish his symbols with an enduring life in the imaginations of men, is either to create a drama of symbols (and that is a myth), or a system of symbols which every new poem he writes explores further and helps to complete' ('The Search for the Myth'; *Penguin New Writing*, No. 30, p. 152). These transition poems of Eliot represent the formative stage of the symbolism that unites the *Four Quartets*, and partly owes its existence to the fertility myths that provided the primary symbols of *The Waste Land*. More accurately, the basic symbol of the death that must be experienced before new spiritual life can be won, is taken over from the early poems, and transposed from the background of the fertility myths to that of Christianity and the Bible. Instead of in the symbolism of the Hanged Man, the reminiscences of the Corn God's burial, and the Fisher King, 'Journey of the Magi' and 'A Song for Simeon' concentrate the notion of rebirth in variations on the theme of Christ's birth.

The first is a reverie from the viewpoint of the wise men, beginning with allusions to Lancelot Andrewes' Christmas Day Sermon on their journey. After the birth of Christ the magi are

> . . . *no longer at ease here, in the old dispensation.*

The hardships of their journey to witness the birth are analogous to the torments that must accompany the destruction of their old gods, and with these gods a part of themselves.

> *this Birth was*
> *Hard and bitter agony for us, like Death, our death.*

This new background is used so that Eliot may relate his own experience of the pangs of growing faith to a specific objective narrative from the history of that faith.

That his own experience is involved is sufficiently obvious not to require elaboration. Nevertheless this passage from *The Use of Poetry and the Use of Criticism*, clearly suggested by Eliot's private memories, is relevant to the imagery of the poem (*Points of View*, p. 53):

'The song of one bird, the leap of one fish, at a particular place and time, the scent of one flower, an old woman on a German mountain path, six ruffians playing cards at nightfall at a small French railway junction where there was a water-mill: such memories have a symbolic value, but of what we cannot tell, for they come to represent the depths of feeling into which we cannot peer.'

The relevance is, particularly, to this passage:

> *Then at dawn we came to a temperate valley,*
> *Wet, below the snow line, smelling of vegetation;*
> *With a running stream and a water-mill beating the darkness,*
> *And three trees on the low sky,*
> *And an old white horse galloped away in the meadow.*
> *Then we came to a tavern with vine-leaves over the lintel,*
> *Six hands at an open door dicing for pieces of silver. . . .*

The memories in each passage are the same in kind, as well as having a certain correspondence of detail.

These glimpses of apparently trivial recollections are integrated with the wise men's discovery of the source of salvation. They are glimpses of the world's affairs seen during a journey which, when ended, will mean that the world can never again be seen in the same way, and that its interests must be put aside. They are, that is, the concrete reminiscences of 'the old dispensation.' The

> . . . *voices singing in our ears, saying*
> *That this was all folly,*

are delusory, seeking to distract the travellers from their journey to thoughts of

> *The summer palaces on slopes, the terraces,*
> *And silken girls bringing sherbet.*

These too are the attractions of the world, finally condensed in the minds of the magi as memories of passing scenes on their way. For this reason the memories 'have a symbolic value', in the way that the imagery of 'Ash Wednesday ' VI has.

'A Song for Simeon' is built on the same relationship between Biblical narrative and personal experience. Its source is in the story of Simeon in Luke ii, phrases from which echo through the poem:

25 And, behold, there was a man in Jerusalem, whose name was Simeon: and the same man was just and devout, waiting for the consolation of Israel: and the Holy Ghost was upon him.

26 And it was revealed unto him by the Holy Ghost, that he should not see death, before he had seen the Lord's Christ.

27 And he came by the spirit into the temple: and when the parents brought in the child Jesus, to do for him after the custom of the law, 28 Then took he him up in his arms, and blessed God, and said, 29 Lord, now lettest thou thy servant depart in peace, according to thy word: 30 For mine eyes have seen thy salvation, . . .

34 And Simeon blessed them, and said unto Mary his mother, Behold, this child is set for the fall and rising again of many in Israel; and for a sign which shall be spoken against;

35 (Yea, a sword shall pierce through thy own soul also,) that the thoughts of many hearts may be revealed.

Spender sees in Eliot's later poetry a loss of the sharp sensuous quality of the imagery in the early poems ('Sensuousness in modern Poetry'; *Penguin New Writing*, No. 16, p. 124). It cannot be on this poem that his judgment is based. The precision of the collocation of abstract and concrete in the opening section strikes at the intellect through the sensibility of the reader, re-animating with the associations of Eliot's own experience, the objective narrative on which the poem is superimposed:

> *My life is light, waiting for the death wind,*
> *Like a feather on the back of my hand.*
> *Dust in sunlight and memory in corners*
> *Wait for the wind that chills towards the dead land.*

What Eliot does here is to translate his experience partly into traditional Christian symbols, and partly into private creations. By this each illuminates and strengthens the other, interacting as fertility myth and a personal awareness of contemporary circumstances did in *The Waste Land*.

The analogical structure of the poem, by which the spiritual significance of Simeon's death is communicated, has the distinguishing characteristic of the opening images. The abstract is expressed in decisively concrete terms—here in the analogy of the physical contrast between the old man near death and the young Christ. The death of Simeon, who has seen salvation, becomes the symbol of the renewing death that may be experienced by all— 'I am dying in my own death and the deaths of those after me.' In this way the poem becomes more than a transcription of a severely personal experience, being rather an individualised version of the background narrative which involves the general Christian doctrine. The organic coherence of the poem is achieved by the exactness with which the sensuous imagery and analogy clothe the intellectual and emotional concepts. The sensuous image, 'My life is light, waiting for the death wind', is echoed in the intellectually conceived description of Simeon as 'one who has eighty years and no tomorrow', and this particular example typifies the plan of the poem. These two Ariel poems make particularly clear the manner in which Eliot effects the transposition of the death symbol of the fertility myths in the later poetry. It ceases to depend on the various customs and practices of primitive religions, and is compressed to the Christian expression of the paradoxical life that comes through death. The incarnation of this faith is in the birth of Christ, which is the ostensible subject of these poems. The explicit Gospel narratives form the spine on which the progression of the poem depends, and round which image, idea, and mood are subtly fused to emerge finally as the individual poetic statement of the narrative's central theme. The background narrative, that is, though essential, is not the subject of the poem.

It is against the same background that the *Quartets* are laid, in that they also demand reference to the fundamental concepts of Christian faith, although there is not the same explicit allusion to the Bible. This suggests that as Eliot emerged from largely un-formed belief in the necessity for sacrifice and asceticism, to the firm establishment of that faith in the Christian tradition, he found the most promising poetic stimulus in direct accession to the prin-cipal repository of Christian teaching. Not a stimulus mainly, but a definitive force that would help to mould and direct the personal element in the new imagery that was then his concern. When the fertility myths were rejected as a background for symbolism, their place was taken primarily by Biblical narratives. It is as though Eliot found his poetic impulses to require in the initial stages a very close dependence on his sources, with which he could dispense as his faith grew more assured.

An illustration of what this means is provided by Eliot's re-expression, in *Little Gidding*, of his conception of the com-munity of the dead, which in 'A Song for Simeon' depends on the analogy of Simeon's experience. In *Little Gidding* it is expressed in these words:

> *We die with the dying:*
> *See, they depart, and we go with them.*
> *We are born with the dead:*
> *See, they return, and bring us with them.*
> *The moment of the rose and the moment of the yew-tree*
> *Are of equal duration. . . .*
>
> (*Four Quartets*, p. 43.)

This is the same theology, but it is a generalised statement, inde-pendent of closely shadowed illustration. Neither has any inherent superiority over the other as a poetic mode. It is, however, not unlikely that the earlier is primarily sustentacular in its appeal for the poet.

In the *Quartets* the process by which the symbols are established, and the poetic myth completed, is continued. Of some of these symbols we have already seen the genesis: the paradox of the Word of God that is given its earthly form in a wordless child; the light; and the rose. It is because of the gradual evolution of this system in the poems here considered that the confident development of the *Quartets* is possible. The myth which they compose has become gradually endowed with a life of its own that has enabled it to move further from the external source in various Christian writings than was possible in the earlier formulative stages. With the last word of *Little Gidding* the final coherence of image and symbol is attained.

This is not to say that the *Quartets* offer the sustained ecstasy of certain and untroubled vision. Such experience is inimical to Eliot's nature, constantly suspicious of 'the drug of dreams', even, we gather, of 'the higher dream'. As 'A Song for Simeon' puts it,

> *Not for me the martyrdom, the ecstasy of thought and prayer,*
> *Not for me the ultimate vision.*

The *Quartets* proceed not through over-confident belief, but through

> *The hint half guessed, the gift half understood. . . .*

They are distinguished from the earlier religious poetry not so much by a change in the quality of their faith as by the more self-contained assurance of the communication, and the greater solidity of symbol.

In this chapter we have seen how some of Eliot's private memories intrude into his later poetry as they had not into the early work, and how this personal element has been integrated with the objectivity of his new-found religious faith. Inevitably, any poet's imagery is basically personal, for it is suggested by his own particular vision of the objects and ideas with which he is concerned. What distinguishes the personal element discussed here from this general poetic subjectivity is that it springs directly from Eliot's upbringing, and the scenes to which he was habituated.

rather than from the fact that each poet will see the world in a different way. When Eliot describes Mr. Apollinax as laughing 'like an irresponsible foetus', the selection of image is not prompted by the influence of Eliot's environment. When, in 'Ash Wednesday', he symbolises the insidious attractions of the world in the image of New England scenery, the more specialised subjectivity is involved. The way in which Eliot tries to objectify this has been discussed—it is based on the creation of a link between the personal images and the objective faith which 'he finds . . . to account most satisfactorily for the world and for the moral world within' (*Points of View*, p. 104).

In the transitional poems a very close relationship between background and personal image is sustained. They are disparate treatments of ideas and moods that are eventually integrated in the *Quartets*. Because of the resulting greater coherence of the *Quartets*, and because the myth is there more strongly founded, there is less need for the elaboration of an analogy for each subject.[1] Briefly, the transitional poems treat analogically those subjects which in the *Quartets* are sufficiently well controlled within the myth to enable Eliot to dispense with individual analogies. The details of this development, and the effects which it has on the poetry are considered in the following chapter.

1. This does not mean that the *Quartets* exist in the rarified atmosphere of abstract philosophical discussion. Nor is it support for V. Sackville-West's assertion that 'such fruits of the imagination as metaphor and imagery' are 'an occasional treat . . . added as an ornament to satisfy what is left of Mr. Eliot's aesthetic conscience' (*Observer*, 22nd October, 1944.) What is meant is that such precise use of analogy as we find in 'A Song for Simeon' and 'Journey of the Magi' disappears. The kind of imagery so notably exemplified in the opening lines of the former poem remains.

Chapter Eight

The Still Point

I. THEOLOGY AND THE FORMAL PATTERN

ELIOT'S attachment to the authority of literary tradition was not, as we have seen, a matter of easy and untroubled acceptance. Because he looked on tradition as the only trustworthy guide for artistic experiment, he sought assurance that it demanded change, and that it contained within itself the means of effecting change. It is the ordered flux of tradition that determines its stability, and a similar paradoxical relationship is at the core of Eliot's conception of spiritual authority. The still point evidently suggests the stillness of eternity, and contrasts with the fevered movement of the temporal. The radiance of the white light that is associated with the stillness opposes the spiritual darkness of the world. Yet in *Burnt Norton* III, light and darkness seem to be equated,[1] contrasted

1. An interesting section, which recalls the distinction made in *The Waste Land* between the spiritually apathetic and those who worship

> *devils rather than nothing: crying for life beyond life, for ecstasy not of the flesh.*
> (Choruses from *The Rock: Collected Poems*, p. 172.)

The darkness in *Burnt Norton* III is a symbol of one way to spiritual rebirth—the despair that may come from thought of 'the disorder, the futility, the meaninglessness, the mystery of life and suffering' (*Points of View*, p. 115). Most men avoid thought of these things, and so are incapable 'of either much doubt or much faith' (ibid., p. 108). The kind of experience symbolised in this section of *Burnt Norton* is 'the analogue of the drought, the dark night, which is an essential stage in the progress of the Christian mystic' (ibid., p. 109).

together with the 'dim light' of the world. The paradox is elaborated in *East Coker*, and we are told that

 . . . *the darkness shall be the light, and the stillness the dancing.*

Within the still point is implied movement, as by the movement of innumerable atoms is composed the stability of objects.

The extension to religious matters, then, of Eliot's search for external guidance, reveals this harmony with his concept of the literary authority. There is a further consistency. Already we have seen how Eliot is prepared to accept humanism as performing the secondary function of awakening religious tradition from the danger of 'petrification into mere ritual and habit'. The same spirit lies behind the unwillingness, apparent in the *Quartets*, to rest content with the emotional satisfaction of momentary revelation, and the desire to explore and analyse the way to spiritual peace. The easier satisfactions of the religious life are completed by consistent examination of motive, by

 . . . *prayer, observance, discipline, thought and action.*
                    (*The Dry Salvages; Four Quartets*, p. 33.)

So the individual talent, given form by the historical sense, criticised the prevalent belief that the transitory heat of emotional inspiration was self-sufficient, and could dispense with the lessons embodied in tradition.

Throughout the *Quartets* the poet seeks assurance that religion can fortify man against the most seductive of earthly delights, and against the most potent instruments of despair. Constantly stressed, therefore, are the evils against which religion operates, rather than the 'calm of mind' which is its benefit. For that reason some would say that the poems are too much concerned with depicting the weakness of humanity, too little with the possibility of religion's conquest of those weaknesses. The poems lack balance, and end inconclusively, offering no solution, attaining no synthesis. The judgment is based on passages which seem, out of their contexts, to be negative and despairing, to belie the possibility of final reconciliation. In fact they provide the constant emphasis that sacrifice and struggle are necessary; that these, and not their reward, should be uppermost in the mind. The passages in question reiterate ideas, in different contexts, and with different bias. The sum, and not any one, of their implications, is what should be considered, just as the symbols' accretion of the various layers of meaning and of contrasted attributes must be considered as a whole.

The mood of the poems strongly suggests that of Johnson's 'Vanity of Human Wishes', and an example of what is meant by the reiteration of ideas vividly recalls the earlier poem. Johnson's picture of the decay of old age—

> *Year chases year, decay pursues decay,*
> *Still drops some joy from with'ring life away—*

does not invalidate the poem's conclusion—

> *Inquirer, cease: petitions yet remain,*
> *Which Heaven may hear: nor deem religion vain.*
> *Still raise for good the supplicating voice,*
> *But leave to Heaven the measure and the choice.*

There is a similar evocation in *Little Gidding:*

> *Let me disclose the gifts reserved for age*
> *To set a crown upon your lifetime's effort.*
> *First, the cold friction of expiring sense*
> *Without enchantment, offering no promise*
> *But bitter tastelessness of shadow fruit*
> *As body and soul begin to fall asunder.*
>
> (*Four Quartets*, p. 39.)

surely one of the passages on which the critics base their attack. The mood of the lines must, however, be collocated with *East Coker's*

> *Old men ought to be explorers,*

and with the resolve of the final section of *Little Gidding,*

> *We shall not cease from exploration,*

which leads to the serenity of the last few lines:

> *And all shall be well and*
> *All manner of thing shall be well*
> *When the tongue of flame are in-folded*
> *Into a crowned knot of fire*
> *And the fire and the rose are one.*

Because she misinterprets such passages and the various complexities of the symbolism, both given substance by continual shift of context, Edith Fry sees in the *Quartets* only 'the negation of submission to authority'.[1] Yet she is correct in her proposal of the basic reason for the appearance in the poems of questionings and doubt: 'he hears the voice of the Puritan conscience in the unfamiliar atmosphere of the confessional'.[2] Not so much, though, in the confessional as in the moments of revelation, which are counter-balanced by somewhat Calvinistic passages on the essential vileness of human nature, and its unworthiness to receive the gifts of Heaven. Two examples illustrate the effects on the poetry of this dichotomy, the inherited Puritanism and the acquired Anglo-Catholicism.

The intellectual content of this passage is subordinated to the incantatory element—derived, one feels, from the impact on Eliot of the tonal qualities of liturgy[3]—and the pattern of sound is the primary factor in the communication of experience of 'the moment in and out of time' which is mystical vision:

> *I said to my soul, be still, and wait without hope*
> *For hope would be hope for the wrong thing; wait without love*
> *For love would be love of the wrong thing; there is yet faith*
> *But the faith and the love and the hope are all in the waiting.*
> *Wait without thought, for you are not ready for thought:*
> *So the darkness shall be the light, and the stillness the dancing.*
> *Whisper of running streams, and winter lightning.*
> *The wild thyme unseen and the wild strawberry,*
> *The laughter in the garden, echoed ecstasy. . . .*
> (*East Coker: Four Quartets*, pp. 19–20.)

The half-suggested rhymes at the end of the lines have the incomplete quality that is in harmony with the fleeting images of the

---

1. *British Annual of Literature*, Vol. 5, p. 14.
2. Ibid., p. 10.
3. On his own reading of the *Quartets* Eliot has recently said that 'for me the incantatory quality is very important', although earlier in the same report the usual proviso appears, that 'the beauty of sound cannot be isolated' ('A Conversation with Ranjee Shahani', in *John o' London's Weekly*, 19th August, 1949, p. 497). Despite the proviso, there can be no doubt that the incantatory element plays a part of considerably greater importance in the later than it did in the early works. On its source the remarks in 'A Dialogue on Dramatic Poetry' on the artistic satisfaction to be obtained from the Mass, give some support for the contention advanced above.

running stream and the lightning. The concept of this revelatory moment is elaborated in *The Dry Salvages*, in a passage which repeats the images of

> *The wild thyme unseen, or the winter lightning,*

and has the same power of incantation. It is in such experience that

> . . . *the impossible union*
> *Of spheres of existence is actual,*
> *Here the past and future*
> *Are conquered, and reconciled.* . . .

Following immediately on the vision is the descent to the problem of reconciling it with the unworthiness of man that is always in the foreground of Eliot's mind. To rest content with the evanescent, unearned, mystical experience is to lapse again into the spiritual sloth. For most men, 'right action'

> *is the aim*
> *Never here to be realised;*

but this must not prevent continued effort, although the knowledge of effort may be the only reward—we are

> *only undefeated*
> *Because we have gone on trying;*
> (*The Dry Salvages: Four Quartets*, p. 33.)

From the incantation that accompanied the vision the mood changes to the more precisely argued consideration of the return to normal life and its problems. The immediate communion with God is the experience of the Catholic, expressed in the more mystical fashion of that religion; the reasoned deliberation which fears the complacency that 'the unattended moment' may bring, issues from the Protestant temperament. It is in this fashion that the two religious attitudes are paralleled in the formal variations of the poetry.

Example may be multiplied. The 'familiar compound ghost's' disclosure of 'the gifts reserved for age' is couched in lucid phrases that vividly recall the eighteenth-century manner:

> *First, the cold friction of expiring sense,*
> *Second, the conscious impotence of rage,*
> *Then fools' approval stings and honour stains.*

The unveiling, in *The Dry Salvages*, of the way in which man may perceive the hidden pattern in 'the drift of the sea' is again in the mystical, liturgical style. The hypnotic, repetitive, yet not languorous word pattern—

> *No end to the withering of withered flowers,*
> *To the movement of pain that is painless and motionless . . .*

culminates in the resolvent

> *Only the hardly, barely prayable*
> *Prayer of the one Annunciation.*

It is followed by the dignified, but considerably more prosaic analysis,

> *It seems, as one becomes older,*
> *That the past has another pattern, and ceases to be a mere sequence.*

To describe these variations as alternatives leaves the wrong impression, for they comprehend many more than two styles. We have seen, for example, the modern idiom of the passage just quoted, and the eighteenth-century manner of the lines on old age; each of the visionary passages has its own peculiar organic form. The two distinct species are separable, however, whatever variations may occur within each. Their modifications and juxtapositioning establish the basic formal pattern of the poems. To elucidate more exactly the theological beliefs that correspond to the formal variations, it is useful to consider Eliot's attitude to the Puritanical religious thinkers.

His introduction to the *Pensées*[1] shows a strong sympathy with Pascal, the defender of Jansenism. The doctrines of this system—which Eliot describes as 'a Puritan movement within the Church'[2]—resemble the Calvinism already associated with Eliot's thought. For a part of Pascal's work to which Eliot is particularly drawn—'the magnificent analysis of human motives and occupations'[3]—

1. *Points of View*, pp. 96–115.
2. Ibid., p. 99.
3. Ibid., p. 111.

we must be grateful to the insistence of Jansenism on 'the degraded and helpless state of man'.[1] The Calvinists, however, insisted on this so emphatically as to consider 'mankind so corrupt that human will was of no avail; and thus fell into the doctrine of predestination'.[2] There the resemblance ends, and to this extreme Calvinistic teaching Eliot, so far as we can judge, does not subscribe.

Louis MacNeice, in his book *The Poetry of W. B. Yeats* (p. 182), advances the plausible theory that the lines

> *The dance along the artery*
> *The circulation of the lymph*
> *Are figured in the drift of stars . . .*

tend to be predestinarian, and links this with Eliot's anti-liberalism. This, although it seems to explain the lines, does not do justice to the subtlety of the thought, which is dependent on the *Quartets* as a whole. The passage from which MacNeice quotes treats metaphorically the interdependence of past, present, and future. What is suggested by the interdependence is not determinism but pattern. The experiences of the world are given meaning and form by the still point, 'where past and future are gathered' (*Burnt Norton: Four Quartets*, p. 9). The present event—'the circulation of the lymph'—is integrated with the eternal 'drift of stars'. And as the past explains the present, so does the present explain the past:

> *The trilling wire in the blood*
> *Sings below inveterate scars*
> *Appeasing long forgotten wars.*
> (*Burnt Norton: Four Quartets*, p. 8.)

By this inter-relationship is formed the pattern—the pattern of history and the pattern of the individual life.

Far from being pre-determined,

> *. . . the pattern is new in every moment*
> *And every moment is a new and shocking*
> *Valuation of all we have been . . .*
> (*East Coker: Four Quartets*, p. 18.)

Following the plan of the *Quartets*, the idea threads and re-threads

1. *Points of View*, p. 111.
2. Ibid., p. 110.

throughout the poems, developing and joining with other parts. In the first section of *Burnt Norton* Eliot says

> *What might have been and what has been*
> *Point to one end, which is always present.*

The inseparable present moment unites past and future. The 'one end' is death, and the success of man in living with this realisation will help to determine the quality of his life. It is, too, an incitement to right action, for

> '*on whatever sphere of being*
> *The mind of man may be intent*
> *At the time of death'—that is the one action*
> (*And the time of death is every moment*)
> *Which shall fructify in the lives of others:*
> (*The Dry Salvages: Four Quartets*, p. 31.)

Here again we can see the necessity for looking on the *Quartets* as an organic whole, and the danger of basing conclusions on quotations considered *in vacuo*.

Eliot, then, does not consider human effort of no avail. The Calvinists did, yet despite this they imposed on their adherents, as did the Jansenists, an extremely strict way of life. In the urgency of belief that man must strive continually to overcome the endowment of Original Sin, Eliot and the Calvinists are united. Eliot would believe, with Hulme, that although men cannot be perfect, they can 'occasionally accomplish acts that partake of perfection' (*Selected Essays*, p. 392). Because of the Puritan influence he tends to dwell not on the peace that can come from synthesis between 'free-will of the natural effort and ability of the individual and . . . supernatural grace',[1] but on the failings of human beings—their 'dishonesty and self-deception, the insincerity of their emotions, their cowardice, the pettiness of their real ambition'.[2] This is the strong Puritan influence in the poetry, and the Catholic is embodied in the emotional faith that religion has a property rising above schemes of morality, in the response to the primary teachings of the Catholic Church—the saving grace of Mary, the purgatorial fire, the transubstantiation in the Eucharist. Clearly apparent in the thought, the two contrasted

1. *Points of View*, p. 110.
2. Ibid., p. 112.

elements in the Christian tradition correspond, in these poems, to two well-defined poetic manners.

This prose analysis is too precisely stated to give any idea of the sense of mystery transmitted by the poetry. It is not simply a matter of saying, in so many words, that in the *Quartets* Eliot is or is not a determinist. In the poems the ideas are not so exactly formulated. This is not to say that they are vague and diffuse, overburdened with unnecessary words and excessive elaboration. All one can say of the difference is that it is the necessary distinction between prose and poetry. Through the poems we perceive something of the melancholy of life, and of its incompleteness. In the end we can see that a pattern unifies this, and that a peace is possible which transcends it. There remains, however, a mystery, a feeling that all has not been explained because all cannot be explained: the mystery is not merely a picturesque decoration.

This may be called the external formulation of the myth of the *Quartets*, the objective system of belief to which they are related. It is based on a synthesis between two contrasted elements in the Christian tradition, and full knowledge of the synthesis can be had only from the poems themselves.

It cannot be over-emphasised that this exposition can be in no way a substitute for the poetry, though it is perhaps more justifiable in this metaphysical poetry than in any other kind. Eliot himself has said that the obscurity of the *Quartets* is 'in the subject-matter . . . inherent in the ideas expressed'. The myth exists in the poetry through the imagery, the symbols, and the rhythms. Exposition such as this has its main interest in its analysis of the sensibility and intellect that are behind the poetry, forming its imagery and contrasted styles—a sensibility and intellect which have substantially the same aims now as when they formulated the nature and function of tradition. The way in which the symbolism gives the myth individuality, and renews its vigour, has now to be considered.

II. IMAGERY AND SYMBOLISM IN THE 'QUARTETS'

Myth, as defined in Chapter Six, was considered almost exclusively as the system of belief to which the poetry was related. As, that is, the philosophy to be deduced from what the poetry said by means of image, symbol, and the other poetic devices. While this was a convenient shorthand for the purposes of the chapter, it does not take account of the full significance of poetic myth. Eliot's poetry is concerned with beliefs already formulated in the Christian religion, so the myth has both an external and an internal life. The former depends on the objective Christian tradition, the latter on the way in which the poetry interprets and expresses this. Now it is not sufficient to equate the poetic myth solely with the philosophy by which it attempts to explain the world and the place of man in the world, to regulate and synthesise the disparate experiences of life.

Before Philosophy, a book on the mythopoeic thought of the ancient world, helps to define the word as it is used here. It gives this account of a Babylonian myth:

'We would explain, for instance, that certain atmospheric conditions broke a drought and brought about rain. The Babylonians observed the same facts but experienced them as the intervention of the gigantic bird Imdugud which came to their rescue. It covered the sky with the black storm clouds of its wings and devoured the Bull of Heaven, whose hot breath had scorched the crops. . . . The images had already become traditional at the time when we meet them in art and literature, but originally they must have been seen in the revelation which the experience entailed. . . . The imagery of myth is therefore by no means allegory. It is nothing less than a carefully chosen cloak for abstract thought. The imagery is inseparable from the thought.'

Poetic myth is not quite the same, for there is not the same insistence on the literal correspondence between image or symbol and fact.

The passage from *Little Gidding* on the dissolution of man's surroundings (see p. 169) takes as one of its symbols the rose from the garden imagery of *Burnt Norton*. The rose represents part of man's temporal experience, and is joined later in *Little Gidding* with the yew-tree, symbol of death:

> *The moment of the rose and the moment of the yew-tree*
> *Are of equal duration . . .*
>
> (*Four Quartets*, p. 43.)

The yew-tree is traditionally associated with the graveyard and has been frequently used in literature with just that suggestion. Haüsermann, in his short work *L'Œuvre poétique de T. S. Eliot*, sees 'allusions . . . à l'if de Tennyson' in this passage from *Burnt Norton*:

> *Will the sunflower turn to us, will the clematis*
> *Stray down, bend to us; tendril and spray*
> *Clutch and cling?*
> *Chill*
> *Fingers of yew be curled*
> *Down on us?*

The allusion is to these lines from *In Memoriam*:

> *Old warder of these buried bones,*
> *And answering now my random stroke*
> *With fruitful cloud and living smoke,*
> *Black yew, that graspest at the stones*
> *And dippest towards the dreamless head.*   (39)

Certainly Eliot also associates the tree with escape from 'the drug of dreams' a phrase which occurs in 'Animula'. Possibly, too, the literary ancestry includes Vittoria's dream of the yew-tree in *The White Devil*. Particularly such lines as these from Act I, Scene i:

> *And both were struck dead by that sacred yew*
> *In that base shallow grave that was their due.*

and these from Act IV, Scene ii:

> *Or, like the black and melancholic yew-tree,*
> *Dost think to root thyself in dead men's graves . . .*

We can see, then, that the yew-tree symbolises death.

> *The moment of the rose and the moment of the yew-tree*
> *Are of equal duration*

because the quality of our lives is determined by our actions at the moment of death—a concept obviously connected with that discussed on page 163. Implied too is the transitoriness of life. Death and life are not literally seen as a yew-tree and a rose, but there is an intimate relationship between idea and image, from which the myth derives its power. Idea and image are, in the poetry, inseparable.

We find the same thing in the myth of *The Waste Land*. It is partly the teaching that man is required to make a positive choice of either Evil or Good, that they lack humility and leadership. It is also the way in which that teaching is communicated: the symbols of water and drought, the allusions, the predominantly urban imagery, for that too is a vital part of the poetic world. Briefly, the poetic myth might be defined as the complete work of transformation performed by the poetry on the real world which is its subject. We have seen how, in the later poetry, the background of the Grail legends and fertility myths gives way to one drawn from Christian writings and tradition. It has already been suggested, too, that there is a clear distinction to be made between the later and the earlier imagery.

The latter is almost entirely urban. Even the natural scene at the end of 'The Love Song of J. Alfred Prufrock' is seen as a social environment, the centre of a fashionable holiday:

> *I shall wear white flannel trousers and walk upon the beach.*

The hyacinths in 'Portrait of a Lady' are in a city park, and the garden in 'Mr. Apollinax' is the formalised creation of a classical age, where statues overlook the affairs of courtiers. The river in 'The Fire Sermon' is that of a town, and the sea symbolism, in contrast to the urban setting, which is observed in precise detail, is abstract, referring to no particular sea. This is emphasised when we consider it in relation to the sea of *The Dry Salvages*, where direct observation creates a much fuller sensuous picture, despite the ulterior significance which adheres to it:

> The sea howl
> *And the sea yelp are different voices*
> *Often together heard: the whine in the rigging,*
> *The menace and caress of wave that breaks on water,*
> *The distant rote in the granite teeth,*
> *And the wailing warning from the approaching headland*
> *Are all sea voices . . .*
>
> (*The Dry Salvages: Four Quartets*, p. 26.)

An exactly similar relationship exists between the opening of *The Waste Land* and the opening of *Little Gidding*. Each presents a picture of nature, a description of a season that has a symbolic value. The April of *The Waste Land* is a generalised April, not a time experienced in a particular place. In *Little Gidding*, on the other hand, the natural scene is immediately observed in greater detail:

> *The brief sun flames the ice, on pond and ditches . . .*
>   *. . . This is the spring time*
> *But not in time's covenant. Now the hedgerow*
> *Is blanched for an hour with transitory blossom*
> *Of snow.*
>
>   (*Four Quartets*, p. 35.)

The earlier nature imagery does not evoke a particular scene because it does not enter at all into the real setting of the poem. *The Waste Land* is exclusively a poem of the vast masses herded in cities, and the water symbolism is taken over directly from the fertility myths. Being abstract initially there is no reason why it it should be precisely labelled. Though different in kind from that of the *Quartets*, it is in its context none the less powerful for that. The *Quartets* themselves are not entirely dissociated from urban life. The London tube appears in *Burnt Norton* and *East Coker*, a street scene in *Little Gidding*, at the appearance of the 'familiar compound ghost'. There is a much fuller use, however, of the rural world and of natural scenes generally. When they appear they suggest, in the first instance, close perception of particular surroundings for their own sake, although they are also symbols, and not infrequently symbols with a literary background.

East Coker opens with a country scene—though a factory intrudes—which emphasises the inevitable decay of houses, men and crops. There is, says the poet,

> *. . . a time for the wind to break the loosened pane*
> *And to shake the wainscot where the field-mouse trots. . . .*
>
>   (*Four Quartets*, p. 15.)

The field-mouse is on its own a reminder of all the natural forces that help to accomplish the fall of buildings, and perish themselves. We recall too the mouse in 'Mariana', also associated with decay and desolation:

> *The blue-fly sung in the pane; the mouse*
> *Behind the mouldering wainscot shriek'd*
> *Or from the crevice peer'd about.*
> *Old faces glimmer'd through the doors,*
> *Old footsteps trod the upper floors. . . .*

The symbol appears again in *Little Gidding*—which summarises many of the symbols—in these lines:

> *Ash on an old man's sleeve*
> *Is all the ash the burnt roses leave.*
> *Dust in the air suspended*
> *Marks the place where a story ended.*
> *Dust inbreathed was a house—*
> *The wall, the wainscot and the mouse.*
>
> (*Four Quartets*, p. 37.)

This symbolism impresses on our minds the dissolution that overtakes man and all man's surroundings—'nil nisi divinum stabile est; caetera fumus'.

Eliot's turning to nature in this manner is not fortuitous. The *Quartets* are concerned with pattern, and it is in 'the perpetual recurrence of determined seasons' that the most explicit symbol of the pattern is found. The decay at the beginning of *East Coker* is one which promotes new birth:

> *Old stone to new building, old timber to new fires,*
> *Old fires to ashes, and ashes to the earth*
> *Which is already flesh, fur and faeces,*
> *Bone of man and beast, cornstalk and leaf.*

'Old faces . . . Old footsteps' return from the past here as well. It is this passage which merges into the evocation of an earlier England.

The lines in archaic spelling allude to Sir Thomas Elyot's *The Gouernor*:

'It is diligently to be noted that the associatinge of man and woman in daunsing . . . was nat begonne without a speciall consideration . . . as for the intimation of sondry vertues, whiche be by them represented . . . by the association of a man and a woman in daunsinge may be signified matrimonie. . . . In every daunse, of a most auncient custome, there daunseth together a man and a woman, holding eche other by the hande or the arme, whiche betokeneth concorde' (Croft's edition, pp. 233–236).

The idea is that the qualities of man and woman combine to form a harmonious synthesis, symbolised in their dancing together. So the perfect governor is one in whom 'fiersenesse ioyned with mildnesse maketh Seueritie; Audacitie with timerositie maketh Magnanimitie . . .' and so on (ibid., p. 238). This hinted pattern supports the notion of the greater seasonal pattern. These dead country dancers symbolise in their actions a design, and maintain the continuance of the earth's flux between birth and death. It is they who are

> Long since under earth
> Nourishing the corn. Keeping time,
> Keeping the rhythm in their dancing
> As in their living in the living seasons
> The time of the seasons and the constellations
> The time of milking and the time of harvest
> The time of the coupling of man and woman
> And that of beasts. Feet rising and falling.
> Eating and drinking. Dung and death.

We can catch in this an echo of *Burnt Norton*'s

> Below, the boarhound and the boar
> Pursue their pattern as before
> But reconciled among the stars.
>
> (*Four Quartets*, p. 9.)

The ending of *The Dry Salvages* is connected with the conclusion of the poem's third section, on the death

> Which shall fructify in the lives of others.

Insinuated too is the idea of its physically fertilising powers:

> We, content at the last
> If our temporal reversion nourish
> (Not too far from the yew-tree)
> The life of significant soil.

By this is illustrated again the way in which the different aspects of the poems' themes are threaded together.

All these symbols are related, explicitly or implicitly, to 'the still point'. The vanished dancers, for example, summon to the mind these lines from *Burnt Norton*:

> *Except for the point, the still point,*
> *There would be no dance, and there is only the dance.*

The conclusion of *East Coker* combines references to both the still point and the ocean, the latter symbol forming the core of the next poem:

> *We must be still and still moving*
> *Into another intensity*
> *For a further union, a deeper communion*
> *Through the dark cold and the empty desolation,*
> *The wave cry, the wind cry, the vast waters*
> *Of the petrel and the porpoise . . .*

These two symbols in particular—the dancers and the ocean—reveal Eliot's desire to assert his attachment to the two traditions to which he is heir. Voluntarily exiled from his native country he turns in the later poetry to the re-establishment of the links between himself and the English tradition and background, and to an oblique affirmation of the influences of his youthful surroundings. It is noteworthy that the passage on the vanished dancers occurs in *East Coker*—the village of his ancestors. Had the manner of the early poems been carried over entire into these poems it is likely that we would have found a less localised presentation of nature. *The Waste Land*, one of whose themes is the destructive influence of cosmopolitanism, finds its imagery in the anonymity of the great cities, in the uniformity of mechanisation: it is precise in its evocation of what is common to modern life in all cities. In the *Quartets* Eliot's establishing of a link between his individuality and his race produces the particularity of the nature imagery. Also, as has been shown, the selection of image proceeds from recognition that it provides an admirable symbolism. The fusion of these two impulses accounts for the changed imagery of the later poetry, and especially of the *Quartets*.

The qualities of 'the still point', central symbol of the *Quartets*, are for the most part elucidated by inference, through such subsidiary symbols as those discussed above. Only in *Burnt Norton* is it directly approached, and then in lines whose main purpose seems to be their lightly touched anticipation of the symbols that will appear in the following poems—the natural scenes, the yew, the dancing, and the journey. It is in very much the same way that Madame Sosostris anticipates the course of *The Waste Land*. Two lines, however, actualise the metaphysical point in the direct correspondence of the wheel symbol:

> *Garlic and sapphires in the mud*
> *Clot the bedded axle-tree.*
>
> (*Four Quartets*, p. 8.)

Philip Wheelwright points out that a 'familiar development of the theme in mediaeval and renaissance iconography is the Wheel of Fortune, whirling men ceaselessly upward to prosperity and downward to misery. But always at the centre of the Wheel's movement, conditioning it, is the axle-tree. Although the visible axle-tree evidently turns . . . there is an axis at the centre . . . which remains unmoving . . . and which "reconciles" the contradictions of the surrounding movement' ('Eliot's Philosophical Themes', in *T. S. Eliot*, ed. Rajan). This is at the basis of Eliot's thought, but there is a more explicit ancestry in Bishop Taylor's:

. . . and a wise man is placed in a variety of chances, like the nave or centre of a wheel in the midst of all the circumvolutions and changes of posture, without violence or change, save that it turns gently in compliance with its changed parts, and is indifferent which part is up, and which is down . . .'

The concept of 'the still point' is considerably clarified by these allusions. They recall to us also the working-out in the poems of the prefatory paradox—'The way up and the way down are one and the same.' This, in turn, is to be connected with 'the figure of the ten stairs',[1] which is 'the ladder of secret contemplation'[2] of St. John of the Cross: 'We observe, then, that the steps of this ladder . . . are ten.'[3] The contemplation which ascent of the

---

1. *Burnt Norton: Four Quartets*, p. 12.
2. St. John of the Cross: *The Dark Night of the Soul*, Chapter XVIII.
3. St. John of the Cross: *The Ascent of Mt. Carmel*, Chapter XIX.

ladder symbolises may include those moments of despair, of descent to an 'inoperancy of the world of spirit' which are, as has been mentioned, an essential part of the soul's progress, and serve to attain the same end as the moments of exaltation. In these symbols of the ladder and 'the still point'—the apex of the ladder, the final attainment—are blended St. John's philosophy of the disciplined ascent from Evil to Good, the apparently contradictory thesis that the ascent may involve a spiritual declension, and the Heraclitean paradox. The negation suggested by the necessity of experiencing despair is echoed in the third section of *East Coker*. This also is based on the teaching of St. John of the Cross:[1]

> *In order to arrive at having pleasure in everything*
> *Desire to have pleasure in nothing. . . .*

Helen Gardner discusses this relationship in her commentary on the *Quartets*,[2] and recapitulation would serve no useful purpose here. Sufficient has been said to illustrate the essentials of Eliot's debt to St. John, and the way in which he integrates the philosophy with his own symbols.

It is possible to define 'the still point' periphrastically as the focus at which all temporal action and movement are concentrated and resolved, or as 'the ultimate point of human aspiration'.[3] Most concisely, however, 'the still point' is God[4] and the power of God, whose 'whole duration (is) but one permanent point, without succession, parts, flux, or division'.[5] It has been stressed that the images which communicate the experiences of

1. *The Ascent of Mt. Carmel*, Chapter XIV. The references to St. John of the Cross are cited in E. M. Stephenson's *T. S. Eliot and the Lay Reader*, pp. 79–80, 88.

2. *T. S. Eliot*, ed. Rajan, pp. 57–77.

3. Wheelwright, *op. cit.*, p. 100.

4. *The Ascent of Mt. Carmel*, Chapter XII: '. . . just so the soul that is to attain in this life to the union of that supreme repose and blessing, by means of all those stairs of meditation, forms and ideas, must pass through them and have done with them, since they . . . bear no proportion to the goal to which they lead, which is GOD.'

5. Sir Thomas Browne, *Religio Medici*, p. 23 (ed. Symonds). The thought of this work often bears upon the *Quartets*. Common to both is their sharp consciousness of 'those four inevitable points of us all, death, judgment, heaven, and hell'. Browne, too, shares the belief that in 'these moral acceptions, the way to be immortal is to die daily . . .' (*op. cit.*, p. 66).

ecstatic religious vision symbolise its transitoriness. The 'running streams' of *East Coker*, the 'waterfall' and 'the winter lightning' of *The Dry Salvages* are brief glimpses only, of the reconciliation involved in the greater water and light associated with 'the still point'. This is partly a reminder that the struggle against Evil is not to be forsaken because of the vision, that the return to reality must be accompanied by a less rapturous, more rational outlook. Also, though, it is because such insight into the pattern imposed by God's will must of necessity be incomplete and not fully understood. Any anthropomorphic presentation of the deity in these poems is rare, but it does occur, I think, in 'Ash Wednesday' and 'Marina', with the same suggestion of the imperfectly seen.

These two are poems of the soul's progress to salvation, to the union with God envisaged by St. John of the Cross: '. . . since God has greater strength, virtue, and activity than the soul, He can communicate His properties to it and makes it, as it were, deified, and leaves it, as it were, divinised, to a greater or less degree, corresponding to the greater or the lesser degree of union between the two. This is the basic conception in Christian mysticism.'[1] The sense of mystical union—fleeting in 'Marina'—is communicated in these lines, where the vaguely perceived face can be only that of God:

What is this face, less clear and clearer
The pulse in the arm, less strong and stronger—
Given or lent? more distant than the stars and nearer than the eye . . .
　　　　　　　('Marina': *Collected Poems*, p. 113.)

'The face' is found again in 'Ash Wednesday', followed by reference to Christ, the Word or the voice of God, and has unquestionably the same significance as in 'Marina':

The right time and the right place are not here
No place of grace for those who avoid the face
No time to rejoice for those who walk among noise and deny the voice.

These passages seem to bear upon the meeting, in *Little Gidding*, between the poet and the 'familiar compound ghost':

1. Quoted in Stephenson's book, p. 79. The main value of her study lies in the references which it gives, references intended as general guidance, not usually related to specific parts of Eliot's poetry.

> *I caught the sudden look of some dead master*
> *Whom I had known, forgotten, half recalled*
> *Both one and many . . .*
> *Both intimate and unidentifiable . . .*
> *   . . . I was still the same,*
> *Knowing myself yet being someone other—*
> *And he a face still forming . . .*

The usual identification is with Mallarmé and Dante and Dante's Arnaut who 'disappeared into the refining flame' (*Purgatory*, XXVI, l. 141, Cary's translation). Arnaut's acceptance of the purgatorial fires is urged on the poet at the end of this section of *Little Gidding*: the scope of the apparition's conversation extends beyond literary to spiritual matters. It seems likely, then, that the impression given by the opening description is intended to imply the presence of God within the multiplicity of the 'familiar compound ghost'—'both one and many'. There is further reason for believing this.

The section that follows the disappearance of the ghost is a meditation on the English Civil War, suggested by the poem's setting. Nicholas Ferrar's community at Little Gidding was visited on several occasions by King Charles—apocryphally just after the defeat at Naseby. It is this which prompts the lines

> *If you came at night like a broken king,*

and

> *If I think of a king at nightfall.*

Now, at the end of the section we are told that Charles, his followers, and their opponents are 'folded in a single party'. This, preceded so closely by the earlier harmony of 'one and many', hints at an identity of the two unities. We are reminded too that *The Waste Land* concentrates the idea of the unacknowledged leader in another king, in these lines:

> *We think of the key, each in his prison*
> *Thinking of the key, each confirms a prison*
> *Only at nightfall, aetherial rumours*
> *Revive for a moment a broken Coriolanus.*

> (ll. 413-416.)

The figure of Coriolanus summarises the symbols of the lost father, the Fisher King, and the underlying theme of the unchanging God—this last is particularly clear in 'Coriolan'. The same idea is involved here. The identity of the two unities symbolises the leadership and power of God. and adds the paradox that earthly defeat is inconclusive. We do not judge the validity of the Crucifixion by the physical death of Christ. Nicholas Ferrar's community was destroyed, and Charles was defeated, but there is an ultimate reconciliation and victory:

> *Whatever we inherit from the fortunate*
> *We have taken from the defeated*
> *What they had to leave us—a symbol:*
> *A symbol perfected in death.*

Through these symbols the presence of the deity pervades the *Quartets*. 'The still point' is God, and represents a summary and reconciliation of all the paradoxical attributes of the symbols, which at once depend on it and help to illustrate its nature—they could be described as a symbolic substratum. The central point of the axle-tree is the symbol which introduces the idea of 'the still point', and its traditional and personal associations are worked out in the other symbols of the poems. The first statement of these associations is in *Burnt Norton*, sections II and IV. Then the revolution of the wheel is paralleled, in *East Coker*, by the revolution of the seasons, in which is implied the constant imminence and fertilising power of death, and the interdependence of past, present, and future. The next major symbols are those of the river and the sea, which have not yet been discussed in any detail, except in relation to the personal element.

The sea too symbolises the unity of past, present, and future. It represents the collected body of history, its confused surface making no distinction between individual epochs. The time which the sea represents is measured and ordered by the tolling bell, whose motion is regulated not by the surface disorder, but by 'the ground swell, which is and was from the beginning'. This changeless force is the concord produced by the surface confusion, implying stability, as the stillness at the heart of the wheel gave meaning to its movement. At the end of *Little Gidding* we are reminded of the inseparable stillness at the junction 'Between two waves of the sea', which is an exact transposition of the axle-wheel symbolism.

'All the rivers run into the sea; yet the sea is not full; unto the place from whence the rivers come, thither they return again.'[1] It is the lives of individual men, the influx of rivers, which compose history. The junction of river and sea—'the sea's throat'— symbolises death. This recurs in a passage in *Little Gidding* which assembles all the other symbols of death:

> And any action
> Is a step to the block, to the fire, down the sea's throat
> Or to an illegible stone: and that is where we start.

The 'illegible stones' are gravestones,[2] the block that on which Charles I died. This brief summary gives only the barest idea of the climactic fusion wrought by *Little Gidding*'s concluding passages. The assembling and reconciliation of the death symbols lead to the final vision of 'the still point', to which death provides the entrance. Death is in this way a beginning, for as the mention of fire in the above passages suggests, death is not the ultimate purgation. Only the fire imagery remains to be considered. It is a constant in Eliot's poetry, but with an additional meaning in the *Quartets*.

The fire of *The Waste Land* was that of lust, contrasted by implication with purgatorial fire. The *Quartets* introduce the theme in *East Coker*. It is hinted in the transmutation of 'old timber into new fires' in the first lines, directly stated in section IV, a series of five stanzas whose form is a variation on that of the Sweeney poems. These verses deal with the basic faiths of Catholic Christianity. Mary appears as the 'dying nurse',[3] the receiving of the Eucharist as a reminder of

> The dripping blood our only drink,
> The bloody flesh our only food:

And, in these lines, the subject that is relevant here:

> The chill ascends from feet to knees,
> The fever sings in mental wires.
> If to be warmed, then I must freeze
> And quake in frigid purgatorial flames . . .

1. *Ecclesiastes*, i, 7. Chapter III of this book is also relevant to the *Quartets*.
2. See *East Coker: Four Quartets*, p. 22.
3. A similarly evasive expression clothes the identity of Christ, 'the wounded surgeon', and of Adam, 'the ruined millionaire'.

At the end of the second section of *Little Gidding*, where the image
next appears, the refining fire is associated with 'the still point'—
the simile used places this beyond doubt:

> '*From wrong to wrong the exasperated spirit*
> *Proceeds, unless restored by that refining fire*
> *Where you must move in measure, like a dancer.*'

The following section hints at the nature of the transformation
effected by submission to the fire:

> *See, now they vanish,*
> *The faces and places, with the self which, as it could, loved them,*
> *To become renewed, transfigured, in another pattern . . .*

This repeats the idea expressed in 'Ash Wednesday' II, of the
garden 'Where all loves end. . . .Where all love ends.' We have,
that is, not the annihilation of earthly love, but its transformation
into the higher love, of God. From the earthly love is purged its
dross, and it is 'redeemed from fire by fire'[1]—from the fire of lust
by the purgatorial fire.

    Little Gidding achieves its climax by the final grouping of sym-
bols. Through the death symbols we are led to those associated
with 'the still point'. The rose—earthly beauty and the attraction
of men to it—is not destroyed but refined, so that it is unified with

> . . . *the crowned knot of fire*
> *And the fire and the rose are one.*

One of the themes of *Little Gidding* is the transfiguration of earthly
love, and this ultimate fire is that of St. John of the Cross: 'For
love is like fire, which rises upward with the desire to be absorbed
in the centre of its sphere.[2] By the unification is established

> *A condition of complete simplicity*
> *(Costing not less than everything)*
> *And all shall be well and*
> *All manner of thing shall be well.*

'All things began in order, so shall they end, and so shall they
begin again; according to the ordainer of order and mystical

1. *Little Gidding: Four Quartets*, p. 42.
2. *Dark Night of the Soul*, Chapter XX.

mathematicks of the city of Heaven' (Sir Thomas Browne: *The Garden of Cyrus*, edition cited, p. xxii).

The eternal imminence of death, the significance which knowledge of this should have for man in his dealing with the affairs of life, the transformation of human into divine love, the illumination of the pattern which is apparent in and yet transcends earthly experience—these are some of the themes around which grow the symbols considered above. They are the primary symbols of the *Quartets*, inter-related, and co-ordinated with the ideas they represent in the manner suggested by this analysis. The *Quartets* are philosophical poetry, poetry of ideas. Linked with a symbolism and imagery that translate the thought into an apparently less direct, but, when the method and organisation are perceived, more intimate and more accurate sensuous apprehension, the arguments of the theologians gain a new vitality of poetic truth. It is by a process somewhat similar that Proust justifies the child's exaggerated description of the impressive staircase in a house strange to him. The exaggeration was in fact the truth, because it conveyed to his audience a more accurate impression of the child's feelings of awe. In the *Quartets* the symbols and images do not reproduce the logical continuity of philosophical discussion, but their grouping does convey the impression of final harmony, to the explanation of which such discussion is. devoted. This is perhaps the true relationship between poetry and philosophy. The poet will evade some of the steps proper to purely rational discussion, but will surrender to his reader a more precise realisation of the feelings and ultimate aims behind the ideas.

This brief reconsideration of Eliot's desire for the expression of unified sensibility recalls the influence of Dante. Enough has been said of Eliot's debt to Dante to render unnecessary any detailed correlation between it and the *Quartets*. There is, however. a further general similarity to be noted. Eliot's poems deal more directly with those 'states of being' presented allegorically in the *Commedia*: the moods of the *Quartets* range from those of the *Inferno* to those of the *Paradiso*, with the final assertion of the latter's ultimate victory. Here again we can see the poet's vision of what in the philosopher would be not an evocation of mood, but a strictly controlled tabulation of cause and effects of the conditions which produce such and such a reaction. Delicately mingled, too, in the poems, with these realisations in sensuous terms of abstractions, are the contrasting passages which comment more prosaically on the ideas themselves. The consummation, however, of all these different elements and themes, is in the final assembling of symbols. We are therefore left with the reconciliation and resolution achieved by what we may call the philosophical idiom of poetry—speaking to the mind in terms of the senses—rather than by the more analytical passages. What has been offered here is not a complete interpretation of the *Quartets* but an exposition of the organisation of symbols, with some comment on their history as it is revealed by the development of Eliot's poetic manner. As a symbolist poet, Eliot's finest achievement is the *Quartets*, where he moves easily among the most complex philosophical labyrinths. In truth, the poems depend on the symbolism, and without an understanding of this, appreciation is impossible.

Chapter Nine
Realism and Poetic Drama

(1)

THE ideal medium for poetry, to my mind, and the most direct means of social usefulness for poetry, is the theatre. . . . For the simplest auditors there is the plot, for the more literary the words and phrasing, for the more musically sensitive the rhythm, and for auditors of greater sensitiveness and understanding a meaning which reveals itself gradually . . . the sensitiveness of every auditor is acted upon by all these elements at once, though in different degrees of consciousness' (*The Use of Poetry and the Use of Criticism*, p. 135). The quotation is from the Harvard University lectures delivered by Eliot during the winter of 1932–33, six years after 'Sweeney Agonistes' two years before the first production of *Murder in the Cathedral*. His career as a dramatist, up to *The Cocktail Party*, covers the period between 'Journey of the Magi' and the completion of the *Four Quartets*. One might expect, then, that the meaning to which Eliot refers will in his own plays be involved, at least in part, with the ideas of the early religious poetry and the *Quartets*. From one viewpoint the plays are an attempt to communicate to the larger audience commanded by drama the themes of these poems. The spectacle of dramatic conflict, and the various levels of enjoyment summarised by Eliot in the passage just quoted, might more readily than the poetry persuade an audience to appreciation of the core of meaning.

Certainly Eliot has never advocated an esotericism developed as an end in itself. Esotericism was looked on not as a desirable and permanent obstruction, but as a means by which something valuable in poetry might gradually permeate society. As Eliot remarks elsewhere in the same group of lectures—

'He (the poet) should normally be glad to feel that the entertainment or diversion is enjoyed by as large and various a number of people as possible. . . . It is one thing to write in a style that is already popular, and another to hope that one's writing may eventually become popular' (ibid., pp. 31–32).

This is not to say that in the plays Eliot seeks an easy popularity, by sacrificing his subtlety of statement and offering instead a debased and blatant simplification. He relies on the inherent attraction of all drama, applying to the problem of arriving at a dramatic method the principles that guided his search for a poetic idiom. Each of Eliot's works is a comment on the others, and in the three plays—*Murder in the Cathedral*, *The Family Reunion*, and *The Cocktail Party*—we find worked out in terms of character and action some of the themes of the *Quartets*. Common to all the plays, most obviously in *Murder in the Cathedral*, is preoccupation with the nature of sainthood.

It is the saint whose death 'shall fructify in the lives of others', although he must refrain from thought of 'the fruit of the action'. Where the ordinary people can hope only for 'the unattended moment' of revelation, it is the occupation of the saint to attain, 'by ardour and selflessness and self-surrender', apprehension of

> The point of intersection of the timeless
> With time.

Murder in the Cathedral is a record of Thomas à Becket's struggle to sainthood. Dramatic concision is achieved by confining the action of the play to the last days of Becket's life,[1] the struggle within him being concentrated and given form in his talks with the four tempters, a type of personification popular in the morality plays to which this bears so strong a resemblance. From the words of the tempters and of the chorus we learn all that is necessary of Thomas's earlier life, and of his former conflict with the evils outside and within him. As Patricia Adair points out in a perceptive essay on the play, something of Thomas's human qualities

1. Eliot has written on the value of the unities. See *The Use of Poetry*, p. 45, *et seq.*

was necessarily rejected in selecting material for a portrait of the saint—

'The dramatic problem, of course, is that the more perfect the saint's self-surrender the more difficult it is to keep him a real man, since it is by our weaknesses that we are most human. Moreover, by confining the action of the play to the closing weeks of Becket's life and so forcing him to play a purely passive role, Mr. Eliot increases the difficulty of making Thomas entirely credible as a man, but deepens the religious significance of the play' (*The Cambridge Journal*, November, 1950, p. 84).

This is on the whole a fair summary, though I am inclined to question the notion of Thomas's complete passivity. The rejection of, particularly, the fourth tempter, involves considerable internal conflict, mirrored, as will appear, in the sermon, and in the second part of the play. Again, although she sees the dramatic problem, Miss Adair passes no comment on Eliot's treatment of it.

It is rather the same problem as that of Horatio for Shakespeare. Horatio is partly a piece of dramatic machinery designed to give or receive information which the audience must have. He is made credible by his manner at certain vital points—in his conversation with Hamlet before the duel, for example, where he attains such dignity and is so intimately involved in the tragedy, that inconsistencies are forgotten and he is seen in the round. In the same way Eliot shows us brief glimpses of other, normal facets of Thomas's character—the flash of ironic humour when the third tempter says

> *I am a rough straightforward Englishman.*

and Thomas replies,

> *Proceed straight forward,*

commenting finally on the 'straightforward Englishman's' complex political sophistries,

> *For a countryman*
> *You wrap your meaning in as dark generality*
> *As any courtier.*

We see him too as a man facing men, rather than as a saint purifying his relations with God, in his first encounter with the four knights. In these ways Thomas is made a credible human being, and while he does appear generally as one far removed from the petty affairs of common humanity, Miss Adair fails to do justice to Eliot's skill in retaining some links between him and the humans who observe the enacting of his fate. These characteristics, too, are not merely 'stuck on', as a film director might individualise a character by giving him a disproportionately large nose. They spring from the same emotional bias, the same clearsightedness and stubbornness of purpose as direct the saint.

The scene with the tempters is the focal point of the play. The first three recapitulate vices to which Thomas has been drawn earlier in his life, and are rejected with comparative ease. The first calls him back to temporal pleasures, symbolised rather as in 'Ash Wednesday', in the lovely echoing lines—

> *Fluting in the meadows, viols in the hall*
> *Laughter and apple-blossom floating on the water—*

suggesting that this is at least a vice for which penance is easily done, and insinuating that Thomas's pride may cost him dearer—

> *I leave you to the pleasures of your higher vices*
> *Which will have to be paid for at higher prices.*

Now is the time for Thomas to recapture an earlier season of joy and irresponsibility. In reply to Thomas's, 'You talk of seasons that are past', the tempter says,

> *And of the new season.*
> *Spring has come in winter. Snow in the branches*
> *Shall float as sweet as blossoms. Ice along the ditches*
> *Mirror the sunlight.*

This brilliantly conceived image for the resurgence in later life of one's younger vices has not the significance of the other seasonal imagery in the play—used as in the *Quartets* to suggest harmonious pattern and to symbolise death and rebirth. Nor is it the same as *Little Gidding's*

> *The brief sun flames the ice on pond and ditches*
> . . . .
> . . . *This is the spring time*
> *But not in time's covenant. Now the hedgerow*
> *Is blanched for an hour with transitory blossom*
> *Of snow . . .*

The parallel is interesting, however, as showing how, in the plays as well as in the transition poems, the imagery and symbols of the *Quartets* were being formulated. The first tempter dismissed, the second and third, also expected by Thomas, offer, the one a return to the temporal power of the Chancellorship, the other a coalition between the Church and a disaffected party. Thomas's answer is that temporal authority has no attraction for one bound to the power of God:

> *To condemn kings, not serve among their servants,*
> *Is my open office. No! Go.*

The fourth is the most subtle. Of him Thomas asks

> *Who are you, tempting with my own desires?*

as he hears described the glories of sainthood to which he aspires, desiring often the

> *glory of saints*
> *Dwelling forever in the presence of God.*
> *What earthly glory, of king or emperor,*
> *What earthly pride, that is not poverty*
> *Compared with the richness of heavenly grandeur?*
> *Seek the way of martyrdom, make yourself the lowest*
> *On earth, to be high in heaven.*

Ironically this last visitor repeats Thomas's own words to the women of Canterbury, urging that affairs are out of his hands, that he must merely adapt himself to fit the pattern imposed by God's will. The chorus interrupts with a description of portents of disaster witnessed by them. demanding once more to be left to their spiritual apathy.

So Thomas's answer to this tempter, to spiritual pride, to aching desire for the glory of martyrdom, is delayed until the chorus has spoken, when he says,

> *The last temptation is the greatest treason:*
> *To do the right deed for the wrong reason.*

Only at the sermon, however, does he analyse what exactly the wrong reason is, showing his insight into the ultimate betrayal suggested to him:

'Still less is a Christian martyrdom the effect of a man's will to become a saint, as a man by willing and contriving may become a ruler of men . . . the true martyr is he who has lost his will in the will of God, and who no longer-desires anything for himself, not even the glory of being a martyr.'

Again, he says to the priests later, as the murderers approach,

All my life they have been coming, these feet. All my life
I have waited. Death will come only when I am worthy,
And if I am worthy, there is no danger.
I have only to make perfect my will.

This is the demand also of the *Quartets*, that nothing must be sought from God, that, as Eliot puts it in the choruses from *The Rock*, one must

    take no thought of the harvest
 But only of the proper sowing.

After his meeting with the fourth tempter Thomas remains always conscious of his weakness, and so is able to exorcise it in submission.

Having achieved purification of his motive, Becket does in his death influence the lives of others, those of the women of Canterbury. After the specious arguments of the murderers, which apart from the blunt heartiness of William de Traci, amount to the complaint that Thomas refused to buttress the state with the approval of the Church,[1] the chorus is seen to have advanced from its former apathy, to have become reconciled to its surroundings and to the necessity for submission to God's will. Throughout the play, despite their being dependent on the earth for their livelihood, they have been out of sympathy with the seasonal pattern and with the life of nature. Evil is symbolised for

1. Eliot's ideas on the relationship between Church and state he has expressed in *The Idea of Christian Society*, in which there is a great deal that is relevant to this, the political aspect of the play: 'To identify any particular form of government with Christianity is a dangerous error: for it confounds the permanent with the transitory, the absolute with the contingent." Not infrequently a government will find it useful to establish just such a confusion in the minds of its subjects. Contemporary parallels to the dilemma of Thomas are too easily found to require mention. Miss Adair's essay deals admirably with this aspect of *Murder in the Cathedral*, one of the ways in which it shows "the same things happening again and again'.

them by animal life, by 'jackal, jackass, jackdaw', 'Grey necks twisting, rat tails twining, in the thick light of dawn'. They see 'Death in the rose', and for them the seasons are 'A sour spring, a parched summer, an empty harvest', with comfort only in the dead winter. In their final chorus they come to see that the animals and all the created world

'. . . affirm Thee in living; all things affirm Thee in living; the bird in the air, both the hawk and the finch; the beast on the earth, both the wolf and the lamb; the worm in the soil and the worm in the belly.'

The feeling of reunion with God's purposes is that of Hopkins's 'As kingfishers catch fire, dragonflies draw flame.' The animal and nature imagery is caught up, in the choruses, with the final reconciliation. Thomas's martyrdom has created 'significant soil', and

From such ground springs that which forever renews the earth.

The specific renewal here is that the people of Canterbury no longer desire only a 'return, to the soft quiet seasons'. The effect of the final chorus is analogous to that of the culmination of *Little Gidding*.

Being out of sympathy with the pattern of the seasons, the people are apathetic too to what this pattern symbolises—the pain of spiritual rebirth. The opening choruses are a complaint against the return of Thomas, in the well-founded fear that with his return will come also a breaking into their comfortably settled way of life:

Now I fear disturbance of the quiet seasons:
Winter shall come bringing death from the sea,
Ruinous spring shall beat at our doors,
Root and shoot shall eat our eyes and our ears,
Disastrous summer burn up the beds of our streams
And the poor shall wait for another decaying October

. . . .

Come happy December, who shall observe you, who shall preserve you?
Shall the Son of Man be born again in a litter of scorn?

This apathy takes concrete form in their wishing Thomas to leave—

O Thomas, return, Archbishop; return, return to France.
Return. Quickly. Quietly. Leave us to perish in quiet.

So their rejection of the return of life with the spring is linked with their repugnance to spiritual rebirth, and to the return of their Archbishop. The change begins after Thomas's sermon, a turning point for him too, being, as I have said, the point at which he clarifies his refusal of the fourth tempter. After it the chorus has this to say:

> . . . *war among men defiles this world, but death in the Lord renews it,*
> *And the world must be cleaned in the winter . . .* '

and later,

> *O Lord Archbishop, O Thomas Archbishop, forgive us, forgive us,*
> *pray for us that we may pray for you, out of our shame.*

Then in the final chorus all the themes are fused in the reconciliation:

> *Even in us the voices of seasons, the snuffle of winter, the song of spring,*
> *the drone of summer, the voices of beasts and of birds, praise Thee.*
> *We thank Thee for Thy mercies of blood, for Thy redemption by*
> *blood. For the blood of Thy martyrs and saints*
> *Shall enrich the earth, shall create the holy places.*

The interest of the play, then, is in Thomas's struggle to self-purification, and in the effect of this on those under him. The political element is subordinate to the struggle within Thomas himself, which, with the sermon and the chorus, largely indifferent to the machinations of the king's supporters, unifies the two sections. It is because this play has so much more in common with the morality plays than it has with the modern stage that so little stress is laid on character. It reminds us too of the conception of Fate in the Greek drama, of which Gilbert Murray has this to say in his introduction to the Eumenides:

> 'Each of us must fulfil his portion; he cannot escape it; he must not exceed it nor trespass on the Moira of another.'

Although *Murder in the Cathedral* is a specifically Christian play, its superficial resemblance to Greek drama is strengthened by the presence of the Greek chorus, participating in the action, and by the fact that the Greeks too were little interested in individual character. In Eliot's play the priests are nameless, part of the corporate body of the Church, and the women of Canterbury are never individualised. We witness the gradual integration of all with the 'eternal design', made possible by Thomas's sacrifice. In the two plays with a contemporary setting Eliot is concerned with the same themes, but here we find more stress on individual character, and consequently more detailed analysis of how the saint's sacrifice will influence the individual life.

To a great extent the situation presented and the action developed in any play are valid only for the particular characters involved. Eliot has expressed his distaste for the fervour with which critics search for a neat bundle of 'philosophy' which may be extracted, imperfectly digested, and regurgitated for the public. In any play with a claim to greatness there is of course a meaning beneath the surface, but when search for it becomes the critic's sole purpose, the result is too little analysis of character, of dramatic technique and fitness, of the elements which make the work drama. *The Cocktail Party* was dismissed by some reviewers merely as an essay in morbid asceticism, and this was entirely the result of a hasty and superficial search for the meaning.

The main ground for the assertion seems to be the manner of Celia's death, and the conclusion,

> *This way, which she accepted, led to this death.*
> *If that is not a happy death, which death is happy?*

Considered out of its dramatic context, a description of Celia's crucifixion near an ant-hill, rounded by Reilly's epitaph, might suggest, to one prepared to look no further, that infinitely painful death was the way to salvation. This judgment, however, overlooks a nice point of character, a purely dramatic problem, and ends by giving a totally distorted notion of the writer's purpose. One of the most important scenes in the play is that between Reilly and Celia, balanced by the comedy of the preceding discussion of the Chamberlaynes' problem. Previous to this scene the only indication that Celia had suffered any deep spiritual change was the conclusion of her talk with Edward Chamberlayne in Act I, scene ii. For the greater part of that act she seemed to exist at no higher a level than the other guests at the party. The first part of her talk with Edward, where they quarrel over Edward's abandoning her, shows her as concerned to analyse her own emotions and reactions, very articulate about her decisions. Even then her only feeling on discovering Edward's change of heart is humiliation. Until, shortly after saying this, she goes on, in words foreshadowing her ultimate discovery that the accepted realities are evanescent wraiths,

> *I listened to your voice, that had always thrilled me,*
> *And it became another voice—no, not a voice:*
> *What I heard was only the noise of an insect,*
> *Dry, endless, meaningless, inhuman— . . .*
> *The man I saw before, he was only a projection—*
> *I see that now—of something that I wanted—*
> *No, not wanted—something that I aspired to—*
> *Something that I desperately wanted to exist.*

Celia, during her examination by Reilly, elaborates these 'hints and guesses', and lays bare her spiritual problem. Not only Edward, but everyone, 'all the world I live in seems a delusion', so that 'It no longer seems worth while to speak to anyone!' Again,

> *it would really be dishonest*
> *For me, now, to try to make a life with anybody!*

Reilly's advice to her, that her choice means 'loneliness—and communion', and Celia's demeanour throughout the scene, suggest that she is committing herself to complete withdrawal from a world that has ceased to have any meaning for her, that she intends to devote herself to a life of prayer and meditation. There is, then, an apparent discrepancy in character between this Celia and the one who, instead, joins the active pursuits of an austere nursing sisterhood and is killed by the natives. That is the point of character. It is, incidentally, interesting to watch the development of her character, for according to Eliot she was in the first conception of no cardinal value to his scheme, being merely a figure introduced to fill out the Chamberlaynes' group. The dramatic problem is to bring home to the audience just what Celia's choice means, of stressing its urgency. To follow rigidly what seemed implied in Celia's attitude would have resulted in loss of tension—she would simply have disappeared from the action, and no true impression would have been given of what her choice involved. To bring this home she is made to die horribly. That she did is not of itself important, but emphasises the importance of her original choice.

This is a more probable explanation of the manner of Celia's death than that Eliot is deriving some obscure pleasure from contemplation of her pain and suffering. On the discrepancy in Celia's character it may be noted that this is only apparent. Coming to Reilly disturbed by her terrifying discovery, she is sure only that life can never again be the same for her—as were the Magi in Eliot's poem. Her immediate reaction is to withdraw from it in devotion to something higher—'an occupation for a saint'. Sainthood finds various forms, and whichever way of realisation is chosen, the character which elects remains unaltered. Celia changes her mind, but the character which drove her to choose originally is radically consistent.

Questions such as these are disregarded or misinterpreted when the critic retires too far from consideration of the play as a record of events and their effects on a specific group of people. Although less common it is equally an error to look on a play as dealing solely with people walled off from life, as a set of problems in dramatic art, even as merely an agreeable way of passing an evening. A play must entertain, but it should also provoke thought and stimulate the emotions. *The Cocktail Party* is a comedy and it does amuse, but to accept only the humour and to pass over the rest in brute patience is a failure to co-operate with the dramatist. In Eliot's own illuminating comparison, conductors may offer different interpretations of a piece of music, but none may produce a travesty of the composer's intention. Similarly with an audience's attitude to a play. The humour in *The Cocktail Party* is a contrast to the serious themes, as in the sequence of Reilly's interviews, and both elements meet in Reilly, who was originally a reminiscence of Hercules in the *Alcestis*. Each arrives at the home of a man whose wife, in the *Alcestis* has died, in *The Cocktail Party* has disappeared without explanation and has in one sense, as Reilly explains to Edward, died to her husband. Hercules, unaware of his host's bereavement, drinks himself into drunkenness before learning the truth. To redeem himself he fights with and conquers death, so restoring Alcestis to her husband. Similarly Reilly has a drinking scene with Edward, more subtly humorous than Hercules', before overcoming the living death of the inhabitants of this fashionable waste land. Hercules uses physical force against death. Reilly fights with the spirit and the mind. Eliot uses the background of Greek myth as he had used allusion and quotation in his poetry, for comparison and contrast.

There is little point in trying to find a precise label for Reilly. He performs, on a higher level, the part of Hercules, and is the dedicated man, partly the desired Coriolanus of *The Waste Land* and 'Difficulties of a Statesman'. Dramatically he unites the different elements in the play, the comedy associated with the Chamberlaynes—not without its serious overtones—and the nobler story of Celia. He overlooks both, directs both, and both are focused in him. Analogous to his part is that of the Canaletto in 'Burbank'. In a somewhat similar fashion Reilly unites the comic and the serious. In what is obviously a comment on the part of Sweeney in 'Sweeney Agonistes' Eliot has said:

'I once designed, and drafted a couple of scenes, of a verse play. My intention was to have one character whose sensibility and intelligence should be on the plane of the most sensitive and intelligent members of the audience; his speeches should be addressed to them as much as to the other personages in the play—or rather, should be addressed to the latter, who were to be material, literal-minded and visionless, with the consciousness of being overheard by the former. There was to be an understanding between this protagonist and a small number of the audience, while the rest of the audience would share the responses of the other characters in the play. Perhaps this is all too deliberate, but one must experiment as one can' (*The Use of Poetry and the Use of Criticism*, p. 153).

Reilly's position is something the same, but, the play being complete, we see him overcome the indifference and misunderstanding of certain of the other characters.

These are some of the ways in which the characters reveal themselves and the dramatist gains his effects. What the characters are doing is establishing a foundation on which they may build their futures. The conclusions they reach are of considerable interest in relation to ideas already deliberated by Eliot in the *Quartets*, as well as in *The Family Reunion*. Before going on to these matters, let it be emphasised again that the dramatic interest is not in the ideas to be derived from the play, but in the struggles by which the players reach an adumbration of them.

The situation taken by *The Cocktail Party* is that different people are faced with the necessity of making a choice. Edward must decide whether or not he wants to begin life again with his wife, and in deciding he will, as Reilly tells him,

> *set in motion*
> *Forces in your life and in the lives of others*
> *Which cannot be reversed.*

Peter Quilpe has to choose between remaining in England to re-establish his largely imaginary relationship with Celia, and going to California. Eventually he chooses Hollywood. Celia has to choose between re-adopting the life in society that Lavinia Chamberlayne has been taught by Reilly to find tolerable, and devoting herself to austere withdrawal from her circle. Her choice is the most important, and it is irremediable. The temptation now is to summarise the play as saying that any choice will determine all one's future. This is not so, for it depends on the level from which the choice is made. Some choices, by the very fact of their being made, will impose on the maker the conditions of his future. So Celia, because she is the kind of person who can choose to dedicate her life, will accept whatever that dedication may impose. Celia's choice is irreversible because she is capable of making it at all. Again, the generalisation must be qualified by reference to situation and character. Contrasted with the supreme spiritual exaltation of Celia is the attitude of the Chamberlaynes who, with Peter Quilpe, represent 'l'homme moyen sensuel', as Celia represents the saint. Their choice, on another level, is equally satisfactory. They become

> *Two people who know they do not understand each other,*
> *Breeding children whom they do not understand*
> *And who will never understand them,*

and

> *in a world of lunacy*
> *Violence, stupidity, greed . . . it is a good life.*

Peter too, in accepting the conditions of his choice, is 'working out his salvation with diligence'. Each of these people, to preserve the limited happiness which is all the world can offer, must accept the conditions of their choice. In this they are sustained by the self-sacrifice of Celia—a point which will be more fully considered later. The thin self-assurance of Peter Quilpe, an emotionally adolsecent and rather affected young man—a characteristic discreetly pointed by his returning from California with the traces of an adopted American accent—melts as soon as he hears of Celia's death, and he says,

> One thought has been going round and round in my head—
> That I've only been interested in myself:
> And that isn't good enough for Celia.

That is one of the themes of the play, the levels of choice, the interaction of character.

Something of the two levels of choice is hinted too in *The Family Reunion*, where Harry dedicates himself to the higher aspiration, and Agatha spends her life as 'the efficient principal of a women's college', with beneath that 'a deeper organisation'. Celia, in a way, may be said to continue Harry's story, for we leave Harry at the moment when he makes his choice and reconciles himself to his destiny. In Harry we see the progress to the decision, in Celia its result. This is much too glib a summary, but it gives an idea of one difference of emphasis between the two plays. Harry is the conscience of his family,

> *its bird sent flying through the purgatorial flames*

to atone for its sins as well as for his own. When he makes his decision and accepts the Eumenides as friendly, he affects the lives of the other members of his family. Charles, whose part in the play has been largely to provide light relief, says,

> I am beginning to feel, just beginning to feel
> That there is something I could understand, if I were told it.
> But I'm not sure that I want to know. I suppose I'm getting old:
> Old-age came softly up to now. I felt safe enough;
> And now I don't feel safe. As if the earth should open
> Right to the centre, as I was about to cross Pall Mall,

and in his last speech,

> *I fear that my mind is not what it was—or was it?—and yet I*
> *think that I might understand.*

Mary too has her insight, created by the influence of Harry, and is given direction and a sense of purpose, taking up the path which she is fitted to follow, as the Chamberlaynes and Peter Quilpe do. Agatha says to her,

> *We must all go, each in his own direction,*
> *You, and I, and Harry. You and I,*
> *My dear, may very likely meet again*
> *In our wanderings in the neutral territory*
> *Between two worlds.*

Mary, accepting this, answers,

> *It takes so many years*
> *To learn that one is dead. So you must help me.*
> *I will go. But I suppose it is much too late*
> *Now, to try to get a fellowship?*

Not all learn that they have been dead. Violet—'I cannot understand it'—and Gerald seem unaltered. Harry's sacrifice and submission, however, have had their effect.

Even these people, apparently unaffected, attain a clearer perception when, freed of the clogging personality, they speak in the chorus as a family community. Then they are granted recognition of the frailty of seemingly stable normality. This appears first just before Harry's entrance, almost as a premonition, and gains force with each of the succeeding choruses. They ask

> *to be reassured*
> *About the noises in the cellar*
> *And the window that should not have been open,*

fearing some 'dreadful disclosures'. Later they acknowledge fear directly—

I am afraid of all that has happened, and of all that is to come—

only to try, on breaking back to their individuality, to fight against the revelation. Violet attempts a 'rational' explanation:

It is the obtuseness of Gerald and Charles and that doctor that gets on my
nerves.

As Harry says to them, they

> . . . *go on trying to think of each thing separately,*
> *Making small things important, so that everything*
> *May be unimportant, a slight deviation*
> *From some imaginary course that life ought to take,*
> *That you call normal.*

The chorus at the end of 'Sweeney Agonistes' is similarly composed of the separate personages speaking in community, and it is when they are so united that they appreciate the lesson which Sweeney has taught:

> *You dreamt you waked up at seven o'clock and it's foggy and it's damp*
>   *and it's dawn and it's dark*
> *And you wait for a knock and the turning of a lock for you know the*
>   *hangman's waiting for you.*
> *And perhaps you're alive*
> *And perhaps you're dead.*

The imagery used by Eliot to convey this apprehension of the thinness of the façade of security in modern civilisation depends on a suggestion of nightmare intruding into everyday affairs—as in this, from the final chorus of *The Family Reunion*:

> *We do not like to look out of the same window, and see quite a different*
>   *landscape.*
> *We do not like to climb a stair, and find it takes us down. . . .*
> *We do not like what happens when we are awake, because it too closely*
>   *resembles what happens when we are asleep.*

There is the same insinuation of normality seen slightly askew in *Murder in the Cathedral* when, in the same kind of imagery, the chorus says that the horror of Thomas's murder is more profound than the fears of ordinary life:

> *Still the horror, but more horror*
> *Than when twisting in the fingers*
> *Than when splitting in the skull.*
>
> *More than footfall in the passage,*
> *More than shadow in the doorway,*
> *More than fury in the hall.*

In *The Cocktail Party*, when Reilly explains why exactly Edward is disturbed by the disappearance of Lavinia, he uses an image recalling the stair image used in the last quotation from *The Family Reunion*:

> *When you've dressed for a party*
> *And are going downstairs, with everything about you*
> *Arranged to support you in the role you have chosen,*
> *Then sometimes, when you come to the bottom step*
> *There is one more step than your feet expected*
> *And you come down with a jolt. Just for a moment*
> *You have the experience of being an object*
> *At the mercy of a malevolent staircase.*

This imagery conveys most forcefully the continually renewed surprise, the disruption of a spiritless sense of security, that come with a fresh vision of life, and which are brought to the people in these plays by the impact of the dedicated person on their lives. So the sense of fear that is born to Charles indicates some measure of spiritual resurgence.

Like Charles, Edward Chamberlayne says, 'Now I think I understand', explaining this in the words,

> *Sir Henry has been saying*
> *I think, that every moment is a fresh beginning;*
> *And Julia, that life is only keeping on;*
> *And somehow the two ideas seem to fit together.*

For the natives too Celia's death has made a difference:

> *Who knows, Mrs. Chamberlayne,*
> *The difference that made to the natives who were dying*
> *Or the state of mind in which they died?*

Celia's death is not an ending, the climax of a series of events important only to herself. It reverberates through the lives of others and marks a fresh beginning. The Chamberlaynes are left with a feeling of responsibility for Celia's death, a memory that will sustain them in their lives. Reilly tells them,

> *You will have to live with these memories and make them*
> *Into something new. Only by acceptance*
> *Of the past will you alter its meaning.*

This may be compared with his earlier advice to Edward on how he and his wife must act towards each other on her return, the finely metaphorical,

> *Don't strangle each other with knotted memories,*

with a past immutably fixed.

As with the other two plays, *The Cocktail Party* is concerned with the pressure of the past on the present, both in the lives of individuals and in history. In the sense of *Murder in the Cathedral's*

> *We do not know very much of the future*
> *Except that from generation to generation*
> *The same things happen again and again—*

and of *The Family Reunion's*

> *It seems that I shall get rid of nothing,*
> *Of none of the shadows that I wanted to escape;*
> *And at the same time, other memories,*
> *Earlier, forgotten, begin to return*
> *Out of my childhood. I can't explain.*
> *But I thought I might escape from one life to another,*
> *And it might be all one life, with no escape.*

There is no escape from the past, as Reilly points out, and as Harry comes to realise when he reconciles himself to his memories, and stops trying to flee them. With him, as the consciousness of his family, he must take consciousness of all his past:

> *How can we be concerned with the past*
> *And not with the future? or with the future*
> *And not with the past?*

Eliot's burning awareness of the presence of the past is one of the reasons which lead him to have some basis in past drama for his contemporary situation—in *The Cocktail Party* the story of Alcestis, in *The Family Reunion* that of Orestes. Thus is illustrated the recurrence of events from generation to generation.

Many of these ideas are to be found in the *Quartets*. The notion of the inter-relationship between past, present, and future that forms a pattern which is 'new in every moment', has been discussed in Chapter Eight. Part of the pattern is the inseparable present moment, uniting past and future, a moment always potentially the moment of death. This evidently returns us to Edward's 'every moment is a fresh beginning', for it may also be the time of death. It comments also on Reilly's,

> *You will have to live with these memories and make them*
> *Into something new.*

Through his experience in the action of the play Edward comes to have what Mary, in *The Family Reunion*, calls 'the knowledge of death', when she says,

> *I believe that the moment of birth*
> *Is when we have knowledge of death.*

Harry, on his return to Wishwood, discovers the truth of what Reilly says to Edward of Lavinia:

> *Ah, but we die to each other daily.*
> *What we know of other people*
> *Is only our memory of the moments*
> *During which we knew them.*

Harry is not blind to the changes taking place in people from moment to moment. Speaking of his mother's retaining the old order of things at Wishwood, he remarks,

> *It's very unnatural,*
> *This arresting of the normal change of things:*
> *But it's very like her. What I might have expected.*
> *It only makes the changing of people*
> *All the more manifest.*

This change of people jettisons nothing, but creates continually a new composition of all that they have been—a theory reminiscent of Proust's idea of the composite personality reaching back to the past. Harry will meet again all his old selves—

> *The man who returns will have to meet*
> *The boy who left—*

199

and he accepts with his own past the past of his surroundings:

> *I am the old house*
> *With the noxious smell and the sorrow before morning,*
> *In which all past is present. . . .*

These are the themes implicit in the plays. Primarily they deal with the different levels of spiritual experience, of the saint and of the ordinary mortal, who is helped to establish his life by the power of the saint's sacrifice to fertilise the lives of others. Harry and Celia are among those having the power to nourish 'the life of significant soil'. All significant life will be directed by consciousness of the permanent imminence of death, of the memories of one's past which mould the fluctuating character, and cannot be evaded, discarded in the lumber room like the last decade's junk. Recognition of a spiritual reality superior to the material creates not a new character but the need to see in a new way all one's past, which is still within one. These ideas are a part of the drama, but discussion of them is not an abstract of the plays, which must depend more on the grip exercised by the dramatic process through which the people involved arrive at the ideas.

In certain of his early essays Eliot has postulated conditions for the creation of a poetic drama which in essence are a generalisation of the feeling that a play is not the 'philosophy' which can be extracted from it, that in fact any play which is intended primarily as a vehicle for a philosophy must fail to be drama. What the dramatist must do is to present an artistic realisation of a view of life which is seen to operate in the action and in his characters. In Eliot's words,

'The essential is to get upon the stage this precise statement of life which is at the same time a point of view, a world—a world which the author's mind has subjected to a complete process of simplification. I do not find that any drama which "embodies a philosophy" of the author's (like *Faust*) or which illustrates any social theory (like Shaw's) can possibly fulfil the requirements' (*The Sacred Wood*, p. 68).

A poem is a world because it imposes a pattern on, and makes a particular arrangement, gives a peculiar view, of whatever is its subject. Similarly poetic drama brings into being in a concrete form a particular way of looking at the world. It is not the illustration of a philosophy, but it will leave its audience with the feeling that they have been in the presence of an ordered world in which certain eternal laws obtain, in which people display certain characteristics and are worked on by certain emotions. It will not depend on exact verisimilitude, on photographic reproduction of the real world and real people. On another plane, for example, the fact that the incidents at the end of *She Stoops to Conquer* were paralleled in real life is quite irrelevant to the question of whether Goldsmith should have used them, and to their success on the stage. The drama will be related to real life, as the messenger in *Murder in the Cathedral*, the police sergeant in *The Family Reunion*, are 'real' people, but it will also have 'its own self-subsistent reality' in the relationships between the various people in the play. In brief, the philosophy is identified with the reality presented on the stage, and is not merely the voicing of comments on life by some of the characters. Poetic drama is a crystallisation of forces which can be seen to operate, though not with such symmetry, inevitability, and clarity, in the real world, and so will represent a 'view of life'.

It is poetic drama which can do this most effectively and surely, for poetry strikes immediately at the heart of a situation or emotion or idea, conveying its essence, stripped of superficialities. In ridding drama of verse, of chorus and soliloquy, we are 'contenting ourselves with appearances, instead of insisting upon fundamentals' (*Selected Essays*, p. 46). The importance of the chorus to Eliot's plays has been shown—it is difficult to see how, without it, he could have communicated the communal, family reaction to Harry's return. A kind of soliloquy appears also, as in the crucial conversation between Mary and Harry, when at one stage their words are more an internal communion than a dialogue. These devices have their fascination and their effectiveness, but most important of all is the use of verse, for it is the verse which, by increasing the emotional tension, makes us accept the devices. Eliot's is a poetry rather like that of Ben Jonson, of which he has said that 'his emotional tone is not in the single verse, but in the design of the whole. But not many people are capable of discovering for themselves the beauty which is only found after labour.' The verse of Eliot's plays is badly suited to anthologists.

It is much too easy a way out for the unsympathetic critic to quote single lines, with the suggestion that they are no more than prose, as James Agate did in his review of *The Family Reunion*. The verse must be seen as a whole, from the slacker, extremely conversational pitch of the lighter passages, to the tightened rhythms of the more emotional. Eliot offers a verse which suggests the contemporary environment, and which, deliberately, for a great part of the play, approaches prose very closely, yet remains sufficiently far from it not to jar on the ears when the more emphasised verse is used.

In *The Family Reunion* Winchell's

> *Coming along in the fog, my Lady,*
> *And he must have been in rather a hurry.*
> *There was a car drawn up where it shouldn't be . . .*

has sufficient rhythmical force to keep it in tune with Mary's tauter,

> *The slow flow throbbing the trunk*
> *The pain of the breaking bud,*

and with Harry's lines, more in the same idiom,

> *To the worship in the desert, the thirst and deprivation,*
> *A stony sanctuary and a primitive altar,*
> *The heat of the sun and the icy vigil,*
> *A care over lives of humble people.*

The pompous banality of the messenger in *Murder in the Cathedral* appears in his prosaic,

> *You are right to express a certain incredulity,*
>
> *The streets of the town will be packed to suffocation,*

which can modulate, in the same speech, into the more harmonious

> *Strewing the way with leaves and late flowers of the season,*

and so keep in touch with the intenser passages. Only in this way can the pattern of the verse be seen, the planned modulation of the conversational basis. The opening talk of *The Family Reunion*, and the conversation between the Chamberlaynes and Reilly, blend without strain with the stronger, more emphatic verse of Celia and Reilly:

> *For what happened is remembered like a dream*
> *In which one is exalted by intensity of loving*
> *In the spirit, a vibration of delight*
> *Without desire, for desire is fulfilled*
> *In the delight of loving. A state one does not know*
> *When awake. But what, or whom I loved,*
> *Or what in me was loving, I do not know.*
> *And if that is all meaningless, I want to be cured*
> *Of a craving for something I cannot find*
> *And of the shame of never finding it.*

Purely because of its poetry, poetic drama possesses a quality which Eliot has attempted to isolate in some of his essays on the Elizabethan and Jacobean drama. His decisions are related to what has already been said of the way in which such drama becomes a view of life. The characters in the drama are inter-related in a pattern such as is formed in a poem by the sequence of word and image. The clearest example of this is the development of the feelings entertained by Mary, Agatha, and Harry for each other, revealed in scenes of contrasted intensity which come almost insensibly to suggest a great deal more than a mere fluctuation of human emotions. Mary's conversation with Agatha in the second scene of part one discloses their failure to establish communication with each other and leaves them utterly out of sympathy. Mary says at the end,

> *So you will not help me!*
> *Waiting, waiting, always waiting.*
> *I think this house means to keep us waiting.*

At this point Harry enters, and he and Mary succeed in making contact, their common ground being at first their antipathy to the attempts to regulate their childhood:

MARY

> *Well, it all seemed to be imposed upon us;*
> *Even the nice things were laid out ready,*
> *And the treats were always so carefully prepared;*
> *There was never any time to invent our own enjoyments.*
> *But perhaps it was all designed for you, not for us*

HARRY
No, it didn't seem like that. I was part of the design
As well as you. But what was the design?
It never came off.

Even here we can catch an implied contrast between the human attempt to impose a pattern, which fails, and 'the eternal design' of which one of the priests speaks in *Murder in the Cathedral*.

As the scene progresses Harry manages to approach a description which finds a response in Mary of his mystical experience, using the image of a brief emergence to sunlight, suggested to him by what Mary has said immediately before, perhaps even by reminiscence of a comparison used by her earlier, in a different context, to describe her feeling that Harry's visionary experience deceives him; he is like

the man who believes that he is blind
While he still sees the sunlight.

In the later passage she asks,

And what of the terrified spirit
Compelled to be reborn
To rise toward the violent sun . . . ?

Then Harry says,

You bring me news
Of a door that opens at the end of a corridor,
Sunlight and singing; when I felt sure
That every corridor only led to another,
Or to a blank wall;

and later,

It was only a moment, it was only one moment
That I stood in sunlight, and thought I might stay there.

It is the sense of community created here between Harry and Mary that makes possible the reconciliation between Mary and Agatha at the end of the play, an end not consciously sought by either. So one comes to perceive not only the pattern woven by the personages in the drama, but also that behind this there is a greater and more subtle pattern. The use of the sunlight imagery also produces this sense of a higher plane on which the characters exist. It recurs in the talk between Agatha and Harry at the end of the play, when Agatha recalls the fleeting moment when

> *I only looked through the little door*
> *When the sun was shining on the rose-garden;*
> *And heard in the distance tiny voices*
> *And then a black raven flew over.*
> *And then I was only my own feet walking*
> *Away, down a concrete corridor*
> *In a dead air.*

Relevant to this is Eliot's comment on John Marston's *Sophonisba*, that '. . . as we familiarise ourselves with the play we perceive a pattern behind the pattern into which the characters deliberately involve themselves; the kind of pattern which we perceive ourselves only at rare moments of inattention and detachment, drowsing in sunlight. It is the pattern drawn by what the ancient world called Fate; subtilised by Christianity into mazes of delicate theology' (*Selected Essays*, p. 232). It is the subtilised Christian pattern that we perceive behind the relationships of the people in *The Family Reunion*. In the events directly portrayed we catch glimpses of what Agatha calls 'the world around the corner'. All this is part of what Eliot has described as the 'doubleness' of poetic drama, an idea at the back of the previous quotation, which he introduces earlier in the essay:

'It is possible that what distinguishes poetic drama from prosaic drama is a kind of doubleness in the action, as if it took place on two planes at once. In this it is different from allegory, in which the abstraction is something conceived, not something differently felt, and from symbolism (as in the plays of Maeterlinck) in which the tangible world is deliberately diminished—both symbolism and allegory being operations of the conscious planning mind. In poetic drama a certain apparent irrelevance may be the symptom of this doubleness; or the drama has an under-pattern, less manifest than the theatrical one' (*Selected Essays*, p. 229).

Partly the subtle echoes of situation, phrase, and imagery communicate the delicate sense of a higher pattern. Harry, talking to Warburton of his father, remembers 'a summer day of unusual heat', when news came of his father's death. Agatha, talking to

Harry, tells him of the time when she first came to know of his father's futile plans for murdering his wife. She had come to Wishwood on

> *A summer day of unusual heat*
> *For this cold country.*

This is not purely a matter of phrase reminiscence. Because of it Harry and Agatha seem to share in some experience beyond the physically perceptible, to share in some other order of being as well. The doubleness is suggested also by Harry's difficulty in communicating his experiences to the other members of his family:

> *But how can I explain, how can I explain to you?*
> *If I tried to explain, you could never understand:*
> *I have all of the right-minded feeling about John*
> *That you consider appropriate. Only that's not the language*
> *That I choose to be talking. I will not talk yours.*

In *The Cocktail Party* too we get the impression of the characters' taking part in some series of actions of which they are not entirely conscious, taking their positions in a pattern not of their own design, as when Reilly says to Edward,

> *Let me, therefore, remain the stranger.*
> *But let me remind you, that to approach the stranger*
> *Is to invite the unexpected, release a new force,*
> *Or to let the genie out of the bottle.*
> *It is to start a train of events*
> *Beyond your control.*

and later,

> *You will change your mind, but you are not free.*
> *Your moment of freedom was yesterday.*
> *You made a decision. You set in motion*
> *Forces in your life and in the lives of others*
> *Which cannot be reversed.*

We are reminded of Eliot's comment that Beatrice in 'The Changling' is the type of 'the unmoral nature, suddenly trapped in the inexorable toils of morality—of morality not of man but of nature—and forced to take the consequences of an act which it had planned lightheartedly' (*Selected Essays*, p. 163).

Tillyard's book on Shakespeare's last plays deals perceptively with the ways in which the doubleness appears there. It is realised in phrase; in a recurrent pattern of imagery—the 'dissolving' imagery of *The Tempest* cannot fail to impress itself gradually on the auditors' minds; in the relationship between character and character; in the contrast between scenes of different intensity. It is precisely in these ways that it appears in *The Family Reunion*, the play which I believe to be Eliot's most successful achievement of the shadowed under-pattern. Evidently the communication of the double pattern depends on qualities peculiar to poetry, and is because of this denied to prose drama, which deals with a slighter and more superficial realism. It was a misconception of the nature of realism which led to the popularity of prose as a medium for drama. The argument was that the spectacle of the characters speaking in verse placed too great a strain on the credulity, and involved too much artificiality. The answer of Johnson to a different argument is apposite here:

'The truth is that the spectators are always in their senses, and know, from the first act to the last, that the stage is only a stage, and that the players are only players. . . . Imitations produce pain or pleasure, not because they are mistaken for realities, but because they bring realities to mind.'

The drama, like all art, is essentially artificial, and the removal of one valuable artifice, the use of poetry, which can comprehend so much more varied, and so much deeper, emotion, carries no equivalent compensation. To illustrate Eliot's argument in 'A Dialogue on Dramatic Poetry', the response of the real person to the situation of Lear when he discovers the perfidy of Regan and Goneril would be an agony and distress of mind too strong to find adequate expression. The emotion that requires poetry for its expression is within him. He is not a poet, but he is striving for poetic expression, though the result may be only an inarticulate cry. Shakespeare's play is realistic in expressing accurately and powerfully what the human feels but is unable to say, in the only medium able to contain such emotion. It is Eliot's achievement to have contributed towards making this possible again by producing a dramatic verse which has grown from the contemporary idiom.

The variation of style in the plays recalls the method used in the *Quartets*, as well as in the earlier poems. Eliot's use of the traditional methods, and his attainment of the defining characteristic of the earlier poetic drama, show that his endeavour is to restore, not to produce a trifling, if ingenious, novelty. In a word, his approach to the problem of establishing a vigorous tradition of contemporary poetic drama is that which led him to formulate the style of his other poetry.

(II)

The conclusions based on this enquiry may be dealt with under two headings—the principle governing the various stylistic changes and dictating the poetic theory; the comment which this makes on Eliot's mind. The latter is not an undertaking that would commend itself to Eliot. His aversion to the custom of considering the main interest of poetry to be its revelation of the poet's personality has been sufficiently shown. Such commentary then, will be restricted to what bears directly on that inevitable degree of poetic subjectivity discussed in an earlier chapter.

The key to all Eliot's work and thought is his personally evolved doctrine of traditionalism. To it most of his predilections, most of what is distinctive in his poetry, may be traced. Some general summary of its evolution will be convenient here. From dissatisfaction with the American literary tradition Eliot was drawn to the European tradition generally, and particularly to that of England, the home of his ancestors. Respect for the value of the literary tradition extended gradually to include some degree of dependence on the general cultural tradition, social, religious, and political. The attraction was mirrored eventually in his adoption of English nationality and in his association with the Anglo-Catholic religious compromise. We have seen, however, the blend between what he had rejected, yet could not entirely deny—the influences of his American background—and his innate sympathy with the somewhat authoritarian Anglo-Catholicism. The later poetry is the ground where the conflict between New England Puritanism and his adopted religion is most clearly illustrated. From this conflict proceeded synthesis, and an answer to the moral problems that had been his preoccupation.

We can see, then, a clearly defined progress from rejection of the inchoate American tradition to acceptance of the worth of Europe's rich culture, and of the pattern that he saw in its development. The questionings and theorisings that accompanied this reveal a mind unwilling to accept too easily, desirous of justifying to itself any undertaking which seems to satisfy its needs. That it seems to satisfy them is not by itself enough. Exactly the same process is at work in Eliot's response to his religious questionings. They are answered by submission to the teachings of the Anglo-Catholic faith, to which he was originally drawn by his desire for a solid basis on which could rest the individual effort of the modern artist. That is to say, the original desire for stability in literature was satisfied by enquiry into the force of tradition. It was this which led him to apply the same process to satisfaction of his spiritual needs. That his original attraction to the religion may well have been partly the result of artistic susceptibilities is suggested by the probability that in 'A Dialogue on Dramatic Poetry' he is expressing his own experience of the aesthetic satisfaction of the Mass, a drama that recalls to us that it was in the church that the dramatic tradition began. His spiritual peace, then, he found in Anglo-Catholicism, child of a flux between two extremes, similar to the flux in the literary tradition. His religion is tempered too by the Puritan inheritance of his American background.

Common to all this is, evidently, desire for stability, prompted initially by the sense of loss born of his feeling the inadequacy of the American tradition, guided on its way by a tenacious remnant of that American upbringing, by the Puritan conscience. An unsatisfied desire for a well-defined background of tradition leads to search for fulfilment of the need. What is eventually accepted as the satisfaction of the need is subject to consistent probing and testing, which do not end with his final acceptance of what he considers the answer to his desires. We find this illustrated, for example, in his decision that humanist thought has a valuable function to perform—that of assuring that religion does not become slothful, and does not lapse into passivity. This questioning attitude he owes to the atmosphere of his American life, the rejection of which began the intellectual and spiritual pilgrimage. The influence of his American birth is therefore twofold.

It is worthy of note that no specifically American scene is presented in the early poetry, which could have its setting in any urban civilisation. This anonymity is modified in the imagery of the later poetry, which takes some of its most effective symbolism from recollections of the New England scene. For the absence of particularity in the early poetry was substituted a background of allusion and quotation which gave depth to, and placed in the perspective of time, the essentials of the contemporary scene. As in the thought, a synthesis was attained, here between various traditional metres and the stamp of a new idiom, ironic, conversational, perfectly adapted to its matter. From the abrupt variations on a distorted blank verse metre, the experiment moved through the compact spareness of the Sweeney poems, returning in *The Waste Land* to the ten syllable base, recalling now the splendour of Shakespeare's evocation of Cleopatra, now the drab account of the typist's experiences, related in a skilfully mannered variation of the Augustan style. This method is retained in the *Quartets*, as is allusion, another acknowledgement of Eliot's traditional bias.

The variations between the early and the later method of allusion have been discussed, and need be only briefly restated here. The similarity between the early and the later method is illustrated in the analyses of the passages from 'Rhapsody on a Windy Night' and 'Ash Wednesday'. Particular uses of the device, as distinct from its general functions of asserting the vitality of tradition and deepening the scope of the poems, are discussed in various sections—the comments on 'Burbank with a Baedeker' in Chapter One, and on *The Waste Land* in Chapter Five, for example. A further development is noted in Chapters Seven and Eight, where distinction is made between the differing uses of allusion to the Bible in the transition poems and in the *Quartets*, a formal development whose importance to the development of Eliot's philosophy has been considered.

Here again, as in the analysis of Eliot's intellectual progress, we can see that experiment rests always on a sure traditional foundation, itself subject to modification and inspection by the experimenting spirit. Both elements in the poetry, the formal, and that concerned with the themes, the subject matter, the philosophy, reveal the operation of the same consistent mentality. It is one deeply aware of the unchanging problems of mankind, acute to perceive and to communicate the sense of its own age, to integrate its findings with the greater pattern of history. A passage from *The Rock* could be applied to Eliot's own 'endless experimenting', which has re-opened long abandoned ground in the poetic tradition, and brought to Eliot himself an increasing mastery over the words that are his medium. The passage also stresses Eliot's steadily more apparent humility, in its regret that humanity's mastery over the material does not necessarily bring any more acute an awareness of the ultimate spiritual reality:

> *Endless experiment*
> *Brings knowledge of motion, but not of stillness;*
> *Knowledge of speech, but not of silence;*
> *Knowledge of words, and ignorance of the Word.*

To attempt to place Eliot in any neatly ordered hierarchy of English poets is an unprofitable enterprise. Nevertheless, some tentative estimate of his position can be made. His poetic theory, opposing violently that in fashion when he began to write, produced a poetry which restored the balance in the recurring flux between an artificial and a prosaic idiom. Eliot's importance to the history of English poetry is that of Donne or Wordsworth. This is not to say that Donne, Wordsworth, and Eliot possess to an equal degree any abstract 'greatness'. Their work is the same in that each, writing at a time when poetry had become fixed too dogmatically on certain lines, brought to it a new outlook, by re-introducing neglected and forgotten artistic methods, individually interpreted. Part of the purpose of my examination has been to show how exactly Eliot achieved this object in the poetry of our time.

We have seen Eliot attacked by the oldest artistic and the newest political prejudices. Against these he has maintained unbroken a consistent and sincere development, both of his technique and of his philosophy. The only justification for his theories can be, ultimately, the success with which they operate in practice. It is hoped that this examination has illuminated both the intrinsic beauty of Eliot's poetry and the integrity of his development. To speak of an artist's integrity is to risk a descent to the commonplaces of vague adulation. Integrity is not, however, so frequently exhibited that we can afford to despise it. Eliot's refusal to sacrifice to easy popularity his artistic and religious faiths must command our respect, even if he does not win our agreement.

Appendix

Appendix

Appendix to Chapter Seven (1) *(Chapbook, 1924.)*

DORIS'S DREAM SONGS

(1)
*Eyes I dare not meet in dreams
In death's dream kingdom
These do not appear:
There, the eyes are
Sunlight on a broken column
There, is a tree swinging
And voices are,
In the wind's singing
More distant and more solemn
Than a fading star.*

*Let me be no nearer
In death's dream kingdom
Let me also wear
Such deliberate disguises
Rat's coat, crowskin, crossed staves
In a field
Behaving as the wind behaves
No nearer—*

*Not that final meeting
In the twilight kingdom*

(2)
*The wind sprang up at four o'clock
The wind sprang up and broke the bells
Swinging between life and death
Here, in death's dream kingdom
The waking echo of confusing strife
Is it a dream or something else*

When the surface of the blackened river
Is a face that sweats with tears?
I saw across the blackened river
The camp fire shake with alien spears.
Here, across death's other river
The Tartar horsemen shake their spears.

(3)   *This is the dead land*
This is cactus land
Here the stone images
Are raised, here they receive
The supplication of a dead man's hand
Under the twinkle of a fading star.

Is it like this
In death's other kingdom
Waking alone
At the hour when we are
Trembling with tenderness
Lips that would kiss
Form prayers to broken stone.

THREE POEMS

(*Criterion*, January, 1925.)

(1)   *Eyes I dare not meet in dreams*
In death's dream kingdom
These do not appear:
There, the eyes are
Sunlight on a broken column
There, is a tree swinging
And voices are,
In the wind's singing
More distant and more solemn
Than a fading star

Let me be no nearer
In death's dream kingdom
Let me also wear
Such deliberate disguises

Rat's coat, crowskin, crossed staves
In a field
Behaving as the wind behaves
No nearer—

Not that final meeting
In the twilight kingdom

(2)   Eyes that last I saw in tears
Through division
Here in death's dream kingdom
The golden vision reappears
I see the eyes but not the tears
This is my affliction

This is my affliction
Eyes I shall not see unless
At the door of death's other kingdom
Where, as in this,
The eyes outlast a little while
A little while outlast the tears
And hold us in derision.

(3)   The eyes are not here
There are no eyes here
In this valley of dying stars
In this hollow valley
This broken jaw of our lost kingdoms

In this last of meeting places
We grope together
And avoid speech
Gathered on this beach of the tumid river

Sightless, unless
The eyes reappear
As the perpetual star
Multifoliate rose
Of death's twilight kingdom
The hope only
Of empty men.

THE HOLLOW MEN

(*Dial*, March, 1925.)

(1)
We are the hollow men
We are the stuffed men
Leaning together
Headpiece filled with straw. Alas
Our dried voices, when
We whisper together
Are quiet and meaningless
As wind in dry grass
Or rats' feet over broken glass
In our dry cellar

Shape without form, shade without colour
Paralysed force, gesture without motion

Those who have crossed
With direct eyes, to death's other Kingdom
Remember us—if at all—not as lost
Violent souls, but only
As the hollow men
The stuffed men.

(2)
Eyes I dare not meet in dreams
In death's dream kingdom
These do not appear:
There, the eyes are
Sunlight on a broken column
There, is a tree swinging
And voices are
In the wind's singing
More distant and more solemn
Than a fading star

Let me be no nearer
In death's dream kingdom
Let me also wear
Such deliberate disguises
Rat's coat, crowskin, crossed staves
In a field

Behaving as the wind behaves
No nearer—

Not that final meeting
In the twilight kingdom
With eyes I dare not meet in dreams.

(3)

The eyes are not here
There are no eyes here
In this valley of dying stars
In this hollow valley
This broken jaw of our lost kingdoms

In this last of meeting places
We grope together
And avoid speech
Gathered on this beach of the tumid river

Sightless, unless
The eyes reappear
As the perpetual star
Multifoliate rose
Of death's twilight kingdom
The hope only
Of empty men.

Bibliography

St. Augustine. *Confessions.*
Athenaeum. Review of *Prufrock and other Observations*, 2nd May, 1919.
'Affable Hawk.' Notes on *The Waste Land, New Statesman and Nation*, 4th November, 1922.
Edmund Blunden. 'Tradition in Poetry', an essay in *Tradition and Experiment in Present-day Literature.*
G. Bullough. *The Trend of Modern Poetry.*
C. M. Bowra. *The Heritage of Symbolism.*
Alec Brown. 'The Lyric Impulse in T. S. Eliot', in *Scrutinies* (ii), ed. Edgell Rickwood.
E. M. Butler. *The Myth of the Magus.*
Roy Campbell. 'Contemporary Poetry' (1931), in *Scrutinies* (i).
R. G. Collingwood. *Principles of Art.*
David Daiches. *Poetry and the Modern World.*
Babette Deutsch. *This Modern Poetry.*
Sir T. Elyot. *The Gouernor.*
B. Ifor Evans. *Literature between the Wars*: 'T. S. Eliot', pp. 91–102.
E. M. Forster. 'The Three T. S. Eliots', in *The Listener*, 20th January, 1949.
   'T. S. Eliot', in *Abinger Harvest.*
Sir James Frazer. *The Golden Bough*, 2 volumes, *Adonis, Attis, Osiris.*
Edith M. Fry. 'The Poetic Work of T. S. Eliot', in *The British Annual of Literature*, Vol. 5.
Robert Graves. *Contemporary Techniques of Poetry: A Survey of Modernist Poetry* (with Laura Riding).
Christopher Hassall. *Notes on the Verse Drama.*
H. W. Haüsermann. *L'Œuvre poétique de T. S. Eliot.*
W. P. Ker. *Form and Style in Poetry.*
René Lalou. *Contemporary French Literature.*
H. J. Laski. *Faith, Reason and Civilization.*
F. R. Leavis. *New Bearings in English Poetry.*
John Lehmann. 'The Search for the Myth', in *Penguin New Writing*, No. 30.
C. Day Lewis. *A Hope for Poetry.*

F. L. Lucas. Review of *The Waste Land*, in the *New Statesman and Nation*, 3rd November, 1923.

Louis MacNeice. *Modern Poetry*.

'Poetry Today', in *The Arts Today*, ed. Geoffrey Grigson.

The Poetry of W. B. Yeats.

Richard March and Tambimuttu. *T. S. Eliot; a Symposium*.

F. O. Matthiessen. *The Achievement of T. S. Eliot*.

Edwin Muir. *Essays on Literature and Society*.

Gorham B. Munson. 'The Esotericism of T. S. Eliot', in *1924*, July.

R. L. Ottley. *Studies in the Confessions of St. Augustine*.

Ezra Pound. 'Harold Monro', in *Polite Essays*.

B. Rajan (Editor of). *T. S. Eliot; a collection of Critical Essays by several hands*.

Herbert Read. *Politics of the Unpolitical*.

Reason and Romanticism.

Collected Essays in Literary Criticism.

I. A. Richards. *Principles of Literary Criticism*.

Michael Roberts. *Critique of Poetry*.

V. Sackville-West. Review of *Four Quartets: Observer*, 22nd October, 1944.

D. S. Savage. *The Personal Principle: Studies in Modern Poetry*.

Ranjee Shahanie. 'T. S. Eliot; Questions and Answers', *John o'London's Weekly*, 19th August, 1949.

Edith Sitwell. *Aspects of Modern Poetry*.

Poetry and Criticism.

'Experiment in Poetry' in *Tradition and Experiment in Present-day Literature*.

J. Sparrow. *Sense and Poetry*.

Stephen Spender. *The Destructive Element*.

'Books and the War', *Penguin New Writing*, No. 11, pp. 126–127.

'Sensuousness in Modern Poetry', *Penguin New Writing*, No. 16.

E. M. Stephenson. *T. S. Eliot and the Lay Reader*.

Kenneth Stevens. Essay in *Durham University Review*, December, 1948.

Times Literary Supplement. Review of *The Waste Land*, 20th September, 1923.

René Taupin. *L'Influence du symbolisme français*

G. Tillotson. *The Poetry of Pope*.

Louis Untermeyer. *American Poetry since 1900*.

H. Ross Williamson. *The Poetry of T. S. Eliot*.

Edmund Wilson. *Axel's Castle*.

Frank Wilson. *T. S. Eliot*.

Index

Index

225

Index